PENGUIN BOOKS

Down *the* Dirt Roads

Rachael Treasure lives in Southern Tasmania with her two teenage children and husband Daniel. Together they are establishing the educational Ripple Farm Landscape Healing Hub to share regenerative agricultural principles and Natural Sequence Farming techniques. Rachael's first novel, *Jillaroo*, blazed a trail in the Australian publishing industry for other rural women writers and is now considered an iconic work of contemporary fiction.

Rachael began her working life as a jillaroo before studying at Orange Agricultural College (now University of Sydney), and received a BA of Communications at Charles Sturt University. She has worked as a journalist on many publications in Australia's rural print sector and for ABC rural radio.

T0363516

Down *the* Dirt Roads

A memoir of love, loss and the land

RACHAEL TREASURE

PENGUIN BOOKS

PENGUIN BOOKS

UK I USA I Canada I Ireland I Australia
India I New Zealand I South Africa I China

Penguin Books is part of the Penguin Random House group of companies
whose addresses can be found at global.penguinrandomhouse.com.

First published by Penguin Random House Australia Pty Ltd, 2016
This edition published by Penguin Random House Australia Pty Ltd, 2017

Text copyright © Rachael Treasure 2016

The moral right of the author has been asserted.

Cover design by Alex Ross © Penguin Random House Australia Pty Ltd
Text design by Louisa Maggio © Penguin Random House Australia Pty Ltd
Front cover photograph by Australian Scenics/Getty Images; back cover
photograph © Natalie Mendham Photography.
Typeset in Adobe Garamond by Louisa Maggio, Penguin Random House Australia Pty Ltd
Colour separation by Splitting Image Colour Studio, Clayton, Victoria
Printed and bound in Australia by Griffin Press, an accredited ISO AS/NZS 14001
Environmental Management Systems printer.

 A catalogue record for this
book is available from the
National Library of Australia

ISBN 978 0 14378 642 9

penguin.com.au

*We at Penguin Random House Australia acknowledge that Aboriginal and Torres Strait
Islander peoples are the Traditional Custodians and the first storytellers of the lands
on which we live and work. We honour Aboriginal and Torres Strait Islander peoples'
continuous connection to Country, waters, skies and communities. We celebrate
Aboriginal and Torres Strait Islander stories, traditions and living cultures;
and we pay our respects to Elders past and present.*

*For Margaret Connolly, my book midwife
and my safety net, and for my children, my children's children,
and so on . . .*

The earth is your grandmother and mother, and she is sacred.
Every step that is taken upon her should be as a prayer.

BLACK ELK, 1863–1950
OGLALA SIOUX

Contents

Introduction

Never in my wildest imaginings of my adult future did I think I would be in my forties, living in a rental property, in a town with my children . . . farmless. But there it was: the bare, brutal facts of a failed dream that a country girl like me had to face. Under the foreign gleam of streetlights, with the press of the energies of unseen people in houses all around me, I would wake in the starless night to gaze at the artificial glow outside my window and the bleak reality that I no longer had a future exploring the same blissful bushland with my children that had seeped into my own soul when I was a child. I no longer had a life of teaching them about caretaking animals and soils, things that I not only loved, but revered and worshipped.

The story of how I lost that future and my farm is more far-fetched than any novel I could dream up. But life is like that. It takes you down roads you never expect to go down, under circumstances that are, at times, stranger than outback fiction and harder to swallow than a John Deere 24-plate disc plough.

I remember the day I went to look at the rental where I now sit and write. My first impression was not focused on the house, but the comfort I took from the fact that it was on a dirt road. Fancy that! A dirt road right in the middle of town! And across from it . . . there were sheep in paddocks yet to be claimed by housing. *Sheep!* I could smell them from where I stood near my ute. Those two things – sheep and dirt – were ribbons of connection not just back to the life I'd lost, but to the future that I hope to create for my funny little family, of just me and two children and the remains of my farming menagerie: a dumpy pony, four chooks and two working dogs, along with an emotionally complex toy poodle called Megatron. My larger horses had been agisted out to other properties, causing me as much agony as a mother sending her children away to boarding school, but I knew I had to make this move if I was going to find some time and space in which to heal.

As I first walked up the front steps to shake the pretty hand of the suited and appropriately heeled real-estate agent, I noticed the outside boards of the house were painted the hue of maggot-infested wool. It wasn't a criticism; just a passing observation from a farm girl who had recently taken up weekly art lessons and was reassessing colours in the world. On seeing the colour, I was suddenly teleported back to my paddocks, stooped over the tail end of a weaner lamb, my bubba children babbling in the ute, while my square, rather manlike, hands gripped shears as I sliced away white crimped wool in search of the activity of the viciously hungry maggots, chewing into the flesh of the sheep. There was something so satisfying about my day, if I knew I had saved one of my flock from such excruciating discomfort. Finding that seam of green stain in the fleece was always the path to revealing where the flesh-eating fly larvae were, and dealing with the problem, pronto.

Now when I direct my farming friends to our rental, I say, 'It's on the dirt road, and you'll see the house – it's "flystrike green".' They instantly get it. To anyone else looking at the colour it may be more glamorously referred to on a paint chart as 'Avocado Smash' or 'Fern Den Lush', but to me – the girl taken out of the country, with the country remaining in the girl – it is and always will be the house of 'flystrike green'. A house I never planned on living in. A house in which I realised I had been grieving the death of my farming life post-divorce for far too long. It was coming up to six years since my marriage blew to dust, so as I stood in the lovely sun-drenched rooms I realised I had to emerge from my own negative clouds and find a new compass to guide me.

The reason my pain had carried on for so long was because when the divorce was imminent in 2010, my father opted for my ex-husband to remain with him in the farm partnership. Dad stood by *him*, not me, and shoulder-to-shoulder the men stayed and laid claim to the land. It was the children and I who had to leave.

For a time, I tried to recreate what I had lost on reduced acreage just up the road from my family farm. In my move from

2000 acres to just under 20 acres, it soon became clear that it was just not going to work. I was trying to earn a living as a writer, pay off a new mortgage, drive children to and from school, along with running a property, when all the while I was running on emotional empty.

And that is how it came to pass . . . me renting a town-bound flystrike-green house that was not my home, but near to my children's schools. The journey to it had left me questioning everything about myself, my agricultural industry and a society that dismissed the power and gift of women and desecrated Mother Nature so brutally.

As I packed my electric fencing equipment that I had once used to regenerate pastures into the suburban backyard shed, along with my chainsaw and fence-post rammer, I also tried to pack away the shame of being ousted from my beloved farm, and tried to find forgiveness for myself and those involved.

The experience has sent me on an inner journey, fuelled by the discovery of a different compass by which to be guided in life. It's not the white man's compass that merely has the four points of North, South, East, West on a two-dimensional geographical landscape. I now view the world by the Native Americans' seven-point compass. A compass that has North, South, East, West and also *Above*, *Below* and *Within*.

Here I was, a person with the soil on her hands and in her heart trying to ground myself in a new place that was utterly foreign to me, with new concepts brewing within, on a dirt road that seemed, at the time, a dead end. But I was mistaken. Life was merely moving me on.

I soon met new neighbours . . . good neighbours. Kind neighbours. Funny neighbours with cool kids, who helped me see that the dirt road I was travelling on was a road that held a writer's seam of gold. A pathway that would give me the courage to speak of healing, for myself as a woman, for society as a whole and, also, healing for our land.

I heard Fred and Rachael before I met them. Musicians of the folk and blues kind, on still nights I could hear banjo sounds drifting over the fence with Johnny Cash's 'train a comin'' as they jammed on their back porch, accompanied by their kids on harmonica and a box for a drum. Our children began playing together in the creek that separated our houses and I soon found myself raising a tiny glass of Slovenian schnapps with them on a sunny afternoon and laughing with them whilst the kids cuddled guinea pigs on a trampoline. Life was starting to feel almost normal, as if we were stitching our lives back together into the fabric of a new community. It wasn't the cloth I would have chosen, but what was patching together was warm and beautiful.

A year into living in the village, Fred and Rachael asked my children and me – 'we three' – and our pony to their backyard wedding. On the day of their marriage, I headed out early to a farm just down the road to pick a good 5 kilos of plump strawberries, from Sophie Nicholls' Littlewood Berry Farm. I planned on piling the fruit high in a large white bowl, fresh, shiny, ruby-red and gorgeous, topped with their little green fringes for the wedding guests. I had bartered with Sophie that if I did a couple of hours' harvesting jam strawberries and weeding for her, she would provide the marital strawberries.

After a meditation in the strawberry patch, staining my fingers pink, hearing the pop of stems as I picked and feeling the living, damp earth pulse beneath my knees, I realised this was my path. To love the land no matter where I was and to share that love with others. The silence of a field. Sky above. Earth below.

Near me cars still grumbled past, planes still roared overhead and the busy life of humans went on, but here I got to feel the silence and the slow turn of the earth. That's why I love farming. That's why I love dirt. It reconnects you to your heartbeat. It helps you see we are all One . . . with every creature, every plant, every soil microbe, every single other being. The web of life and our place in it can be rediscovered in a paddock, in the bushland, on a ridge top, along with joy for simply breathing. We can remember we are made of the same stuff of stars and of soil. For me, being in a paddock means anything is possible.

But the strawberry patch stillness couldn't last. I had work to do. I had to go home to shampoo the pony! Our chunky little patchy brown-and-white Gemma had been given the honour of being 'bridesmare' for the wedding ceremony and was needed for the photos.

On the front lawn with the hose running over her, my daughter and I delighted in the froth of shampoo, rummaging our hands lovingly on Gemma's summer-smooth pony skin. This again was a blessing of now. There was no time to grieve a lost farm at this moment or carry baggage of bitterness. I was meant to make this earth-walk this way, hard as it had been. While the sun shone down on bubbles and giggles, love swept through me. As it says on a doormat that was given to us as a housewarming gift, 'Home is where the love is'.

Soon Gemma was plaited with lavender ribbons and purple stock flower, and my children and I frocked up in our 'Gladwraps', as a friend once put it. We were about to head off for the wedding photos, but being the cricket tragic I am, I thought I'd take a quick peek at the telly before we left – just to see how Australia was going in the Test. The Kiwis were answering back in their second innings with a solid knock on the WACA's sun-baked pitch. But instead of finding out the score I saw the players, like seagulls flocked together, walking off the ground. My ten-year-old son turned to me with concern in his gumtree-green eyes and a quaver of fear and uncertainty in his voice.

'Something terrible has happened in Paris, Mummy,' he said. My heart plummeted. Harming anyone or anything for political, economic, religious or any other reason lies beyond my comprehension. I knew there would be mothers on the other side of the world grieving the loss of their children, and children the loss of their parents. Losses far greater than mine. Perspective in place, I pulled on my best cowgirl boots, switched off the TV and hugged my children to me.

As we set off, me in my new flowery dress and our little pony in tow and the kids with the cricket set, I tried to keep the certainty in my heart that the world really is a good place . . . if we humans allow it to be and if we choose to see it that way.

In the backyard at the wedding, a crowd of bluegrass, blues and Irish folk musos held their beloved guitars, harps, violins, fiddles and flutes aloft to make a walk-through archway for the couple. Holding hands, Fred and Rachael made their way to a rustic gypsy wagon to tie the knot. It was there in the crowd I felt again the presence of my compass in my Australia. A place of peace, of love, of Aussie humour and goodwill. If I had to move to a town, I thought, it may as well be one as friendly, beautiful and peaceful as this one.

The crowd laughed as the couple exchanged banjos and an in-house muso joke, saying 'with this tone ring, I thee wed'. When the bride kissed the groom, laughter and applause rose up into a blue summer sky, and as their children hugged their now-wed parents I hoped that the sound and sensations of all that love and goodwill would waft into the skies and reach Paris and Syria, and to all those torn by war. I hoped the sounds of love were arcing to the natural world and animals too, caught in the crossfire of rigid human beliefs and hatred.

That night my life began to expand, renewed. At the wedding, I met a couple – both nearly ninety, married for over sixty years – who told us stories of seeing the last thylacine when they were little. In the paddock next door a mob of kids used plastic electric-fence posts as javelins in their own mini rural Olympics and then played cricket until it was too dark to see the tennis ball. I sang Irish ballads with people I'd never met. I relished the crowd of down-to-earth folk, as a man in shorts, with odd woollen Tasmanian-made Mongrel socks, one knitted in green and the other in rainbow hues, danced on the back lawn. Eating mountains of fresh, wonderful food, everyone spoke of peace, freedom, getting along, honouring the earth and each other, and before the night was done, there was not one strawberry left in that giant bowl.

The Clearing

I began my rural journey as a knotty-haired tomboy playing in the singing creeks of southern Tasmania with frogs, tadpoles, skinks, mud and rocks. I had holes ripped in the knees of my hand-me-down boy jeans and would spend hours gazing at tiny living creatures in clear, sparkling water that shone and warbled over moss- and algae-covered creek stones. The Tasmanian land at Runnymede that my father was involved in was undergoing rapid change due to the fact its new owner, a civil engineer, had brought in some big machines to sculpt the landscape from that of marsh and bushland into a farm.

Right from the start there was conflict within me. I was a girl who loved the fairy glades of ferny rocky creek beds that offered a backdrop to my imagination, and yet all around were the ravages of the dozer blades that had fallen ti-tree, wattle and peppermint gums, and dozed sags, ferns, tussocks and rocks. The remnants of a beautiful bushland were windrowed into long giant heaps and left to dry. Then months or years later, on an autumn day when the wind was right, we would gather as a family and watch the burning. I would see graceful huntsmen she-spiders scuttling from the smoke, watch silver-sided skinks panic from log to log and hope with all my heart that any possums, quolls or Tassie devils sleeping in the piles would escape the furnace. Around the heaps the soil had been disced by iron ploughs, then harrowed and then sown with firstly turnips and swede, then later with improved pasture species that were delivered in giant bags from seed companies, and mixed with hard little white lumps of superphosphate fertiliser that was mounded in small mountains in the paddock. Back then the government helped subsidise superphosphate so it was literally bought by the truckload.

I would look at the rocky, black clay soils and sometimes-sandy loam patches that were now the home to a flock of Polwarth sheep on virgin pastures and wonder at it all. Through the innocent eyes of a child, I innately knew the brutality of the men's action, but was reliant on the teachings of adults that this was a great and masterful thing. I would ask my father why they had to doze all the bush – why couldn't they just graze the animals in grassy patches amongst the trees? I don't think he ever saw my naive viewpoint, but I was, after all, *just a girl*, whereas my brother was earmarked for greater things due to his status of older sibling and boy.

My father did try to bring clarity of mind to his blue-eyed, rather confused daughter by pointing out the young sapling stands of timber that the dozer driver had been instructed to leave for shelter for the sheep. Later, he would show me how wonderful it was that the turnips were edging their way out of the exposed soil and indicate how the sheep had nibbled the core of the turnip out so that a shell, like a half-buried skullcap, remained in the ground. The stench from sheep on a turnip crop is something to experience – like gas from an ancient swamp – and those farting ovines told me it wasn't natural for the animal, nor this land. Maybe in England, but not here. Wandering off, I would go stand in the remaining shelter belts of young trees and shut my eyes and try to recapture what the landscape had looked like before the clearing, and picture the diverse plants the sheep would've preferred. Who would want to eat turnip all day long?

To me what was once a garden of Eden had now been 'tidied up', as Dad always put it, into a 'farm' that looked for all the world to me like a war zone – similar to the footage I'd seen as a toddler on the TV news when reports from Vietnam were beamed into our lounge room. Back then even in black-and-white I could visualise the colour of blood and the pallor of men at war. Amidst the remaining saplings I felt a similar war-torn grief from the land. I could see in my mind's eye the landscape as it had been: the way the sunlight had filtered through treetops in a silver-and-gold sheen of light. In those sunbeam curtains in the bush, little moths and butterflies had flittered about and I'd be mesmerised in this world as the tussocks shone and lit spider webs drew me towards them in fascination. There were songs and secrets to be heard, whispered in the leaves of the gums above me as the breeze blew, because I was the kind of child who heard such things. But now all I saw were the pushed-up butts of logs, roots held in the air like clawed fingers reaching as if they were desperate to be rescued by the sky above. I would frown against the sun beating down on soil that was once a shaded, secretive and pristine landscape, and wonder at the adults' choices.

Sometimes as we walked over the new paddocks, I noticed little waterways where I'd once met a blue-tongue lizard or a little brown frog were all but destroyed, dozed over, and the contours of the land reshaped to suit the investor farmer's straight and tight fence lines. I've since been to those shelterbelts where I used to ride my pony. Little Tristan, patched with dun and white, would walk up to his knees in kangaroo grass, snatching at seed heads with his velvet muzzle. We'd jump the fallen logs the men never bothered to snig out, Tristan's ears pricked, his black tail swishing. Now, over thirty years on, those same shelterbelt trees have just about all died. What hasn't been cut for firewood are grey bones on the ground, and the native grasslands that used to grace the area have all but been grazed out and replaced with British varieties of pasture-like cocksfoot, clover, phalaris and rye. There are no lizards or frogs to meet nor even much birdsong left, save for a flock of introduced cockatoos that have taken over in great numbers, looking like white washing on a loaded line when they sit screeching in the few remaining long-dead ringbarked grey gums.

Even the marshland on the lower country, where as kids we would wade through floodwaters catching long snake-like shiny black eels, is now devoid of pin rushes due to the large drainage system created by big machines. With the recent weather patterns of low rainfall, the area barely floods and I sometimes wonder how those long-buried eels survive in the silted-up dam beds, if at all. Tenaciously the native hens, or bush chooks as we call them, still remain on the marshes in their army-green feather jackets and stalk about on their ready-to-run stick legs. But the canopied world that I would play in before the dozers came has long been destroyed. The land now has a same-same blandness of very little natural life. To those who hadn't witnessed and felt the pulse of it over three decades ago, you wouldn't notice its absence now. These days, to the everyday viewer, it would simply look like what we now term 'farmland'.

Despite this early deep insight and conflict in my childhood mind that we were damaging the landscape, I came to embrace agriculture, adore sheep with a passion, and love farming with all my heart. My father was the son of a farm labourer. Through tenacity and sheer hard work, Dad made good and became a Hobart solicitor, specialising in company law. Eventually he put enough of his hard-earned dollars aside to buy a small farm to enjoy on weekends with us kids. But for me, weekends weren't enough. I had a double dose of country in my veins, with my mum being the daughter of Derwent Valley farmers who had land connections running back to the Tasmanian highlands at Bothwell and the coast at Dunalley. I wanted more than weekends! I wanted to be immersed in the land right from the start. Agriculture, writing stories about it and studying it daily, was to be my only path.

But in watching the demise of soil health and in turn human health over the past thirty years, I'm finding that my old love for rural culture is strained. I mean no disrespect to my forebears, nor my father, nor men and women who have toiled to clear this land, but I am hoping to reach for a new future for agriculture through new farming methods. I see a future that is balanced, one that honours the land in the way Indigenous cultures do, so there is a placement of reverence upon it. So that we can all survive as a species and have a planet that is thriving, not dying.

I can see agriculture splitting, like the way a road does . . . there are three routes: one is that of an old meandering highway like we still have here in Tasmania. It's a road on which the traditional farming family travels. This is where the (usually male) farmer hands the land down to (most likely) the eldest son and they jokingly deem the son's inheritance into farming as a form of 'child abuse'. This is due to the lack of profits and perceived life of struggle on ever-declining soils, with rising costs like fuel, herbicide, pesticide and fertiliser (a post–World War II system that is based on using leftover chemical by-products from war and that is described as 'best practice' by Australian government advisors).

The second road, which is more like a six-lane highway, is the corporate system of agriculture, whereby technology, profit-driven commodity production and overseas investment drive methods of producing food that is not so much 'food' as it is filler for marketed 'product'. It's a fast-paced, sterile, straight-lined road to travel and those who don't keep up with the speed of it fall away. Diversity in nature and healthy ecology have no place here, and even though you may find more women in this system, there is no sign of Mother Nature's feminine principles of cyclical and slow. I've read articles that claim that in Australia we are now producing oranges that contain zero vitamin C due to farming practices that are more concerned with profit than human health. Nutrition in food produced in this autobahn-style of farming has been steadily in decline since the 1950s so that when you shop in the fruit-and-vegie section of the major super-markets, you may be shortchanging your body on much-needed vitamins and minerals, even though you think you are making a healthy choice. In this system we pay supermarkets cents per kilo, not cents per bodily goodness, and it's costing us dearly.

The final road – the road I want to travel down and the road I want to take you down – is the dirt one. The road less travelled. Down this road are the slower travelling methods of farming that will nurture clear-flowing waters that have been filtered by healthy, fecund, breathing soils that underpin a multi-layered farming system. Methods that not only produce chemical-free, nutrition-filled food, but that embrace ecosystems as a whole and build human communities on farms and in rural town-ships. In these systems there's not only room for women, but also children. And there's also room for food infused with love. What could be healthier?

I was raised in a household where meals were cooked and presented to the breadwinning man at the head of the table, business shirts were ironed as stiff as his briefcase for him, and children were silenced and shut away in their rooms at news time. It was all in order to serve the man of the house. His peace and happiness was paramount. It was classic fifties stuff that carried through into the late sixties when I was born. I learned early that those women not wearing aprons, and the ones who were young and pretty enough, were objects for men's sexual enjoyment. As a six-year-old, hidden behind the couch, I saw enough on the TV of Benny Hill chasing half-naked women and Alvin Purple's sexist soft porn to find out where I stood in the world as female. It was not a good place.

With an older brother who had a different relationship with my dad, gender stereotyping hit me hard and early. They share a language seeded around masculine, knock-on-wood 'real' world things like share portfolios and company law. It's a language some women can learn, but I've never wanted to. My reality innately had those extra points on the compass.

What was real and tangible to me was possibly airy-fairy stuff to them. Right from the beginning, I was never going to be the girl I was expected to be. I was never going to be a lawyer or a doctor type. I couldn't do numbers to save myself. I was never going to make a Hobart society wife either. I didn't like dolls or dresses.

Instead I drifted with clouds and dandelion seeds blown in the wind. I was distracted by colour and light. I shrank into a shell of terror from the outside world and emerged in glowing light in my inner world, knowing I was made of the Divine. I conversed with fairies and angels. I liked cowboys and Indians and torn jeans. Along with my complexities, I was a grumbly tomboy in a world where pretty, demure, compromising girls were rewarded. Adding to that I was born a creative, and dubbed 'a mad writer like your grandmother'. Still, despite feeling a fringe-dweller to my own family, I acknowledge the love in which I was raised. It was love made jagged by the era, but it was love nonetheless.

As I fly back in time and hover over that clearing that I witnessed as a child, I know in my heart that if a woman had been in charge of converting that land into a farm, she would have gone about it vastly differently. The landscape's beauty and diversity would've been retained, and all the creatures would've got to share in some way.

When I found myself at the age of forty-one, without the paternal support I craved trying to escape a toxic marriage, I sought the refuge of a single room on my friend's farm next door. Crammed into one bed with my kids, I realised the depth of my lack of self-worth. I was ill equipped to reason with the blokes who had ousted me and negotiate a better way forward with them. In my world, women had been conditioned to put up and shut up. So I did. I gave in and walked away with nothing. That's what a woman does when their core belief is 'I am not worthy'.

On paper, I was better qualified as an agriculturalist and had worked hard on the practical implementation of farming since I'd left school. Hadn't I proved my stripes that I belonged on my farm? That I was capable? Was my father doing the best he could, thinking he was protecting me from the workload farming brings by keeping my primary school teacher ex-husband on the farm instead of me?

In 2003 when I returned as a married woman to my father's hobby farm of 800 acres, it ran a motley lot of Merino wethers. Dad said fondly that some of the sheep were 'old enough to draw a pension'. Those big smelly wethers, thinning from age with crispy dry wool, came with yellow teeth worn down to stubs like dehydrated corn kernels. Whilst my then-husband worked off farm, I set about converting the farm from a profitless tax deduction into a respectable farming business. I convinced the blokes that we ought to lease more country, so that our flock grew to 2000 sheep, a mix of wool and prime lamb production, run on over 2000 acres of pasture and bushland. Also, there were my Hereford girls I'd bought from a jillerooing mate of mine. Quiet, regal beauties, who produced pixie-faced calves that kept coming, so soon we had a herd of thirty gorgeous bovine ladies. To drought-proof the business, and silence the ongoing 'not enough rain, not enough feed' loop of complaint, I steered us into a partnership with our neighbours and put in a hydroponic fodder shed that had the capacity to produce up to 2.5 tonnes of sprouted barley per day. It was fresh, easily digestible, regular stock feed that I weaned cattle onto and fed to our sheep regularly so our wool was sound and our lamb weights would be good for the trade. It meant I could take pressure off our grazing land too, and slow our paddock rotations down so the landscape could rest. We also began to sell the fodder to horse owners as well. It was lush, vibrant stuff that we pulled out of the trays like long green shag-pile hall runners after eight days of growing time. Twice weekly I bundled my little son into the ute to do 'Fast Grass' deliveries to horse owners whilst my daughter was at school. I remember the days fondly as it was around the time my little blond-haired cherub boy was learning to count. And count he did, as we drove to the rumbling of the diesel engine of my Holden Rodeo.

'Ninety-six, ninety-seven, ninety-eight, ninety-nine . . . *One hundred*!' he would say breathlessly. 'Phew! I did it.'

'Good boy!'

'Now I'm going to start again, Mummy!'

'Okay,' I'd say, pulling a 'is he serious?' face. 'Great!'

'One, two, three . . .'

They were busy but wonderful times, filled with purpose and a vision. Plus, for a born nurturer like me, there was something so satisfying being with my child, delivering grass to racehorses who were stabled most of their lives or kept on bare paddocks. I knew their acidic grain-tied guts were gaining relief from the feed we were supplying.

Dovetailed into life was my love of training working dogs,

which I bred and sold at the Victorian Casterton dog auction. For Mothers' Day, with a royalty cheque from one of my novels, I bought myself some portable sheep yards that I erected outside the front of the house. I could train my pups, wave to my kids on the deck as they played in the sandpit and even sip a beer while the dinner was on, all the while coaxing a young pup into a confident life of sheep work.

We'd also put in horse paddocks and, with the help of friends and neighbours, built a round yard. For a time a black glossy waler stallion became part our family and we began to breed a few stock horses. I was also generating off-farm income from writing novels and channelling that into the farm. Life was busy, and blissful because my babies were with me – both my two-legged and four-legged kids – and I was holding on tenaciously to my right to write, despite spousal grumbles. Life held the potential to be extraordinary for all of us. But there was one sticking point. The men in my family. They couldn't seem to share nor see my vision. Dutifully, I fulfilled my perceived role of wife, mother, daughter. I was constantly on call for them, in the house, the farm office, the yards, the paddock and the shearing and fodder sheds, always there for my babies but constantly putting my needs as a woman last. Over time, I felt like I was cracking from not being watered. Like the grassland, I was being pared back to something I wasn't and wilting from lack of nurture. The men would come into our home bringing with them clouds of negativity that, like the rain-less clouds outside my kitchen window, just made me sadder. The more I looked at my internal landscape and then to the external landscape, I knew the old farming and social systems weren't working. Like me, the land and the animals were struggling.

Instead of doing the same thing over and over again and expecting a different outcome, I began to seek methods that would help solve our problem. I'm not saying I'm an heroic farm girl like the girls in my novels . . . Some days in my writer's head I was distracted, dreaming up descriptions of sheep moving across pasture, and I would forget to check a trough or shut a gate. I'd be lost in my creative thought. But there was one thing absolute about me when it came to the farm. I was utterly passionate about it and my life on it. However, I was yet to learn some blokes are terrified of passionate women.

In my research, I began to see the parallels in the treatment of the land with the treatment of myself. The feminine of the land was being neglected and so too was I. I wanted to change how we farmed our land and keep the chemicals away from my children. I wanted to be honoured in my new status as mother. Yet motherhood had seemed to disempower me in the world of men. It hadn't given me the extra standing I thought it would. I was pushing for change but the men in the family were having none of it. My quietly rebellious mum was like me, mute in a culture that had taught women to 'disappear' themselves.

By the time my second child started school I was exhausted. I withdrew into myself. I shrunk into a pall of gloom inside the home, only coming alive again when I was in my beloved bushland with my dogs and children by my side, or escaping to my writing world.

I recall a female farming mentor of mine drawing me aside. With her older woman wisdom, she must have seen that I was being drained energetically. She looked into my weary eyes and said my name as if she felt sorry for me. As my son and daughter dabbled about in a mud puddle, she must've seen how I nervously kept an eye on the mood of the men. I remember her hand on my arm, and the glint in her eye.

'Have you got a Fuck-off Fund, Rachael?'

'A what?' I looked at her, puzzled.

'Every woman needs a Fuck-off Fund,' she said matter-of-factly in her Tassie drawl. 'Are you putting any money aside for yourself? Just in case. I have. I know I'll never leave him, but it's nice to know I could fuck off any time if I wanted to.'

I reeled at the horror of the thought. I had never entertained the idea. When I married, I married for love and for life. But some inner alarm in me dinged. What could she see that I couldn't? When it came to money, I simply trusted that there would be enough, that what was mine was ours. I hadn't been the type of woman to spend money on clothes, redecorating the house or Sunshine Coast holidays. All my book royalties were tied up in cattle yards, sheds and farm equipment, and the red hides of Herefords or dogs and horses.

But what that woman foreshadowed became real. By 2010 my husband remained fixed in the farmhouse that was central to the farm business with my dad's blessing, and I found myself on the farm next door, camping in my best friend's spare room with no money and nowhere else to go. My father hadn't heard me . . . that I wanted to be a full-time farmer who wrote a bit, not a full-time writer, missing a farm for the rest of my life. Throughout the whole mess, my mother just doggedly got on with being a grandmother to my kids, and swallowed the ugly situation and remained silent.

As I lay in that bed, crowded either side by my sleeping children, I wished I'd heeded that woman's advice. My daughter had plaster casts on both legs at the time as treatment for her cerebral palsy. I'll never forget how she would kick me awake as she slept fitfully. We would laugh about it in the morning, but during the sleepless night I knew I didn't want to say goodbye to that childhood place . . . my sacred world of majestic trees I worshipped, bushland groves that sustained me and mountain skylines that gave me my compass point on the earth. Above all, I knew I didn't want to farewell my beloved, beautiful animals: sheep, cattle, horses and dogs I adored with all my heart. There would also be the loss of sharing those precious moments with my children on that place. Would my children be visiting a motherless farm for the rest of their lives?

In the three months we lived in my friend's house, Dad came to the door once. I don't know why. He never really spoke much. But standing beside him, looking like Dad's second-in-charge, was my ex-husband. I remember feeling the same energy a horse must feel when it is compelled to bolt for its very own survival. At the time I kept thinking, *Why did Dad have to come with him?*

As if an answer to a prayer, within months my 'Fuck-off Fund' arrived out of the blue in the form of a modest book advance for a collection of already written short stories. My publisher at the time had no idea just how much she saved my sanity and my life. The money was enough to help put a deposit towards a two-bedroom uninsulated house – a real 'fixer-upper' – in a dying rural community. I had no idea how I would make regular mortgage repayments on it with a vocation like writing, but I knew the children needed a home and stability, so I dived in with blind faith. The house sat on a patch of flat ground on a steeply sloping 20 acres just 6 kilometres up the road from my family farm and just 1 kilometre from my children's tiny country school. The school had only eighteen children and was only just surviving the threat of closure. I thought if I stayed nearby in the district, maybe my father or my brother would eventually ask us back home to the farm. My waiting slid from months to years.

I thought back to when I was a child, seeing the brutal clearing of the land and remembering how I could never understand the masculine economic rationale. In the same way, I couldn't understand my father's silence about me and the kids having to leave the farm to make way for my ex-husband. I also didn't 'get' why my former husband would choose to remain in my childhood district and stay in business with his ex-wife's family, nor did I see how my brother seemed okay with all of that. All I can know is that for those particular men, their intentions were right for them, in their world – a patriarchal world that holds all the power in our society. Nowadays I hold no blame for them. Only a deep gratitude for the lessons they delivered to me.

Since losing my place I have had recurring dreams of homelessness and never being able to find somewhere to lie down and rest. I now have some sliver of a sense of what it must've felt like for those Indigenous families ripped from their heart-places within the landscape. I grieve for my Aboriginal friends now more fully than I ever have. In the same way I grieve for long-remembered special trees I used to touch on my dawn jogs and for the gentle breath seen from newborn lambs on frosty mornings. Rocks, favourite strainer posts, sags that always looked like wallabies, on and on my love-memories flow for that place. But why keep trying to go down a road of memories that is now so forever blocked? I asked myself, where does that much crying and self-pity get you? My continuing flow of salty tears would eventually only bring salinity, and salinity gives you barren ground! It was time to move on.

With no money for livestock and fencing, I had to find another way on the 20 acres I had bought in a panic. Little did I know, by moving to that cold house on the hill, with the tired, overgrazed and ploughed paddocks, I was about to embark on the best and worst journey of my life . . . I would be starting all over again, hoping desperately that I could remain in my beloved agricultural industry somehow.

The Wonder of a Working Dog

I once had a kelpie pup I named Taxi. I thought the name would be a great laugh. I imagined the farmer who bought him standing in the midst of a paddock calling out, 'Taxi! Taxi!'

He was a sharp little pup with prick ears, a shiny black coat and those little tan blobs above the eyes that make kelpie faces so endearing. Taxi was one of several pups I would train annually to sell at a working-dog auction and festival in Casterton, a town dubbed 'the birthplace of the kelpie', situated halfway between Adelaide and Melbourne. I loved packing the dogs into the ute on that Queen's Birthday long weekend in June and sailing over Bass Strait to drive to the event. Because Taxi was so utterly gorgeous, as were the other dogs I sold at auction, with my big heart I found it far too gut-wrenching putting all that love and time into a little power pack of canine sheep-shifting fur to sell to an anonymous buyer in a crowd of hundreds. The shouting auctioneer, the dog's ears flattened to the noise, sidling near the handler's legs with nervous glances, and the excruciating moment when the time came to hand over the lead . . . After my babies arrived (the ones without the fur) I was not made of enough steel to keep doing it. It felt to me like I was selling my own children to the highest bidder. I've left that style of selling to others, but a lot of great dogs go through that auction system in Casterton and on to wonderful owners. It's a chance for farmers who don't have the time or the know-how to put the foundations on a dog for working stock to buy some of the best-trained dogs in Australia.

Over the past twenty years, the Casterton auction has also lifted the value, status and meaning placed on working dogs, which is a great thing. Sadly, I've seen incredible cruelty in the rural industry too; dogs bashed semiconscious in sheep yards by angry men until the dogs' spirits were crushed as much as their skulls. Or sheep dogs half-starved, riddled with worms, hauled on chains and zapped by electric collars so brutally that they would fling themselves on the ground yelping in a state of panic. The cruelty didn't stop at dogs, however. I saw horses whipped, yanked, tugged and belted by furious women until the horse's soul eventually seemed to fly from its body, the poor creatures continuing to walk the earth with eyes of the dead, their giant horse hearts still beating. I've seen men, besotted with football on the television, knowingly leave ewes with lambs stuck in them to die under blinding sun while flies laid maggot eggs into their flesh and crows clustered to peck at their eyes. Then there's the billions of microbes in the soil that no one thinks about. Living things butchered each time a plough slices the turf and turns the creatures to the sun. Billions upon billions of living beings fried by sunshine or stubble burning, or wiped out by herbicide sprays or ground grazed bare. The very same animals grazing the land bare also suffering under management systems that leave them malnourished and shelterless. Agriculture can be a brutal, greedy, human-ego-filled place.

But thank goodness that culture is changing. As a species, I believe we are evolving into kinder creatures. Many farmers, livestock workers and dog handlers I know are looking to life's guiding compass – the part within – and many are ready to ask themselves, 'Am I honouring these animals that give me income? Am I honouring the land that I run them on that gives me a home?'

It's at places like the Casterton Kelpie Muster you see the level of skill, intuition and evolution of the human spirit coming forth with gentler ways. Those men and women who have learned to switch off their egos and turn on their empathy with animals are often the ones who top the auction with the most confident and balanced dogs. Those people paying money in the thousands for dogs are also acknowledging the preciousness of the creature they are purchasing, and the skill needed in their training. I am glad we are evolving into softer beings when it comes to our four-legged companions. There is awareness now within the industry that you don't have to be a yee-haaing cowboy around animals to get the job done.

Most meat consumers don't want that either. One of the movies my kids and I watch over and over is *Temple Grandin*, starring Claire Danes. It's a story based on the real-life woman Temple Grandin, who altered the American slaughterhouse process to a kinder way, using her insight into what animals see, hear, smell and feel, generated by her autism. It is brave people like Temple who are making changes to the agricultural industry for the betterment of all animals. We have our own quiet heroes here in Australia who are champions of kinder treatment of animals, like Bathurst-based Graeme Rees, who teaches the most mind-rigid men and women the art of low-stress stockhandling. Graeme became a mentor to me and, after spending time in the stockyards with him, my whole perspective changed on stock flow, and with it my life changed for the better.

Along the path I've travelled with working dogs and livestock handling I've met some of the best, most centred humans, and like the dogs I've encountered, they have all been my greatest teachers. Dogs have taught me to be a better human. They have taught me patience, to temper my temper and to love unconditionally, along with other acts of present-moment mindfulness: like stretching in the mornings, dozing in the sunshine and smiling frequently at the smallest of things. Dogs have opened up my world and given me a richness to living that is ineffable. I owe them big-time. They are my constant companions.

Before my children arrived, for a time I had eleven dogs. Most were roly-poly pups in litters, but others were at various ages and stages of training. Each one was a divine being wrapped up in fur. My desire to become a working-dog trainer began early. When I was little, on Sundays we would pull up in the Ford station wagon outside the manager's farmhouse on my dad's mate's farm. The manager's wife was always cooking a Sunday roast in her electric frypan, the smell drifting out from the house making me wonder at the dedication of that woman. I'd been going to that farm almost every weekend since I was a baby and it fed my hunger for all things agricultural. Until my dad had earned the money to buy the farm next door, we spent our time there, joining in on whatever was happening.

There was one specific event that cemented in me my fascination for a working dog's natural willingness to round up almost anything that moved – including small children, like me! The manager was moving sheep near the shearing shed. I must've been very small because I remember my short little legs could barely keep up over the stony uneven paddock. I was so excited to see the yellow-brown dog with its crazed eyes and lolling tongue blur like a catapulted stone across the pale butter-coloured grass around the fringes of the mob. The sheep were full wool, their cloven hooves en masse eddying dust up around me, so that my vision became one of dreamlike mist.

I remember the elation within me and how it lit my little face into a beaming smile. I was incredulous to be this close to the action. To be set loose on a Sunday away from the confines of the house and into the world of dust, men, dogs and sheep, my hair blowing into stubborn knots that my nana would later brush out, tut-tutting over my 'tomboy' nature and asking me why my mother hadn't tied it back. But I loved to be witness to the almost wordless world of the men. Such strange communicators! Standing side on. Pauses as wide as the paddocks that stretched before them. It was the place of roly wool sheep, ribby-sided dogs and lung-thumping rides in the ute over newly worked ploughed ground. It was the place of lizards on rocks, snakes in sags, taddies in the creek; of sheep, horses and mild-eyed cows. It was a place of bounty to me. I loved to help in the huge vegetable garden that Dad and his mate cultivated every Sunday, containing beans, broccoli, spuds, artichokes, peas, silverbeet, beetroot, carrots, cabbage, spinach and swede. In the evening on the way home we'd cut up a whole side of lamb, me packing chops into boxes with Dad as we stood in the breezy meat house, Dad hacksawing away down a sheep's spine as it hung from a hook. Next to the shed sat the offal pit: a place of fascination, dread and lip-curling grossness for a kid. But I loved it all . . . even then, as young as four or five.

As I stood in that holding yard that day, I saw the sheep come towards me, their faces vanilla-ice-cream white, fresh from crutching shears. How was the dog doing that, I wondered? I don't remember the dog's name but I do remember the manager's red face and his voice getting louder and louder, shouting the dog's name over and over again. Then the dust got thicker and before me a wall of wool, as solid as grey stones, began toppling towards me. I could hear my dad calling urgently. He was shouting that I should run but it was too late. The mob hit me and swallowed me up. My soft baby cheeks met with rubble stone, my teeth and lips crashed on rocks, and the acrid stench of sheep shit enveloped me. Some of the sheep ducked and dived out of my way, so close I could see their fear in those pale-yellow eyes. Some didn't have time to dodge me and I felt myself pummelled on the ground, winded by the fall and pained by the harsh press of those sharp panicked hooves. By the time the sheep storm had passed and dad had hoicked me up by my arm, I was bruised, crying, shaking. I smelt like the underbelly of a shearing shed. Still, it didn't put me off sheep, or working dogs.

'Why did the dog do that?' I asked later.

'It was a young dog. It went the wrong way,' Dad explained. But I somehow knew it wasn't the dog in the wrong. I could feel the chaotic energy: the terror of the sheep, the unhinged unrestrained force of the dog. The yelling of the farm manager. It didn't feel right. That was the moment that set me on a path of discovery into stock psychology. I became fascinated by the synergy between man, beast and dog . . . one that would uncover the fact that dogs never 'go the wrong way'. Only humans do.

My early memories of man's management of dogs included driving through the farming area of Cambridge, near Hobart airport. Of course it's all cloned giant big-buy stores now and the paddocks are smothered with consumerism, but I remember my surprise and delight at seeing rows and rows of sheep dogs tied to steel pegs. I thought it was some kind of dog show.

'What are they doing?' I had asked Dad, eyes glued to the array of leaping, barking dogs jerking on chains as we drove by.

'Hydatids testing,' my father said. I was well familiar with hydatids; a worm that forms cysts in the offal of animals, predominantly sheep, and when eaten, can infect dogs, dingoes and humans with worms. A government-funded school education program had been circulating the Tasmanian classrooms. Sitting at our old wooden desks that still had holes for ink bottles, in my green checked uniform, my eyes had grown wide in horror and fascination at the diagram they'd given us. Circular arrows connecting a sheep to a dog and also to a human who had a see-through stomach and head showing the worms within. It had a sinister feel to it.

'Always wash your hands after playing with dogs,' we were told sternly. When we brought the information home, Mum was able to tell her gruesome stories about her farming family members who had contracted hydatids, or the old-timers she knew who'd died from it.

'If the surgeon slips and cuts the cyst, millions of worms burst out and infect your body even more,' she had said dramatically. 'Your uncle had it once, and his sister . . . you can even get it in your brain.'

It made my little stomach squirm, but still, it didn't put me off dogs.

The hydatids testing went on for weeks, because I remember the next time we drove past, Dad had met the farmers from our Runnymede district there and I found myself on the testing strip, where I was not allowed to pat the dogs. Warning signs were in place. The dogs seemed to sense this was some kind of death camp. They were going nuts on the ends of their short chains that had been hammered into the ground in rows on steel pegs. Farmers, in dull, earth-coloured clothing like the soil itself stood about waiting for results. The vets in white coats had a *Dr Who* feel about them and seemed menacing to a young girl's eyes, like they were being cruel.

'What will happen to them?' I asked, watching the dogs excitedly yapping and flinging their bodies against the chains. They were mostly sheep dogs, collies of some type, or the Tassie breed of Smithfield with shaggy coats and pale eyes. There were fewer kelpies in those days in Tasmania. Back then, the kelpie was viewed as more a 'mainland style' of working dog, more suited to hotter, larger properties. Mixed in with the sheep dogs were also farmhouse dogs, so little Jack Russells, Australian silkies or corgi bitzers joined the mix.

'If they test positive, they'll be put down,' Dad said. 'They want to eradicate the disease from Tasmania.' He went on to explain the words 'eradicate' and 'quarantine'. But I had stopped listening. Once realising 'put down' meant killed, I began to cry. I thought of the dogs I had known in the yards at Runnymede and wondered if they would pass the tests. I thought of the farmers who would grieve the loss of their working mates. Would the manager on the farm cry about his dog if it had hydatids?

I don't remember if people wormed dogs then, and I have no idea how many dogs were put down, but it's made me as an adult become a stickler for disposing of sheep's guts properly and worming my dogs.

It wasn't long afterwards that, I discovered my name, Rachael, meant ewe in Hebrew. My brother had laughed at me for it, but I felt like a piece of life's puzzle fell into place. Sheep and dogs. I grew up knowing I wanted to work with those animals and to write about them. So as soon as the school bell rang for the last time, I was off down a dirt road, journal in my bag along with worn old farm boots with hobnails that pressed into the soles of my feet, bound for my first job as a jillaroo on a grazing property.

In my ugly maroon Toyota Corona I zoomed teenage-driver style along the winding dirt roads, dodging brush-tailed possums and Tassie devils towards Tasmania's central highlands and the dolloped grassy high hills between the historic sandstone townships of Bothwell and Ouse, to a property called Ousedale. I soon discovered the locals liked to educate travellers that the Scottish word Ouse rhymes with 'moos'. In the store I found postcards and tourist items stamped with the slogan 'There's more than moos in Ouse'. There sure was! At least for me there was. There was a whole new world on those tussocked hills that felt so much better than the ivy-clad walls of my former private school. As a would-be shepherdess with the name of 'Ewe', I couldn't have found a better first job. Nor a better mentor in Phil Nye, my first boss. He was young but he was the best stockman, teacher and farmer an eighteen-year-old girl fresh out of school could hope for.

It had been my mum's middle sister, Auntie Susie, who prompted the whole experience for me. The year before, she and Uncle Colin had taken me to visit my cousin and their eldest son, Ian, at Orange Agricultural College. I was hooked when I saw the campus, college farm and the syllabus, not to mention the crowds of fresh-faced young ag industry students who looked so free compared to how I was faring in my final year of school. To get into the course, applicants had to have at least a year of practical work under their belt. To help get me into the college, Susie had put in a few calls to her farming network and knew she had found kind and understanding bosses in her friend Louie Nye and her son Phil. I was offered 80 bucks a week, petrol thrown in and board and lodging. A bonus offer was I could take my pony Tristan with me as my very own stock pony. I was beyond excited. My life now heralded brighter days as I threw off the brown school tie and itchy woollen tights of girls' school forever and donned a flannie shirt, boots and jeans.

Phil, no matter how hard the work, or how long the days, would always smile when he spoke. Sometimes he would look shyly down to the toes of his boots, yet I came to see his mannerisms weren't ones of shyness, but incredible self-possession. He was calm from the inner to the outer and his stockmanship and horsemanship reflected that. Even when he was frustrated that a cow had crossed the river to the neighbour's place or a sheep had broken through the fenceline to thieve some of the lucerne crop,

Phil would still hold a smile in his eyes, gritting his teeth with challenge. His voice was soft and soothed horses and mesmerised dogs. What a contrast to that shouting manager I had known as a toddler!

I loved the isolation of the farm by the river that sometimes had more than eight gates to open on the long winding road in, depending on where the stock were. The Nye family were often forgiving of my youthful naivety and, I'm sure, my misguided views of the world, but as a first job it was my dream come to life. It was here I saw such a stark contrast to the stockmanship I'd experienced as a child. Phil communicated all he needed to to his horses with a simple touch or step towards or away from them, with the lift of his hand and the click of his tongue. His dogs looked at him as if he were some kind of deity to bow before. Not in fear. But in adoration.

I came to learn through Phil that farming men do let their working dogs come inside, they do cuddle them by the fireside and play with them and give them food treats. All the old-timers who had told me off as a kid for patting their working dogs could now go jump, as far as I was concerned. The proof was in the pudding in Phil's dog Joe. By day that dog worked like a trouper for his boss and by night snored like a dozer on his patch of rug beside the fire.

This steady-moving, methodical relaxed man went on to become one of the best in the world at teaching horses to trust humans, and was taken on as one of the first Pat Parelli instructors in Australia. Years after I'd left Ousedale my mum sent me clipped pictures of Phil riding his stallion at a gallop, saddleless and bridleless. I have since learned that every experience we live, 'good' or 'bad', is a gift. I had seen the worst of stockmanship and I'd seen the best. I knew I wanted to travel the road Phil was on in terms of communicating with and handling animals.

It was no wonder that years later, after agricultural college and then a degree in communications at the university in Bathurst, as a young journalist for the *Stock and Land* newspaper, I found myself at the steep, green-hilled, windswept home of Paul Macphail at Welshpool who didn't just 'train' dogs, but *educated* them. Along with the dogs, Paul reshaped the minds of humans too. And I was one of his pupils with my first ever working dog, Dougall.

Dougall came as a surprise gift from a former boyfriend in the mid-1990s after a lifetime of me longing for a dog, but my parents refusing. Al was a beautiful, tall boy from Orange with blue eyes and thick dark curly hair. Not only was Al an electrician – a sparky – with a tool belt around his lithe hips, he was a motorbike rider, whitewater rafter, water polo player and an all-round nice Aussie bloke. But if I thought the guy was gorgeous, Dougall was even better! (More faithful, to start with.) He had a parental mix of a wandering red kelpie father from up the Molong Road and black-and-white border collie mum. He arrived to me as a tiny tricolour puppy in an airline crate when Al came to see me in Tassie. As Al grabbed his baggage from the trailer towed in by airport staff, that young man gave me the surprise of a lifetime.

I had no idea the dog would be mine as I peered into the giant dog crate and cooed at the minuscule sheepdog puppy with frightened brown eyes wedged at the back. Suddenly, Al wrapped his big hand around the handle and lifted the crate up.

'He's yours,' he said, a smug 'good boyfriend' smile on his face.

'Mine? Really!' Tears welled in my eyes in shock, surprise and delight. Al had just revved over a family boundary that said I couldn't have a dog. Unplanned, I at last had my own working dog!

Dougall was as nutty as a Picnic bar and having come from a litter that consisted of just one – him – he was slightly left of centre but burst himself inside out to please me. Whilst Al didn't stay by my side over time, Dougall did. He slotted into my world and became my constant companion. At the time I was still living with my parents, saving for an overseas trip, so my mum and I snuck him into the house and he was there for three months before my father even knew we had a dog.

Dougall lifted my heart to a place of joy and made me braver than I was. For a time I had to leave Dougall as I adventured overseas. A good friend of mine whom I'd cheekily nicknamed 'Filthy Fee', a sheep-groom based at Conargo in New South Wales, babysat Dougall for a year, and there he got to enjoy billabongs, sheep work and a visit to the Conargo Hotel now and then. When I came home I was hired as an Australian Broadcasting Corporation rural radio reporter, and Dougall had to be hired too. Before the ABC let me loose in Sale, Victoria, I did a stint of training in Burnie, Tasmania. Here Dougall sometimes came on air to bark to listeners when giving my rural report. He often had to be shushed when he played too robustly with my colleague Elaine Harris' seeing-eye dog, Dorrie. The golden lab and the sheep dog would rumble in the offices outside the broadcast booth while Elaine and I were on air, sometimes sending an office chair whizzing across the carpet, or Dorrie delivering up a giant 'Woof!' right when the weather was being read out. Dougall became a bit of a hit within the ABC, and was asked to Christmas drinks, travelling up in the glass lift for a rooftop soiree in Melbourne and talking with cricket commentator Tim Lane.

Those ABC days in Sale were the time I met my future husband, who was then running droving trail rides on his family cattle-grazing runs in the snow-gum country above Dargo. Dougall gave him the tick of approval so he was accepted as a boyfriend. Not long into my work at the ABC I was offered a job with Rural Press as a Gippsland dairy reporter, writing mostly for *Stock & Land*. I was so in love with the written word that I left the radio and, together with Dougall, took the journo job.

I was asked to cover a story on Paul Macphail's 'Working Dog Education' program. Of course I had to take Dougall to the interview too. Here I saw clearly Dougall's lack of breeding and sheep-work finesse, but he made up for it with unshakeable loyalty and obedience to me. This turned him into a very handy dog that on command would back, bark, gather runs, roll over, play dead and ride with me on a horse through the High Country, not to mention doing party tricks and dancing. He came home from rural shows with blue ribbons and prizes of bags of dog tucker for his dog high jumping efforts, his record almost 3 metres, scrabbling up a wall of boards to be with me on top of bales of hay on the back of a ute. As the time wore on, I became obsessed with getting better at stock handling and I returned often to Paul's, practising my handling skills on Dougall and using Paul's better-bred dogs with more style to learn further. Watching. Listening. Soaking it all in, always with the view to returning to Dad's farm one day where I could be the best sheep farmer and dog handler I could be. Paul and I became friends, so after I moved back to Tasmania with my fiancé, I began to facilitate schools for Paul and help him out demonstrating pups at Agfest, a three-day festival run by the Rural Youth organisation every May in Tassie.

At one of the schools during a lunch break, Paul asked me to step outside the shearing shed with old dog man Wes Singline, who was visiting the school.

'Show Wes Dougall's trick,' Paul said to me with a grin, nodding down towards my dog. I glanced at Wes, nervous to be showing my eccentric canine to a man who was renowned for his dogmanship.

'Dougall,' I said, looking down to him, 'go back. Go *waaaay* back!'

With his funny 'one ear up, one ear down' look, Dougall bounded away in an anticlockwise cast around some sheep in a holding paddock. Just when he was on the fringes of the mob I shouted, 'Dougall! Roll over!' Dougall, at full pelt, flung himself into the air, in a perfect body-flipping commando roll. He found his feet, and kept casting. I called again, 'Dougall! Roll over!' He gave another spectacular thrilling tumble, then regained his race to get to the other side of the mob of sheep, perfectly on balance to where I was standing. I raised my hand and without a word or a sound, he sat. Then I whistled and he set about mobbing the sheep and bringing them to us.

On seeing the commando roll cast, Wes was shaking his head, wheezing laughter.

'In all my years,' he chuckled, 'I've never seen a dog do that! Not in all my years.'

I've never seen another dog like Dougall either. No two are ever the same. He saw me through, that dog. By my side on travels around Australia with my job as a journalist, he also came to work on a cattle station in outback Queensland, tailing cattle. He was an intense worker. Just before wet season, water points were few and far between on musters on the Rolleston property. Dougall worked so hard his back legs cramped so I had to carry him for a time on the front of the saddle until we reached a trough. In 2002, with my other dogs, Diamond and Gippy, Dougall walked down the aisle with my bridesmaids on my wedding day on a riverside paddock. He travelled with me, on towards becoming a wife, a novelist, and falling pregnant. But dear Dougall left me a few months after my daughter arrived inside me. It was as if he was making room in my life for her. I'm not sure if he died from overwork on a hot day, or if it was snake bite in the yards near the shearing shed that took him from me. I was inside at the time crafting my first novel, *Jillaroo*, and my fiancé had borrowed him because he didn't have his own dog and there was sheep work to be done on my cousin's place. I can still hear that last haunting cry at the vet's before Dougall died. A mournful moan of 'I don't want to die. I don't want to leave you.' He was a do-anything, go-anywhere dog and the grief I felt in losing him was beyond description. I still miss his comical presence, even today, well over ten years later. After we drove home from the vet with his body wrapped in a sheet, my Auntie Susie sat me down and Uncle Col gave me a shot of whiskey, while my cousin dug a hole to bury the dear boy, who was still only seven years young when he died.

It was Dougall who led me to Paul Macphail and it was Paul who led me not only into the colourful world of working dog breeders and dog schools and trials, but also into a journey of self-discovery and self-awareness. Out of the blue, Paul gave me a book called *You Can Heal Your Life* by Louise Hay. On its cover were rainbow colours and a photo of a lady's smiling face dolled-up Yank style with short blonde hair. At the time, I wondered what on earth that book had to do with dog training, but as time wore on I saw it had everything to do with it.

'I think you need this book,' Paul said. I took it from him, a little perplexed. But after I read it, I knew Paul could see I was blocked in a lack of self-love and confidence. I couldn't become a better handler if I was 'unconscious' to the inner workings of myself. I don't think Paul will ever know what he began in gifting me that book. It turned me into a scholar of life and a seeker of what it is to be human. I began to search for more and more information on how humans function in the world. At the time, the contents of the book were a revelation to me. After I first read it, I began to post sticky notes on the mirror as reminders to myself about self-love and life's riches. I began to see how I had given away my power to society's false beliefs and put myself last behind others. I began to consume other similar books, and search the internet for even more information, then I would weave my new understanding throughout my novels and into my life.

Through meditation and practised mindfulness I became witness to my own behaviour and how it was reflected back at me through dogs, horses, people, my health, my landscape and livestock. I began to want to change the beliefs I'd absorbed as a child and learn to love myself fully and trust the world and the process of life. There comes a point where you have to own the circumstances you find yourself in. It has nothing to do with other people, and everything to do with yourself. Dogs reflect this to us clearly on so many levels. We can never blame them for going the wrong way. We take them that way.

I have Paul to thank for the path of enquiry. It's not only made me a better dog woman, but also a better mum and, I hope, a better person. In the same way I raise my dogs, I never tell my kids they are naughty or bad. I correct their behaviour if it needs it, but I praise them constantly and deliberately. Never do I hit them or stifle them with diminishing words. Like with puppy training,

I may use tones in my voice to reach the parts of their brains that need to learn social and safety boundaries. With guiding young animals it is about pressure and release, just as it is with children, and love, love, love. Like my pups, I want my kids to be curious and waggy-tailed about life. Not cowering, robot-like, too afraid to express themselves, ashamed of themselves or limited by labels.

The most recent road trip we three took was again a ute journey crammed in between school terms. The kids and I stuffed the ute full of swags, bags, our two kelpies and the poodle. We were headed from Tasmania to Hamilton in western Victoria for a two-day working dog school with my long-term Casterton auction friends, the masterful dog trainer Ian O'Connell and his amazing, energetic wife, Kay.

Why did I choose this kind of holiday for my kids instead of a trip to a Gold Coast theme park or a beachside resort? It's because I want them to know you don't have to follow everyone on the major highways of life. There are different paths to travel, and different ways to view the world. The choices will be up to them and their imaginations. And I also wanted to give my young country kids a foundation of awareness about dogs and livestock from one of the best handlers in Australia. Given that I was no longer on our farm with them to teach them such skills, Ian was a perfect mentor to show my children the kind way with animals.

So there they were, my beautiful children, aged eleven and twelve, sitting in a shearing-shed classroom, in front of a whiteboard, with Ian standing before us all. To quickly sketch him in,

Ian O'Connell was the founder of the Casterton Working Dog Auction over twenty years ago. He is a champion dog trialler, and yearly attracts payments for his young dogs of more than $12 000 each. Beyond those very human tags of accomplishment, he's peaceful with people and animals, and imparts his knowledge with a deft, gentle touch. He's also hilarious.

In our morning session at 'dog school' Ian had two young kelpies, Sally and Boris, tied up to the steps flanking the raised board where the shearers normally work. There were no sheep in the shed today, only eight young male rural trainees from the Rural Industry Skill and Training Institute (RIST) and a few other young agricultural workers and one woman. The kelpie pups were lively and curious, but Ian had instilled in his two young prodigies an inner compass of confidence and calm. Their bright eyes were soaking up the situation they found themselves in, and then gazing back in adoration at their human hero. In front of Ian, sitting at desks beneath the corrugated-iron roof, were young future farmers, equally as keen as the pups to soak up information. Behind them, idle for a time, was the stack of computers containing their course content. For the next two days Ian would be making sure the computers were put away and the students encouraged to focus on the dog they had on the end of the lead and their own ways of being. How they walked, how they talked, what they were conveying to their dogs in their voice and body language. The inner to the outer.

After our morning session we gathered to see Ian's training

principles in action in the yards. Here, the kids were witness to Ian's deep wisdom, infinite compassion and brushstrokes of genius as he humbly demonstrated perfect synergy between man, dog and sheep upon land. All the components were pieced together in a beautiful dance of mindfulness and self-control. No hard cussing. No harsh treatment. No panic. With Ian and his pups it's all praise, praise, praise, along with pats and pampering, even if it all goes pear-shaped and the pup gets it wrong and sheep scatter. It's all positivity. You can feel it. I watched my children light up when they saw Ian in action with the nimble but sensitive Sally, and the bold-as-brass Boris. He tempered himself to suit the temper of his trainee.

When it was my kids' turn, they grabbed their dogs with glee. I could tell they had a sense of apprehension and nervousness, but like the pups, were keen to at least try. Our veteran dogs, Rousie and Connie, hadn't had any stock work in years, not since leaving the farm. In the backyard of the rental they have the occasional task of putting the chooks to bed some nights, and they do it with great seriousness and skill. Rousie was only just starting out as a working dog when we had to leave the farm, so I'd barely had him around sheep. I had no idea what he would be like with my son working him. Connie had more miles under her collar, so I teamed her up with my daughter who, due to her cerebral palsy, can sometimes be unsteady on her pins.

Dear old Connie, who is deaf and a bit blind, slightly batty with age and impersonates a labrador with the size of her girth, was still a champion the moment she set paw inside the round yard. She worked the sheep for my daughter like a dream, crouched down, slinky wolf-like and steady. I saw the serious face on my daughter as she lost all sense of what was going on around her. For her it was just her, her dog and the sheep that huddled at her legs. As the dog drifted around the sheep, I saw my girl catch the buzz . . . of working a dog and ovines quietly through the yards. Ian looked on, pleased. It was his breeding he was witnessing in Connie. Ian had given me Connie as a pup, well over a decade ago, as a thankyou gift from the community of Casterton for writing my novel *The Stockmen*. It was a story about both the Casterton Kelpie Festival and my fictionalised version of the history of the kelpie and Jack Gleeson, the Irish stockman credited with founding the breed. When I was on the farm, Connie and my border collie, Diamond, were my main girls in moving sheep. I couldn't have done the mum thing and the stockwork without them, and each time Connie steadily did her job, I would send out a thank you to Ian for his amazing gift in her.

I was originally going to call the pup Cassie after the township of Casterton, but at the last minute I changed my mind. Ian had been such a champion, giving me the idea to write a novel about Jack Gleeson and cheering my efforts on as a mum, dog woman and writer, that I named the pup Connie – short for O'Connell. The next step for Ian and me is to have a film producer see the potential in *The Stockmen* as a movie. We want to make Jack Gleeson and the story of the kelpie breed part of our nation's psyche and what better way than to put the story on the big screen!

A few days after Ian's school, when the kids went to visit their rellies in Gippsland with their dad, my old mate George Pickles, who is a stock contractor, offered me a day's work drenching sheep so I could give the dogs a bit of a go and reconnect with my favourite place on earth – the stockyards. Rousie did me proud, and as we drenched nearly 2500 sheep on a back road near Hamilton I was in seventh heaven. George did me proud too. Instead of a bustling noisy day, we worked steadily and calmly in relative silence, apart from the air compressor for the drenching machine. The day flowed. The sheep flowed. My heart healed a little more.

As we hoisted the stock contractor's gear onto the back of his truck and loaded the dogs, George gave me one hundred bucks. It was the best hundred bucks I'd ever earned.

My son is bursting at the seams to breed kelpies and border collies and train them like his mum did when she had a farm. We talk about it each day, and each day we get closer to our wishes being fulfilled. I know that the divinity of a dog that will be the leverage to get us three back onto a farm.

Catching the New Farming Wave

Picture a road that hurtles you along like a theme park ride. It has a narrow blacktop strip and faded curving double white lines that twist like ribbons in the wind. It dips and turns, spiralling up, falling away, winding up again through deep green tunnels where sunlight strobes through bushland in a maddening flicker. Above you there's the surprise of towering steep-sided cliffs whizzing past, and below, just a couple of metres away from spinning wheels, is a sheer bush-covered drop that is treacherous enough to turn your stomach just glimpsing it. A sudden gap in the bush reveals a view to the most glorious waters that offer up many Tasmanian moods, depending on the day – slate-grey seas or blues borrowed from the tropics – but each time it is breathtaking.

We would tackle this road when visiting my Auntie Susie and Uncle Colin on their mixed-enterprise farm in Tasmania's north-east, near the tiny town of St Marys. At the time they lived at the top of that mountain climb along a much more subdued, flat, pale dirt road, which ended at an eagle-nest cliff face. Here my mum's sister Suze and her husband Col milked an array of dairy cows of varying breeds but mostly old-style shorthorn, and in a paddock they fattened pigs, who bedded down inside a straw-filled shed at night. On the river-flat paddocks, they ran a few beef cattle and some coarse-wool sheep. Both of them tended a farm vegie garden that was like an Eden to a child in its beauty and bounty, with finger-staining strawberries and crunching green peas. The farmhouse was always alive with kids and cooking and the back step busy with cast-off boots, poddy lambs, cream cans and persistent cats. It truly was the best foundation that immersed me in a multi-enterprise farm business, made up of life and love. Because of it I've never let go of that dream to create a farmscape that supported both ecology and economy.

Even as a keen, but wild, agricultural college student at Orange in New South Wales when we visited farms for our 'case studies', I would view them through the lens of my formative years. Our college was showing us the latest and greatest agriculture on offer as we headed into the 1990s. Impressive though the farms were, I still felt uncomfortable amidst state-of-the-art large commercial piggeries, laser-levelled rice and cotton fields and the huge battery farm chicken sheds. This larger, more intensive style of mono-cropping and industrial single-species meat production sat at odds in my gut. I could see that while the fellas loved the big machines, big inputs and computerisation, and we were taught about futures and grain trading, along with global economics and the importance of deals with China, I always thought that bigger was not always better. To me, local trade and local community support made more sense . . . even though it may have made less cents. This industrial style of system left many questions unanswered for me. There was little room for nature and her cycles, particularly in breeding and reproduction of farm animals. In the modern methods we studied at college, man seemed to tamper with everything and the aim was 'better genetics' and 'increased production', not healthier food. At first I thought maybe I was a 'backward Tasmanian', but during the almost three decades since my rural college days, I've seen agriculture morph into an unrecognisable industry, and our population has never been sicker or more obese. I believe it's because we are getting out of balance with our food systems. There is a chronic absence of agricultural understanding from our political leaders and educational institutions, and increasingly our society is blinded by science that supports corporate agriculture and masculinised economics. Mankind is now mass-producing product for *markets* based on profits, instead of humankind growing food for *people* based on love and need.

These days, Susie and Colin's small multi-layered family farm may be considered 'quaint' by some, but as a Tasmanian I would describe my uncle and aunt's farm system as 'balanced', and that in turn generated recipes for good health for all those who ate the food from it. Their lives were rich beyond measure from the pure food, landscape and simplicity by which they lived. Even though their work was constant, it wasn't solely about financial gains and status. There always seemed time in summer for family, whether it was waterskiing on the coast with friends, kayaking on the river, bushwalking to stunning views on mountain tops or bike riding through national parks for their four kids. In winter there was skiing, or bonfires. Sometimes I got to tag along, and those were my happiest childhood days. Adventures to town occurred occasionally for my cousins with a load of livestock to sell or a ram to cart home in the back of the stock crate. The long road along the valley to the selling centres meant the farm was relatively isolated, and a lot of their customers would buy produce direct from the farm, including homespun wool that both my aunt and uncle still spin on wheels, fireside. Colin's wheel is electric and Susie's has the old-style foot treadle. That simple vignette sums up the difference between the styles of men and women perfectly when it comes to farming! When women are absent from farming systems, it's all electric. That's why, I believe, balance between old and new, masculine and feminine, needs to be returned to our agricultural landscape.

As I sat witness to the changes in farming, I began to think maybe I was becoming idealistic . . . a woman hankering for 'the good old days', but during one of my meanderings on the internet, trying to find a way to make the most of the twenty acres I'd moved onto, I came across a family in Virginia, America, called the Salatins from Polyface Farms. What I discovered was a new movement gaining momentum over there, and it seemed like exactly what I was hankering for. I was so elated when I saw the YouTube clips of Joel Salatin that I signed up immediately to go and hear him speak. Of all the places . . . he was coming to my home state of Tasmania! The island at the arse-end of the world. It felt like it was 'meant to be'.

Seated in the audience next to my cousin Claire, Susie and Colin's youngest, we listened to Joel, his son Daniel and daughter-in-law Sheri speak about their booming business on Polyface Farm . . . 'Poly' meaning 'many'. It was refreshing to be hearing the story of a farm made up of not just one crusty old farmer in a field but many faces, young and old, male and female. The increasingly famous Salatins were leading the charge in meeting the demands of more and more consumers seeking food grown with ecological integrity. Thanks to new thought leader and best-selling author Michael Pollan, Polyface Farm received wide exposure via his book *The Omnivore's Dilemma*. Since then, Joel Salatin has been dished up to mainstream media and has gone from being a relatively unknown visionary pig farmer to a *Time* magazine cover boy.

On hearing Joel speak, I suddenly realised I didn't need my 2000 acres to be a farmer. He told us of a thriving flower business on just a quarter of an acre. Joel offered example after example of people thinking outside the square and bringing innovation to their land and their lives. My heart bloomed that day. The innovation he spoke of spurred me on more than ever to aim for a farming life again . . . on my terms . . . or should I say, on Mother Nature's terms. What Joel and his family have created on Polyface Farm is far from a nostalgic step backwards to the 'good old days'. Instead it's a whole new movement, one that attracts hundreds of people seeking internships on Polyface each year or, as Joel calls them, 'young stewards of the land', as they search for a way forward into a new wave of food production. Pure enthusiasm can be felt just being in the presence of Joel and his family.

The Salatins are very progressive, using technology for social media, marketing and management, yet they are stringent in their respect of Mother Nature's processes. Because of the spray-free food that is grown with faith and love, their business is in a rapid growth phase, with about 5000 health-hungry families buying directly from them. Not only are diverse species of animals run on the farm, but the way the animals are run enhances the soil and ecology in vertically stacked, compatible enterprises. Also they are inspiring a grassroots global revolution of value-adding and direct selling to customers . . . one that has seen Joel tangle with the red tape of bureaucracy. He's amusing and compelling when he speaks of the top-heavy corruption in corporate food systems that we are now suffering from and experience each time we shop for untampered food or even sip our water.

Joel rejects the notion that farmers need to concern themselves with the problem of feeding six billion people on the planet soon. He reckons a farmer only needs to wake up, get out of bed and love what they do, then focus on feeding their local village.

It sounds simplistic, but Joel is right. If we ate in season, bought local from farmers who farm regeneratively, and did away with the giant companies who feed us with crap masquerading as food, then I believe the world would eventually right itself.

During my childhood my brother and I helped feed our local village. We would pedal about our neighbourhood selling surplus vegetables that we'd cultivated on the Runnymede farm, making not only a tidy profit to spend at the shop – in my case on cricket and horse magazines – but also providing our neighbours with fresh, nutritious food. One older lonely widow also seemed to like visits from cheerfully grubby kids on bikes, and many times we were given the additional bonus of a Tic Toc biscuit.

It's only relatively recently that we Tasmanians have been subjected to corporate farming. I'm witness to our land and rural enterprises being sold to offshore buyers. Family farms have been moved aside due to the supermarket stranglehold on vegetable, grain, meat, fish and milk production, and those farmers who do remain are generally using the high-input systems of fertiliser, pesticides and herbicides that are destroying not just the land but their businesses.

Chatting to Joel during a break at his seminar, I soon found his energy was contagious. His positivity and wonder about farming was to a degree evangelical, but I came away with the flame of my love for farming rekindled, my heart healed a little more and hope flooded my being. Here was a farmer – a male – farming with a seven-point compass that included the four earthly directions, but also the other three directions of above, below and within. He was a man of faith. During my talk with him, I also discovered him to be a man, a husband and a father who nurtured his 'female' land, along with his wife, his children and his mother. A noble man with a sense of humour and a quick smile. In his book, *Fields of Farmers*, Joel explains:

> *The miracle of life, whether it's a chick hatching, cow calving, or seed sprouting, draws us irresistibly to the wonder of our nest. That so many people think this visceral relationship with life's daily wonders is not attractive or appropriate for technologically advanced sophisticates indicates a profound hubris and lack of understanding. We are all utterly and completely dependent on soil, honeybees, raindrops, sunlight, fungi and bacteria. Neither the greatest scientific discovery nor the highest gain on Wall Street compares to the importance of a functioning carbon cycle or dancing earthworms.*

Reading Joel's words, I recalled the sun-drenched or rain-sheened paddocks at St Marys, and the farm my uncle and aunt cared for, along with their kids. I became a novelist for the exact reason that Joel expressed. So often farming and the people in it are belittled, simplified, brushed aside as less important. So often within our industry we talk everything down into doom and gloom and depression. I studied agricultural business and communication so I could weave the two together and not just showcase our contemporary industry and its richness, but also to entice young people into a career there. Holistic agriculture has been absent from our educational institutions for far too long, yet farming is a life-affirming vocation. With innovation and vibrant thinking and appreciation, farming can be profitable, emotionally rewarding and a place for abundant living on all levels. It is the foundation of a healthy life for everyone . . . from the farmer through to the customer.

As I stood amidst the crowd of people at the Salatin event, I saw that thoughts are contagious, and the Salatins had thoughts that were worth catching. On that day, I caught the new wave of farming belief – that we can all prosper in systems like Polyface Farm. 'All', including everyone from men and women, to children and microbes.

Recipes for Restoration

In a smoky room in a restaurant called Carnivores in Nairobi, Africa, a cluster of waiters came to stand by me and surprised me by singing 'Happy Birthday' in rich, melodic accents. I was turning twenty-five and I'd just experienced a bizarre meat-heavy meal, sliced off giant skewers directly onto the plate.

'Crocodile, madam?' the waiter had asked. Then later, 'Antelope?' It was a vegetarian's and animal-lover's nightmare but I found the experience a once-in-a-lifetime Kenyan moment. Touring Africa had challenged me on many levels, but I didn't realise just how much until after I returned home. It was then I discovered for the first time the tangible link between good food, good thoughts and good health. My almost year-long backpacking trip that took me to twenty-seven countries around the world set me on another long journey – one of illness.

I found myself once again up on top of the sheer mountains

near St Marys, Tasmania, travelling with my Auntie Susie. She was taking me to a little village of Falmouth to go see the vet. After Africa I was like a car with a flat battery and just couldn't start. No doctor could pinpoint the cause of my illness and after months of being so crook I couldn't work, my Auntie Susie intervened with Tim McManus, a former Department of Primary Industries veterinary officer. Going to stay with him and his gracious, always grinning wife Elaine was a last-ditch effort in finding out what was keeping me so ill. Tim knew exactly what to look for, and led us to a South African pathologist who was working in Hobart, and was well familiar with water-borne parasites and other nasties offered up in Africa. It turned out that my blistered hands after rafting the giant, wild rapids of the Zambezi River in Zimbabwe is not good for one's health! I had contracted bilharzia, a type of blood fluke picked up in warm waters that burrow into your skin and then inhabit your bloodstream and liver. Erk! Once I was treated – ironically and hilariously with the same treatment found in dog wormers – I wound up with chronic fatigue. Again it was the vet, Tim, and Auntie Susie who picked me up and set me on the road to recovery with wonderful recipes for restoration.

A fresh-food diet, exercise and a busy mind were what the vet ordered. At the time, my auntie and uncle had moved out of their St Marys property to make way for their children, all keen on farming. They were now living in a basic cabin on a cheap bit of dirt they called Pebble Plain and were gradually converting it to a grazing property. I spent days on my aunt's fledgling farm in the hills above the Fingal Valley, eating the food they grew. Then I would ride that wild roller-coaster road down to the sea, where I would walk the beaches and coastal dunes and boulders with Tim, studying the world around me with his scientific knowledge feeding my mind. I'd breathe in the blast of fresh sea air and forget my worries. On the final day of my boot camp to wellness Tim made me climb a shale mountain called St Patrick's Head that divides those wild roads in two. It was a mental mountain climb as much as a physical one.

After that, my life and my body moved on. Tim cured me with an apple a day and barley sugars in my pocket, along with good old-fashioned outdoor rambling and enquiry into the environment around me. Auntie Susie kept me busy too, whether it was restoring old furniture, plonking me on my old faithful pony Tristan, or penning up sheep. They fed me on home-hunted roo from animals who knew no stress and from a garden based on Bill Mollison's permaculture principles. The brush-tailed possums were so high in population then, Uncle Colin had created a little island in the dam outside their house. They had a possum-proof bridge and gate to it. Because of this ingenious setup and the moist soils on the island, they had vegies aplenty, and with such good food, my body soon found its compass to wellness.

I was not surprised a few years later when as a rural journalist, still carrying barley sugars in my camera bag as a back-up for flat spots of energy, I came across a famous lecture by a man named Joel D. Wallach. A farm boy from the USA, Joel watched his father treat his livestock cheaply with good nutrition. Calling the vet for drugs was too expensive, so his farming father kept his animals healthy through food and additives of minerals. I pictured all the heavy mineral blocks I'd set down in my time, with the sheep flooding to them with as much excitement as if they were headed to a footy final.

Later, with a degree in agriculture and as a trained vet, Dr Wallach noticed how the human medical system was taking us further and further away from nutritional treatments for human health. His point was that you couldn't patent and sell food nutrition easily if you were a drug company, so they steered society away from nutrition as a solution to ill health and a prevention to disease. Manufactured drugs, however, could be owned and sold through doctors trained by universities who were sponsored by the very same companies. When Dr Wallach began to speak up with some of his scientific findings based on his vet work, the medical profession mocked his 'lowly' vet status and his insights. In response, Joel trained in human medical science, became a naturopathic doctor and launched his famous and brilliantly titled lecture 'Dead Doctors Don't Lie'.

The point of the title is that the doctors – the people who are meant to guide us about our health – on average die ten years earlier than other people in our population! This is based on American statistics, which stunned me, and I'd bet the stats would be similar here.

The good news is holistic doctors are on the rise and more and more we're questioning the 'commercial lean' of our medical system. Like Joel Salatin's customers, doctors are seeking out food grown with love and integrity as healthy treatments to assist wellness for their patients, ahead of simply prescribing drugs. But back then it was interesting that I'd not only been cured by a vet, but I'd been given the keys for greater awareness about my own responsibility for my health via the nutrition in the food I ate, from none other than . . . a vet.

When I spent time at my auntie's, I noticed I always went home leaner and lighter, happier and brighter. For years I thought it was because I was more active there, but the truth was at home I jogged a minimum of 7 kilometres a day and played hockey and was extremely active. My diet was okay, eating vegetables and meat produced from the farm, yet I would regain the weight at home. This puzzled me. It wasn't until this year that I found the missing piece of my puzzle about weight loss and health. When I was at home in the city, I wasn't happy. My exercise wasn't about health. It was about running away and the extra weight was about emotional protection. I lived with a chronic level of stress, feeling as if I never fitted in. City living also rattled my nerves and stress hormones will put weight on you as fast as you can say 'Mars bar'.

Since moving off the land to our rental, I'd been comfort eating like crazy and no matter how often I tried, the mental patterns on loop about my 'eviction' from my family farm kept playing in my head, and my 'victim' status seemed to remain stamped on my forehead. I thought it was time to do something about my self-defeating mind chatter and eating. I went in search of holistic doctors who could help me. Based on past experiences, if I hadn't found one, I'm sure I would've tried the vet!

First I located a doctor who kept me even-keeled with acupuncture, then I found a GP who was an holistic doctor, as colourful as she was cool. Both doctors had the conventional medical system down pat, but were as open and as enquiring about life as I am. At one point, when I visited my new technicoloured GP, I found myself lying on her floor with my feet up on her wall with her reclining in the same position next to me saying, 'This is nice, isn't it?'

I looked to her as I lay on my back on her doctor's surgery carpet, and thought to myself, *I'm lying on the floor with my doctor with my legs up the wall! She's not in an office chair writing me a prescription – she's on the floor with me! She's a real human! She knows what it is to have a body and how to exercise and move it to heal it. Hallelujah!*

With both doctors to help me there was no need for pills to 'fix' my mental loop about my farmless grief. Many other doctors on their fifteen-minute-session treadmills would have simply written me a script for antidepressants. As a writer who needs to 'feel life' to write about it for others, I would've binned the script anyway. Instead I opted for six hypnotherapy sessions with her. I have no idea what happened or how it worked, but it's like the doctor took pruning shears to my neural networks and 'snipped' the tangle of brambles in my brain that kept taking me back over and over the grief of the past. After my third session I remember this weird sense of calm as I walked out of the surgery – weird because I hadn't felt calm in a long time. After collecting the kids from school, my son asked, 'How was the doctor today, Mummy?'

'Great!' I answered. 'She hypnotised me and has turned me into a tomato plant.'

Both my children laughed, a little too nervously, and I could see them checking me for leaves and red round fruit, and then assessing Mummy's mental stability.

Then I explained, 'A tomato plant is still. It's like a seed. It does nothing but trust that it will grow. It takes what it needs in water and nutrition from the soil and it turns itself to the sun for energy. Without even thinking, it grows steadily and slowly on its own time, and bears fruit. No stress. It just is. I'm like that now. Still, like a tomato plant. I like being a tomato plant!'

The kids laughed but there was something in them that seemed hopeful that the doctor was at last giving me the support I needed as a single busy-as-all-get-out farmless mum. Now it's a running joke with the children, and each time I am doing my 'get to school speed wobble', the kids chant to me, 'You are a tomato plant. Remember, Mummy! You are a tomato plant!'

Weirdly, a few weeks after that hypnotherapy session with 'Dr Tomato Plant', I planted a rhubarb crown in a nice pot, in good soil and mulch. I watered it. Mysteriously, the crown died and instead in its place up came . . . drum roll . . . a tomato plant. This summer we've been dining on its perfect little red balloons of fruit every day, and each time I see the leaves stressed from lack of moisture, I water it and remind myself to do the same. One must water (care for) one's self . . . something we women forget.

Dr Tomato Plant also had me buy a diet book she described as 'very good'. I'm a short, stocky, strong girl who has learned to accept the Tasmanian genetics I was handed, so I reluctantly bought the book, but I'm so glad I did. It has given me the piece of the puzzle I had been missing around the issue of food and weight gain for years, which stretches back as far as the windy road all those years ago to my childhood.

The Slow Down Diet by Marc David has turned my ideas around on food and my relationship with it. When I sit down, or in my case, don't sit down to eat, I've been slowing down my metabolism. Constantly in 'flight' mode, my system metabolises what I eat as fat. Marc David reveals the intimate connection between stress, digestion, metabolism, weight and health. I saw how I was eating fast, always on the run, and I realised that as a child, I always sensed tension at our table. Not good for a healthy metabolism, despite the farm-fresh food on offer all my life.

In comparison, at my aunt's at meal times, there was laughter and there was time. For each other. For the meal. For digestion. And even though Auntie Susie was crazily busy, she always sat and ate with us. I watched her milk house cows at sun-up and feed poddy lambs on her way to giving hot barley mash to the chooks, then

Susie would head off across the paddock and over the Harefield Road to join Colin in the dairy for the twice-daily milking.

She would still put her energy into feeding my cousins and me with vegetables from her garden, butter churned by her own hand, bread kneaded with her strong knuckles and baked in a wood stove that was fuelled with timber she had axed herself. There were oat biscuits made from the basics of sugar and flour, with honey mixed through them collected from their own hives. I used to love pulling the handles of the big vermin-proof tubs in the kitchen to see the vast quantities of sugar and flour within. It wasn't until all of us kids were in bed, that she would join her husband fireside and begin to spin wool by hand to sell, giving the piglet or lamb that was nestled near the wood stove in the kitchen a feed before she went to bed.

They were humble beginnings in farming in the seventies in Tasmania, but the hard work of my auntie and uncle has led to setting up their children in farming, and they get to experience the rich challenges of an agricultural life and the freedom and constraints farming provides. I'm sure it wasn't as idyllic for my aunt as I've recalled it. She would've worked herself to exhaustion, and then had to manage the kids. I remember all of us getting into trouble for flicking dollops of mashed spud on the ceiling, but she must've liked our cheekiness on some level, as the brown stains remained there for years as a reminder to all of us of the good times and fun we had around that kitchen table. Mealtimes at their house were a joy, our digestion serenaded afterwards by music Uncle Colin played on his squeezebox, piano, organ or harmonica. Happy tunes of living. Instead of the nightly dread of television news.

In the mornings, I recall too the way my cousins would load up their breakfast bowls with porridge, much the same shape as St Patrick's Head mountain, and coat their oat mountains in thick layers of brown sugar like rocky screes on the slopes, with lashings of milk from the house cow that had dollops of cream still within, landing like blobs of snow. They were and still are thin as whips, those boys.

By the time I reach my fiftieth birthday in a few years, I wish to be somewhere equally as wonderful as my auntie's table, or an extraordinary place like Kenya. And on that day, I shall have good health thanks to good food, good thoughts, good friends and plenty of laughter. I shall eat with the turn of the earth, and allow myself to stop and breathe. Big meals as the sun rises, small as it fades. Shared meals with simple recipes and good company, because that's what makes our lives rich and healthy beyond measure.

Truffle Treasure Hunt

You can search the finest menus of the fanciest upper-class restaurants of all the land and you'll never find it on offer . . . a truffle, chicken and cheese sandwich. That's exactly what my mates and I would chow down on, sitting on the dropped tailgate of a ute, fingers grimed with dirt and a feather-eared dog nearby looking up at us hopefully.

For a good few years in the early- to mid-2000s I was one of only a handful of truffle-dog handlers in the country and had honed my skills as a perfumist and harvester of that delicacy: the elusive black truffle. Originally from France, these little black underground blobs that look a bit like pin-pricked polished dollops of horse poo bring in big bucks at the fancy-pants white-tableclothed restaurants. I was lucky enough to be hired as a harvester by Perigord Truffles of Tasmania, a fledg-ling company with a big vision to supply black truffles in the off-season when the Europeans were in their summer.

When I first began my job, most of us Tasmanians hadn't heard of truffles, confusing them with chocolates. Locally, we could pluck crayfish out of the seas and barter our own wild venison or wallaby meat without having to fly interstate to a five-star restaurant. Our tastes were pretty much limited to our island and the seas that surrounded us. We didn't know about the significance of the truffle in other places. But the world was changing and Tasmania was opening up to new markets. As a young journalist on the *Tasmanian Country* newspaper, I'd driven north-west of Hobart into the Derwent Valley to interview Nuffield Scholarship winner, Peter Cooper, a co-founder of Perigord Truffles of Tasmania. Driving past old hop kilns towards the equally old sandstone homestead, I had no idea where this interview would lead me, but eventually it led me to the end of a dog lead.

It was in his country kitchen that Peter waved a truffle under my nostrils to sniff for the very first time. I couldn't help wrinkling my nose, and frowning in confusion. Delicacy? To me the ugly thing smelt like a confusing combination of stinky socks, chocolate, melted butter and old-man sweat. But like good coffee, caviar and fine wine, it's an acquired taste, and now I can't speak or write about a truffle without salivating.

'Some day, once we've grown the business, we'll be looking for dog handlers to harvest them,' Peter had said during our interview. As I scribbled notes my mind buzzed. I was not a desk or office girl, and I knew journalism and my place in the Hobart newspaper offices was only temporary. My goal was to write a novel and bide my time until I could convince my dad to let me come home to build the business on his farm. A job as a dog handler harvesting truffles seemed like my dream job in the meantime, so as I listened to Peter talk, I tucked the idea away in my mind as a far-off fantasy.

Fast forward a few years and I happened to see a tiny ad printed in the classifieds of the *Tasmanian Country*. Perigord Truffles of Tasmania wanted dog handlers! Living in a $10-a-week farm cottage on my cousin's farm I was writing my first novel *Jillaroo* and gathering work in from anywhere so I could pay for my addiction to writing. The job would suit my living-day-by-day lifestyle perfectly. I sent my application off straight away.

It wasn't long before I was driving past those old Derwent Valley hop kilns again with a sense of excitement. I would not only meet 'my dog', that I would be in charge of housing and handling, but I was also to meet 'Dog Man' Steve Austin, whom Peter Cooper had commissioned to train a team of truffle sniffer dogs. Steve is a high-energy, passionate trainer and when in action he reminds me of a kind of Steve Irwin of the dog world. I can still hear his convincing exclamation of 'Yes!' each time the dog got it right and hit on a scent target. I've used his communication techniques on my own dogs in training.

Just like Steve Irwin, Steve Austin is a bit of a legend. He's trained dogs to seek out rabbits, rats and feral cats on the near-impossible-to-get-to Macquarie Island, 1500 kilometres south of Tasmania, whilst the dogs range past and ignore the carpet of birdlife who nest there. From the outback to the rainforest, he's taught dogs to find cane toads, feral cats and foxes in the most difficult terrain so as to protect our threatened native animals. He's even got squads of dogs protecting us from the rise of illegal narcotics flooding our society. Equally importantly he teaches dogs to seek out mines in war zones and find missing people in the aftermath of natural disasters. Often his dog students are misunderstood canines on deathrow, unwanted and untrained, imprisoned miserably behind mesh and about to be euthanised. Even back then, in my early truffle days, before Steve's career fully bloomed internationally, it was an honour to meet him and spend a day as one of his pupils. He was an unforgettable personality. As I sat with a springer spaniel I'd only just met, I found myself behaving just like the dog . . . wanting beyond measure to learn and to please Steve and to extract an enthusiastic 'Yes!' from him.

Converting my working-dog knowledge to sniffer dogs was not easy. The learning curve was steep, but when the student is ready, the master will appear, and I had waited years for this job to surface. You couldn't have had a more willing student than me, nor a better master than Steve to teach me about dogs. From the truffle point of view too, Peter Cooper was a master at helping me define the perfume of a truffle and decide if it was ready or not to 'take'. I came to love the smell of truffles as much as my dog loved them, and felt myself wagging my tail as much as him when we locked onto a zigzagging scent trail and found our target. It was exciting beyond belief. I was in my element.

Just a waft of a truffle nowadays sets my senses alive. Not just because it's a specialty food, but because of the memories it evokes of my learned art, the hours of searching in beautiful Tasmanian countryside in sometimes harsh conditions, and the euphoria a woman experiences when it's just her and her dog in the landscape, and in particular, finding one of the precious black truffles as if it were the Holy Grail.

Today in Australia, truffles aren't so unknown and can be found widely in food stores. Sometimes they are infused in golden oil contained in tiny bottles, bottles so small they look like they belong in doll's houses, but still with big price tags. Or you'll find their little flea-like shavings peppered through gourmet salt.

From Sydney to New York's finest restaurants truffles are placed at the highest-priced end of the menu, shaved over pasta or creamy potato or melted through a cheesy risotto. Or in fancier guise, on one menu I read, 'Black pudding with morel and truffle puree and wagyu tenderloin poached in truffle jus'. I mean, really? Is that entirely necessary? Impressive though the dishes are, I liked the way we enjoyed truffles. Simply. In outdoor surrounds.

Each week in winter I would travel north for two days of harvesting and stay with my fellow harvesting workers in their homes. If we harvested truffles one day, we would sneak an unsaleable one that may be damaged by insects into the fridge with some free-range eggs overnight. The flavour of the truffle would infuse through the shells of the eggs as if by magic and by the next morning, before we'd loaded up our dogs, we'd be sharing truffle omelettes for breakfast. On our seasonal 'cut out' – meaning our last day of harvesting for the winter – our boss Peter would provide us with a giant wheel of King Island brie sliced in half with slivers of truffle set within. We would crunch down on biscuits with the melt-in-mouth truffle-infused cheese, fingers stained black or red, depending on the soil type in which we'd been digging.

These tailgate-truffle feasts out in a paddock, amidst long winter grasses, with sheep over the fence looking on, always sat in such contrast to the transformed truffle that was served on a large white restaurant plate in Sydney, Japan or the Netherlands. I'd imagine the scene sometimes as I handed over my bounty for Peter to clean and package up on ice for the airport. I could see my diner cloaked in subdued atmospheric music and romantic lighting. Starched table napkins would be sitting stiffly on the diner's lap, after the waiter had flamboyantly and flourishingly placed it there, the starch causing the napkin to remain angular like the flying nun's habit. The waiter proudly reciting the menu as if it were some glorious poem and not just the convoluted dishes that a genius chef had devised. A second wine waiter bringing out a carefully selected wine that complemented the truffle, and pouring it into wine glasses alive with the reflections of candlelight and so clean the glass would sing simply from a fingertip touch. The wine waiter would then bow slightly as if he'd achieved some kind of artistic accomplishment. In other words I'd envisage a scene a whole world away from mine, with my grubby jeans, tangled hair jammed under a cap, nose smudged with dirt and gumboots caked in mud. My fingernails alone would have had me thrown out of such a place.

Once it was rumoured the truffles we were harvesting that day would be flown to Princess Mary, who was on a yacht somewhere for her birthday. I imagined her in her royal bikini of navy-and-white polka dots, sunning herself on Mediterranean waters, then when the sun was sinking towards the azure horizon, I imagined her frocking up all princess-like for her Tasmanian truffle delight. I love the image in my head of my fellow Tasmanian-born Princess Mary on a sun-drenched deck, anticipating the arrival of a truffle I had grubbed out of the ground a day or so before. Her world and the world of fine restaurants sat in such a stark visual contrast to the place I was in, handling the truffles. Kneeling, sometimes in slushy mud, sometimes in a hard-as-rock frost, whilst my dog rolled with delight in whatever stinky or dead thing he could find amidst the trees.

I also can't separate the scent of truffles from the smell of Devon meat, or Belgium, as we call it here in Tasmania. You know the sort you see in red plastic tubes in supermarkets selling cheap? Cut in small squares, my dog, a springer spaniel named Tiny, would go nuts for it and would work all day hunting truffles for the fatty stuff. I tried him on chicken, on dried liver and other rewards, but he was a sucker for junk food so Devon it was.

I also came to discover there is something magical about a trufferie. A trufferie is the 'orchard' into which we would enter, sterilising our boots and dogs' paws before we went through the wallaby-proofed gate. (Yes, wallabies like truffles too.) It took me yonks to be confident enough to say the word. Trufferie. In my broad Tassie accent I would say 'Truff-fer-ree', like 'referee'. But it ought to be said with a French roll of the tongue: 'True-fur-ree'. *Ah! Mais oui!*

We'd drive through farmland and arrive at the properties, entering a secluded world where rows and rows of oaks, hazelnuts and the evergreen ilex had been planted, their roots infused with the truffle fungus. I came to know the different soils in the different trufferies in that job, witnessing it at close quarters on my knees, bowed down in worship. I would see that secret world of filaments of underground fungi, of tiny creatures, and smell the scent of decay that fed the whole system. Delicate lace roots tangled and entwined with woody tree roots, birds above me watching me curiously. It was a magical time. And above all, there was my harvesting team of dog women, earth girls and out-and-out larrikins who have since become my lifelong friends. Not only did the money come in handy during the bleak wait for a twice-yearly royalty cheque to turn up, but the job gave me great networking opportunities with other farm women. We'd do working-dog deals, source hay for one another, point each other in the direction of agistment paddocks in dry times, or to where a good line of cheap sheep or cattle could be bought. We became a farm-girl sisterhood. Girls who talked cattle prices and rainfall, not shopping and shoes.

Looking back, it seemed as if the earth orchestrated our meeting because those women were my mainstay as I sailed into the foreign seas of singledom and farmlessness. Those truffle girls were the ones who came to paint walls in the refuge house. To offer food parcels. To treat the children to a trip to the zoo. To text a funny joke. To tell me they loved me. To give me a place to stay when I needed to get away. They were women of my kind. We were a bunch prepared to trudge in gumboots for kilometres up and down rows of trees in a mid-winter Tasmania, being towed behind a dog, and no matter how frosty, or how suddenly hot, or how rainy and windy, we'd dig our fingertips through soil and shove our faces into the holes we had dug. All of us, with our trained noses sniffing along invisible perfume seams for hours, just to find truffles. People think it's the dog that digs up the truffle. But that's not so. One scratch from a dog's claw and the precious item could be damaged and degraded. Our dogs were quickly called away from the booty of truffles they'd find. Some dogs were known to eat truffles. It was an expensive mistake we would never let happen. Although I think it did happen once or twice with Chips, who was a big, strong, clever dog and often gobbled one down, leaving Deb cranky with him and swearing like a trouper.

Amidst the rich-smelling leaf litter some truffles could simply be found on the surface of the ground. But this was rare. Most times a dog would 'hit' on a target, meaning he would zigzag forward, his floppy ears wet from the grass, helping to waft the scent to his nose, and then suddenly he would scratch on the surface. I had to watch my whirligig springer spaniel, Tiny, like a hawk and be focused on his every move. I would then reward him verbally and with a chunk of Devon as he sat straight-backed and keen-eyed, sweeping the ground with his plumed tail. I would drop to my knees and ever-so-carefully inspect the area with just about every sense of my body. Closing my eyes I'd inhale above the freshly scratched soil, hoping for a clue. Sometimes tiny mounds could be seen, the soil loose and friable, and I knew I'd bagged one straight up. Other times it was a frustrating task of digging, shoving my nose into excavations, clumping handfuls of soil to my nostrils to see if I could still detect a scent. Sometimes the trail would go cold and precious time was wasted when a truffle remained hidden, like buried treasure in the ground.

I remember Jeanie kneeling on the wet grass with hillocks of soil all about her like a gopher gone mad, her dog dozing in the weak winter sun. She had looked up to me, palms to the sky as if pleading with the Truffle Gods, and said with reddened cheeks, 'I know there's one there! *I know it!* I just can't find it!' She pulled up just short of a sob. Given that top-quality truffles were worth about $3000 a kilo to our boss back then, we would be reluctant to leave a spot where we'd caught a scent. We could be walking away from a beauty. It was addictive and alluring. At times it was physically challenging due to the steepness of the hills and the pull of the dog on the lead, or the wildness of a freezing mid-winter's day, but it was the worst when you could smell a truffle but not find it and the perfume told you it was now or never and that same truffle that you failed to uncover would be on the turn the next time you were back in the trufferie.

All of us were farm girls back then, supplementing our income from our part-time seasonal work, but really deep down, all of us knew we'd joined a sisterhood. The truffle harvesting and camaraderie between us and our dogs fed our souls, as we happily trudged on a frost-crusted earth in search of black gold.

A Knight in Shining Farm Boots

It was 2009. I was emotionally as parched as the landscape around me. The dams were low. Rain wasn't falling. People's spirits were slumping too. It wasn't so bad for us. We had my then-husband's teaching income, my book royalty cheques arriving every now and then, and we'd spent enough time drought-proofing ourselves with the fodder production shed and reducing our stocking rate so it was just a matter of getting by until it rained. Faith and optimism would see us through, or so I thought.

Even still, those fellas kept pointing out what was wrong. It was exhausting. With the inner work I was doing sparked by Louise Hay's book given to me by Paul Macphail, I could see that even without rain, our lives were rich beyond measure and so many things were oh so right! Why couldn't the fellas see it? Why couldn't they speak it? Couldn't they hear themselves? Didn't they know how deadly it was to talk your world down when you can just as easily talk it up?

As I tried to find my footing as a new mother in a man's world, I had grappled for answers about the men's view and their disregard for what was magnificent about our lives. The more I practised Louise Hay's spin on the world, the more I was led, as if by an unseen force, on a pathway of books that kept appearing before me like stepping stones. Other books came to me on new science, philosophy, spirituality, farming, history, feminine awakening and faith. Through such books and lectures, in particular epigeneticist Bruce Lipton's work and the writing of Esther and Jerry Hicks, I was learning that it is our thoughts and the words that we speak that form our reality and govern everything – particularly the health of our bodies. With my daughter's condition too, I was seeking out health methods that truly addressed the inner and the outer lifelong condition she faced. We began to see a Bowen therapist to help her with her high-tension little legs. That dedicated practitioner also set us on a journey towards other modalities of healing that were not only helping my daughter but healing and awakening me as well.

I realised what I was learning wasn't spiritual whoopee-la-la stuff that can so often be dismissed by practical realists found in my farming culture, but I was actually learning about quantum physics and the new science of epigenetics. Very concrete concepts proven in laboratories at legitimate universities around the world. (The only PhD I'd ever claimed to obtain was a Post

Hole Digger, and with it I watched soil and rocks spewed up from the earth as we put in some great fences with it. Being so close to the soil and life and death of animals leads you to what I think is the best outdoor university life can provide.)

Because of this new awareness and hunger for a new way, I began to practise being witness to my daily thoughts and the words I spoke. I began to see the energetics others were attracting around me.

At the time I had an 'in-law' who would come and stay with us often. Instead of kicking back and blessing the fact he was sharing a pie at the bakery in sunshine with his family, he would rant about the price of the pie, the weight of beef within it and the minuscule amount of money for the beef that would've been paid to the farmer. Doom and gloom and misery-gutsing on a sunny winter's day with glorious, healthy children in our company. I found it sickening. Literally. Particularly when I had paid for the pie for him and desperately wanted everyone around me to be happy, to be grateful, and to love life.

When we were out and about this particular in-law would introduce me to people, saying, 'This is Rachael. She not only writes fiction, she speaks fiction as well.' As I was smiling politely, shaking hands, inside me I was bleeding from that cruel remark. Each time he said it, it cut me to my core. Not only was it the ultimate put-down for an honest person, but it revealed just how little respect and understanding a dominant alpha male had for a woman like me. I may come across as idealistic, but my positive speak and big-vision paintings with words are a very deliberate intention about my place in the world and the change I wish to inspire. I still ask myself today, Why did that dear soul have such a compulsive need to dominate, belittle and silence me? Was it because I was female and I had a public profile? Was it because my philosophies did not sit well with him? Was it because he knew I had an inner power building inside me . . . the power of a woman coming into her own, finally, at forty, knowing her real place in the world? Even if what I said sounded like fiction to the more bitter and cynical around me, I knew that by speaking love, light, positivity and optimism and directing my focus towards what was possible and what I was grateful for, I could in fact change my reality. I wanted the men around me to get that too, so their lives could flourish. I also knew the old belief systems of agriculture didn't need to be adhered to, and that we could find a new way forward.

Along with the extra work drought brings, I had young children to care for, livestock to feed daily, a fledgling fodder business, writing deadlines to meet and our little school facing closure . . . again. It was all life's stuff, which I knew I could handle, but I couldn't do it without being nurtured, or without support, nor without being honoured as a woman and a mother and without being protected. I felt increasingly that energetically dark shadows were drifting into my space from those around me. There was never any offer of solutions. It felt like a never-ending cycle of 'not enough rain, not enough chores being done, not enough bookkeeping tended to, not enough tidying up, not enough of anything'. I felt I was simply 'not enough' for those men around me, and with the tendency in me to want to keep everybody happy, no matter how much I gave . . . it was never enough.

To keep myself going emotionally, I would set off at dawn, iPod ear buds jammed in my ears, jogging in the glistening bushland with my dogs at my heels before the kids were awake. The rhythm of my steps on rough terrain set a background tempo to Esther and Jerry Hicks' *The Law of Attraction* that played as an audio book.

With the sun rising over the bushland I began to see I had a power deep within me that I had dimmed due to my childhood programmed beliefs. I saw how I diminished myself to make those around me feel comfortable and in the process enabled them to never truly respect me.

On those runs I was becoming a woman starting to shake off her chains of self-bondage, and I began to discover those slow changes didn't sit well with those around me.

I could now see that despite the glorious children that trundled around us, despite the free-range-egg-and-bacon pies I cooked, or home-grown farm-fresh meals I'd set down on the table, or the wool clip I'd just classed and sent to market, or the cattle I'd just drafted, or the bestseller I'd just released crediting my husband for his support, or the way I'd try to make myself feel attractive with my post-baby body for him, I felt I could never make him happy. Nor did my efforts seem to ease my father's, or father-in-law's, focus on what was 'wrong'. I began to feel like

I was losing myself. At the time, I was reading theories in quantum physics that our belief systems actually alter our very own biology within our bodies. It explained why I was getting so sick frequently. While a tiny seedling of a new way of thinking, believing and being was beginning to sprout inside me, outside of me everything seemed to be drought-dead. I was a woman, a mother, hungry for care.

In these sorts of times, the support of other rural women is crucial and, thankfully, never far away. Whilst my husband was away from the farm teaching, I employed my neighbour Maureen to help me with the domestics so I could continue my vocation of being both a novelist and a farmer. Sally across the road was always there with something delish to eat. Just over the boundary fenceline there was my champion Lu, along with her stablehand girls Steph, Sexy Sal or Ange-flange ready for a laugh. A few ks up the dirt road there was another cluster of good, fun women.

But I was still at a loss as to how to 'fix' things for my family on the farm. When my neighbour Janice McConnon called to say she had secured some funding through Natural Resource Management South (NRM South) to bring some guest speakers to the Runnymede Cricket Club I slumped with the weight of obligation to support community events. The cricket ground was basically a paddock with a brick shed in one corner and surrounded by a gloomy, ominous plantation of blue gums in dark rows on what was once a farm. I wondered what on earth a guest speaker could do to help a district as desolate as ours? It would be easier to just stay home.

We'd already had Lee Kernaghan blow in with the dust to the Woodsdale Footy Club to sing from the tray of a truck and give us some respite from the roundabout conversations and despair about no rain. That gentle, beautiful man in a big black hat gave us not only his time and kindness, but also the generosity of his signature, taking up a thick texta and signing hats, CDs and also the bonnet of a ute. He even, upon request, signed 'Mattress' Bourke's Jack Russell, the little dog delighting in all the fuss. Now, here was Janice again imploring me to come to yet another 'depression drought-buster' night, and out of sheer exhaustion I wanted to say no to her.

She's a beautiful woman, Janice. A stalwart of the community, who not only works on the farm beside her husband and two kids, but dives into the farm kitchen to provide meals, cups of soothing tea and cheer to all. She's also a master networker on behalf of the community and a practised diplomat – something needed in a small district like ours! She's the sort of lady who could run BHP and a small country with one hand tied behind her back, whilst moving a mob of sheep at the same time. At community events Janice glides gracefully into a room like a ship with full sails and even in dusty farm clobber looks regal yet kindly, like a good queen who leads others to achieve feats they never thought possible.

Janice was responsible for bringing the Bendigo Community Bank to our nearest town, and the profits from that bank have been channelled back to us locally. She'd been working with me tirelessly to protect and preserve the Levendale Primary School, which yet again faced threat of closure. I am sure, to this day, it was Janice's heavenly sponge cake that convinced the man in the suit from the Education Department to keep the heart of the community beating for just a few more years.

And so it came to pass that I found myself a week or so later mustering the energy to walk into the fluoro-lit, beer-stained carpeted club rooms to listen to guest speakers I'd never heard of. Little did I know my entire life was about to change that night. I was about to find Australia's knight in shining farm boots. A man who could give me, and many others, the answers I was desperately searching for about our soils and farming methods. A man who has since given me heart and hope, not just about our district that was dying, but about the future of the entire planet.

That man is Colin Seis, a farmer who lives about 20 kilometres north of Gulgong in New South Wales. If you don't know where Gulgong is, think Mudgee. If you don't know where Mudgee is, think over four hours' drive north-west of Sydney. If you don't know where Sydney is, I can't help you.

Col had come to Tasmania at a time when it felt to me as if we were at war. Our culture and our environment were under attack. The school was in the last death throes after strangulation via city-based people-politics and policies, and our community was feeling threadbare due to the exodus of farming families from the area. This had been caused by government-supported tree companies, propped up by superannuation-fund investors, that were buying up the family farms and moving already depleted and depressed people out. It had fenced us into a future of low population, and a district that no longer grew food. Choppers were spraying atrazine, the European Union-banned chemical, from the air over our roofs where our drinking water was collected, and over my clothesline where my toddlers' clothes would hang. Superannuation-funded dozers were clearing native bushland in creeks and waterways to make way for the rows of monoculture trees because the government passed legislation to make it possible to do so.

Possums and wallabies were being massacred by their thou-sands as 1080 poison-baited carrots were cast about the landscape to take pressure off recently planted genetically enhanced trees. I couldn't even run my kelpies and collies in the crisp morning dawn without worrying they'd eat a carcass of some poor thick-furred creature that had managed to squeeze through the fence to the sanctuary of our bush runs, only to die in agony, laced with deadly poisons. We foreshadow the devastation that will certainly come when fires take hold of the plantations, now seven years on and as tall as two-storey buildings, and as neglected as derelict housing-commission suburbs since the tree companies went bust and pulled out all their workers.

On the television in my lounge room, which thankfully faced away from the plantations, I'd catch advertising on the benefits of tree growing and how 'green' a person could be by investing their money there. It was not so much rage I felt as I watched such untruths, but a fear – that we had got so off track with our inner guidance and that economics all around the world was destroying soils: the stuff that sustained us. I tried to apply the 'look for the positives and find a way forward' approach, but the tree companies kept coming at us. To add to the grief of what was going on around me, my darling friend down the road had birthed a little girl, who died after just five short days of living, with a rare physical defect. Later via internet research the heart-broken first-time mum discovered that the particular physical defect in her little baby was linked specifically to that same chemical, which has been banned in the European Union. What I was witnessing in my world was terrifying.

At the information night, I sat my exhausted arse down in the moulded plastic chair and crossed my arms, preparing to have a meditative kind of snooze, to escape for a while, whilst the guest speaker took to the front of the footy club rooms beneath the shields of winning teams and names of past cricket club presidents. Behind him was a pull-up screen and a projector beamed the NRM South logo. Before me I saw a grey–blond-haired man, with kindly blue eyes and a quiet, gentle voice. As he began to speak, I was jolted awake. The more Colin Seis spoke, the more I felt as if he were an answer to my prayers. An angel dressed in tidy farmer clothes, yet there he was, as normal as any other farmer in the room really, but his concepts and story were something altogether revolutionary to me. The crowd was mostly there because of the beers and because we all found it hard to say no to Janice, but within minutes he was winning them over as 'a good bloke' and 'one of us'.

'We've got it wrong,' Colin said. 'It takes months and even years to sequester carbon out of the air into trees. Don't think I'm knocking trees. I'm a Landcare member, I've planted thousands of trees on my place, and tree planting is good, but with trees the carbon is stored in the wood. We need it in the soil.

'In six months, a farmer can sequester more carbon via growing long grasses than a tree plantation can in six years . . . and what's more, the carbon is stabilised in the soil. If every farmer in Australia did it, we'd soon fix this climate change problem. And the ecology would be balanced too.'

As I listened I wondered why more people didn't know this. Why was so much farmland being bought up and put into trees as if it were a good thing? If long grasses on farms were the answer, why weren't governments advising and assisting farmers to grow grasslands so we could address climate change and keep people on the land and in rural communities?

As a journalist for Rural Press and ABC rural radio I'd been to plenty of farmer meetings over the years – field days, lectures in country halls, conferences in hotels and information days at universities. I'd heard speakers address farmer groups many, many times. Most of the speakers were not farmers. Most had something to sell or promote. They were giving scientific results, information or guidance on data that had been funded by fertiliser companies, chemical companies or academics wanting to secure their salaries and research funding. Some were failed farmers who had joined consulting companies. The practising farmers who did speak at these events were usually roped in to help sell whatever idea or product that profited not him but the company or university organising the event. Now here was Colin Seis 'speaking our lingo'. Not the stuff of academics or agri-corporates . . . but 'our speak'. Farmer speak. In his gentle laid-back manner he drew me in and lit me up. My entire life changed that night – more than I could ever know at the time. I glanced over to my then-husband leaning on the bar with the other men, hoping he was hearing it too and would want to travel with me along Colin's road of thought.

That night Colin introduced us to the term 'regenerative agriculture'.

'What's the point of aiming to be sustainable,' Col had said, 'when what we're doing now is not sustainable? Agriculture is in big trouble. For the last sixty years agriculture has lost the plot. Monoculture crops, high rates of fertiliser and pesticides are the norm around the world and it's been an ecological disaster. The recommended solutions are often to use more fertiliser, herbicide, insecticide, but we never address why more are required.'

At this point Col paused to make sure his fellow farmers were coming with him.

'I'm not an organic producer,' he stressed. Colin must've known these old-school blokes were not ready for any of that hairy-armpit, knit-your-own-undies-from-alpaca-hair, bongo-drum kinda stuff which organics had previously been labelled by the more conservatives.

'I'm not promoting anything tonight. I've got nothing to sell you. I'm just showing you what I've done on my place, because many of the things we do in agriculture make someone else wealthy, not us. We're the silly buggers on the end of the line and we're the losers. But we don't seem to ask the question, "Why do we need to use all those high input products?" The usual answer is to achieve good production, but why do we need high inputs to achieve good production?'

Col pressed a button and on the screen flashed an image of a farm in black and white.

'My father in the 1930s grew good crops with no pesticide and very little superphosphate. He didn't have insect or fungal attack. So why can't we grow crops like that now? Why do our crops suffer from attacks?' Col paused and looked about the room. 'Because we've stuffed our soil. We need to ask why are our farms crashing? It's not to do with lack of fertiliser. It's not to do with the lack of rain. It's because our farms don't function in an ecologically sound way. Carbon in soils is dropping so we put on more fertiliser; insect attack is happening so we put on more pesticides; weeds come so we put on more herbicides. We put more and more product on. I call it "the moron principle". We don't need those things. We can get off them. It's all related to ecology.'

There was a scattering of nervous laughter, but there was an uncomfortable truth in what Col was uncovering for those of us in the room. I wished my father was there to hear this, but he never came to these things. Col wasn't here to muck about. He literally has a planet to save and he was trying to reach the blokes who owned not only the land, but also often closed and traditional mindsets. The men in the room were also in love with their farm machinery, so when Colin dropped the next bomb I almost cringed on his behalf.

'Ploughing began in Mesopotamia about 10 000 years ago,' he said in his gentle Aussie voice. 'We've been cropping the same way since the Egyptians or the Sumarians. We haven't changed agriculture since then. Maybe we got agriculture wrong in the first place? Now, that's a good question to throw at you. Really all that I've done is find a different way of practising agriculture.'

I could feel the tension in the room grow. In my district ploughing was almost a recreation and a religion, and some blokes were yet to wake up to the fact that it compacts soils and kills the life within it. There was something the blokes loved about kicking up dust behind tractors. It was a social faux pas to tell a fella to ditch his plough and let it rust away out the back of the machinery shed.

'Why do we plough?' Colin asked. 'We kill everything to grow the crop. But really ploughing is a disaster. I'd like to see every plough in this country buried. Ploughing leaves the soil with no carbon and gives you hard, compacted, lifeless soil. Herbicides used in the process affect human health and, what's more, kills perennial pasture.' Just when I thought Colin was losing the audience, he drew them back by showing slides of his farm and the first tractor that the Seis family bought. A proud moment in their history.

'Industrialised agriculture started in the 1930s and my grandfather and father were early adopters. It was very profitable for my father and he carried on with it for twenty years straight and stuffed the farm.' To prove his point, Colin showed photos in the 1930s of a suited man standing in shoulder-high grain crops, then by the 1950s that same bit of land was photographed. It was bare and there were gullies of 10–12-foot-deep erosion sites.

'The soil would no longer grow crops,' Col said. 'We describe that kind of country as "farmed out". It was "microbically" dead so my father decided he'd fix the problem. He was one of the first pioneers of the pasture improvement phase and was an innovative farmer. So I grew up in high-input agriculture where Dad used introduced grass species like clover and rye, high levels of fertiliser and set stock grazing. The system worked well in that era and Dad was using the best science at the time. But eventually the place became weedy and unproductive. On today's figures I worked out it would cost us over $80 000 a year to maintain what he was doing.'

Colin said because his dad began the high-input methods of modern farming early, the farm's soils crashed so by the 1970s the stalling health of the soils and the costs began to beat his father.

'The soils were acidic, there were salinity outbreaks, trees were dying and we were going broke.' Col then explained to his audience he wasn't there to prove his father wrong, but it was a fact.

He said he hears a similar story wherever he goes in Australia and around the world. I thought back to when I was little and the mini-mountains of superphosphate that were dumped in piles ready to be scooped up and spread on those Runnymede paddocks sown down to 'improved' pasture species. It was the same story.

The emphasis of what Colin was saying was on the big screen before us. Country that was oh-so tragically familiar. Barren, short-grassed, dead.

'What's changed? Bloody nothing! If we're not ploughing, we're still nuking the country with pesticides. We've just got bigger machinery and we stuff the place more effectively. That's about the main change.'

Again I felt the collective prickle of the audience. But there was no escaping the fact that Colin was telling us we had a desperate need to change because agricultural techniques were failing all over the world and we were propping it up with genetically modified plants and manmade inputs. People in the Western world are getting sicker and sicker from the monoculture mass-produced food that is grown and processed into something that looks like it comes out of a science lab. With the current 'drought' people in this district innately knew it was all struggle, so how could they change? Again Colin provided an answer by next showing what he'd achieved on his own property.

'It's not *the* answer,' he said. 'But it's *one* answer that has got me off the treadmill of ineffective farming. Change means we have to admit we've been doing it wrong for the past thirty years, but we know change is not that simple. The advice of science has not been correct, and we can only work with what we know.'

The way Colin did change to become profitable is the most extraordinary story, and as he told it to the room, everyone came on board to listen. The beers stopped getting bought at the bar, and gradually the body language of the resistant farmers began to alter.

'My incentive to change was not by choice but by necessity. We had a major fire in 1979. We lost everything. It was a million-dollar fire and in one day we lost machinery, sheds, fences, houses and livestock. I was what's termed "instant broke". I knew I had to find another way of doing it. I couldn't switch to "low-input agriculture". I had to change to "no-input agriculture". We had no money. It was a survival thing.'

I hadn't known when Colin delivered this story for the first time the depth of the horror and the scarring from that fire that he'd endured both physically and emotionally. Everyone in the room lived with the threat of fire, so the empathy levels and admiration for Colin suddenly escalated. He told us his neighbour had been in the same boat being burnt out too so, as most Aussie blokes do when they've had a bit of trouble, they sat down to have a few beers. Together the two of them came up with the amazing concept that is now known as 'pasture cropping' – where annual crops such as oats or wheat are sown directly into dormant or 'sleeping' perennial pastures. No need for ploughing and no need to destroy the perennial plants to crop. And so much cheaper than the traditional way.

'You gotta be drunk to think of something that stupid,' Colin said of their decision to give it a go.

'In the early nineties Australia had begun direct-drilling crops into soil but it meant nuking everything with Roundup,' Col continued. 'My neighbour and I wondered why we had to kill the plants just to sow a crop. Why not drill when the plants are dormant?' Colin looked at his audience with his elfish, cheeky grin. 'Why haven't crops been planted into grass before? No one's been drunk enough to think of it,' he joked.

'No one was more surprised than us when the first crops we sowed bloody well worked! But no one before had really looked at how nature worked in a grassland and how She runs it so warm-season and cool-season plants are compatible. No one had taken much notice of what Mother Nature did.

'We think the lack of rain is the problem, but it's the humans who are managing the soils and the animals that are the problem. Grass plants have a big root system if left long. Most of our pastures are grazed short so the soil structure crashes and we're not accessing nutrients, so the whole food system crashes. On my place, we wanted to run the animals just like Mother Nature runs them on African grasslands in the wild, and run the cropping just like you'd manage a vegie patch. Mulch for moisture and to control weeds, and feed the soil and control temperature with lots of organic matter and ground cover. We thought, *Why don't we do that out in the paddock?*

Why didn't we? It all made perfect sense to me. Colin had

encapsulated in words what my gut had been telling me for years. I'd been pushing the men on our farm to stop spraying thistles and other weeds with chemicals. I'd been trying to convince them to apply alternative fertilisers to our increasingly rock-hard paddocks. The soils beneath my boots always felt compact and resistant, and the stock seemed to have a tail end of unhealthy animals in the mob, and I just didn't agree with what the men did with landscape. Not resting it long enough, choosing grasses that died in summer, and clearing and burning too frequently. I could see lack of rain was not the problem. Dad ran the farm as if it were a parkland. The tidiness of it had sat at odds with me for a very long time, having watched animals graze and their preference for diversity whenever they escaped the confines of their paddocks.

Here was Col about to deliver the explanation about our continent and our false belief in 'drought' that I had innately suspected all along. I thought of the cynical fertiliser reps, contract spreaders and agricultural product traders I'd tackled in vain to help me find another source of fertiliser. I hadn't understood why the fellas in my life insisted on buying in the fancy seeds that had been advertised in glossy brochures and when they went to the trouble and expense of sowing them, they turned up their toes in the dry. Even when the grass was at its best, the sheep only wanted to get out of the paddock into my garden or onto the road to nibble at just about every plant on offer there. The glossy-brochure green-lab plants in the paddock just weren't what my sheep and cattle were after, no matter how much science and expense went into creating them.

I went home that night with a light bulb switched on in my heart and head. As a last-ditch effort to spark change, I invited Colin to visit our farm on his next trip to Tasmania. He generously gave me half a day of his time, toured our farm, viewed our livestock and pastures, offered advice. Being a kelpie breeder and trainer himself, he even spent time watching my dogs work sheep in those portable Mothers' Day yards outside my farmhouse. He had a lovely gentle drift to him and offered such wisdom and insight. But oddly, from my perspective, the men in my family didn't seem to see they were in the presence of someone who would become one of the most significant agricultural change-agents this country has seen. And he was right there on our farm . . . offering us advice! What a blessing! But on the day Col came to see us, I remember feeling embarrassed that I was the only one listening to him intently. I couldn't understand why.

Against the grumbles of the fellas, I began to implement some of Colin's recommendations, by mobbing up sheep to rest more paddocks, and planning a better grazing rotation to encourage native grasses to return. But before I made much progress in the change of our management, my marriage went belly-up and the kids and I had to leave the farm.

In the months that followed, as I tried to find a home for us, I remembered Col's words from that very first night I heard him speak. I clung to his statement like a life buoy: 'Agriculture needs more women in it,' Col had said matter-of-factly. 'Women are nurturers. We blokes, we fix things with bulldozers. We need more of that nurturing influence in agriculture.'

This one statement gave me such hope. Hope that there were men out there in the world, the ones who hold the power, who were brave enough to say it. Brave enough to take a stance and pave a way forward for the recognition of women's wisdom and for the protection of Mother Earth.

Walking the Talk

It was the first day of spring 2010 when I got the keys to our new 'home', and as I stood holding them in my hands, I knew a miracle had occurred. We authors have the dodgiest of incomes so I bless the kind broker who put his trust in me to set me up with a mortgage – albeit a small one, compared to the grand 'mainland' prices people endure. Despite the prospect of a new house, a coldness came to me in the fact it wasn't my home. The bite of winter hadn't been as keenly felt in my friend's spare room. Warmed by her love, she and I would make jokes about her husband having two wives as he trundled downstairs in the mornings. One was stacking the dishwasher and the other making school lunches – what a lucky man! With the kids despatched on the school bus, I would go back to writing and she would head outside to argue with a ute that routinely wouldn't start. During that dark time, I'd always had my friend's light.

I'll never forget the grace and generosity of my lifelong soul sister. She ran me baths, lit candles, made me song mixes and kept me exercising. It was scary to be leaving her support, but I knew we had to get out from under her family's feet.

Our 'new' house was 6 kilometres up the road from my childhood farm, which was starting to flush with new growth and where lambs were arriving, without me there to check them. I kept my eyes fixed on the road ahead. What a symbolic day for new beginnings, I told myself, but as I stood looking at the paddocks I'd just blindly bought, I wondered where to start. The house, thanks to a bunch of friends and my good ol' Uncle Colin, was about to undergo a revamp. It wasn't long before it was having its mottled brown carpet pulled up and the pink and yellow walls were enjoying a whitewash from kind friends. The life-battered dwelling was more than a little tired, and mirrored the land surrounding it. The 20 acres we found ourselves on so unexpectedly was suffering from corby grub attack on the over-grazed hillsides, ferns were running rampant over bare sandy soils in some sections, and on the creek flats there was an area that had been cropped for potatoes that lay barren, compacted and bare. Steeper banks seemed only to grow wattles. I had no money for fencing, livestock, improvement to the stock water systems, re-sowing pastures or machinery. Heck, I didn't even know if I could pay a mortgage! All I had were two horses, a pony and faith that, with time, all would be well.

First, I focused on the beauty of the land. The treed hillsides, the preciousness of a lone daffodil in the paddock and the bird song of mountains. The cheeky currawongs, strutting in their glossy black suits, and tiny blue wrens showing off to their taupe girlfriends. I didn't know it at the time, but that pleasant orchestra of nature would later be shattered by the sounds that drifted up from a valley that was cluttered with neighbours. If there weren't gunshots at two in the morning, or creepy local married men knocking on my door for no apparent reason, there was the daily screech of some banshee in the distance roaring expletives at her kids from over yonder.

Where had I landed?

Steeled with the knowledge that thanks to Colin Seis I had all the tools and the willpower to keep going as a woman who could find her compass on this land, I vowed I would leave the property in a better state than I found it. I began to foster the notion within myself that I, like the land, deserved nurturing and care. If I could bring the land alive, I could somehow heal myself along with it.

Along with Colin Seis' wisdom, I'd been studying YouTube clips about restoring grassland using grazing animals as described by South African-born ecologist and farmer Allan Savory. I had also been to several lectures by Col's mate, holistic farm management expert Graeme Hand, who had been trained by Savory. Dressed as neatly and handsomely as a farmer's clothing catalogue model, Graeme arrived at our new little property to teach a group of us in the valley about grazing pressure and what to look for in terms of plant growth and decomposing leaf litter, and when to move stock off a paddock to rest the ground. Graeme even taught me to 'poo score', judging the health of the animal via their manure. To put my new knowledge in practice I nervously splurged and bought myself a solar electric fencing unit, whilst my cousin Claire and Uncle Colin gave me some tread-in white posts and a roll of electric fencing tape to get me going. Because I didn't have sheep or cattle anymore, the only grazing trial animals on hand were the horses. Using them behind moveable fencing meant I could help all those different sections of the topography – the wattled hills, the ferny slopes, the patchy pastures – to recover.

Slowly, over time, I began to restore the land function and ecology on our property, which the kids and I dubbed 'The Heavenly Hill', but who was I kidding? I was talking fiction and I knew it. Heavenly Hill? This new place, although picturesque, was far from heavenly to me. I grieved for my old farm with an ache and felt in some kind of living hell no matter the mindfulness or the meditations. Here I was practising the old adage of 'fake it til you make it', and by giving the place that name I hoped I would find heavenly love there for myself and the kindness of family again. It was, on some lonely nights when the kids went to visit their dad, hell to be there, coming to terms with what I'd lost, but I was determined to make that strange place a happy home for my children. I monitored paddocks, taking photos, moving fences, assessing my horses' health and walking the land daily after putting my babes on the school bus. My social life was wrapped up in the informally gathered and stupidly named Levendale 'Arsture Poppers' – a group of locals willing to trial what we were learning. We began to gain traction, with more people coming to look at what we were doing on our small farms.

One of our group, Pip Wagner, modified a direct-drill seeding machine to Col's specifications so that we could trial pasture cropping. I paid Pip in beer currency to drill an acre of the tired spud-cropped land on the creek flat with oats. Colin had taught us that oats, an annual plant, kickstart soil function by unlocking sugars and nutrients in the soil and encouraging mycorrhizal fungi. It's this fungi that has a special relationship between the nutrients in the soil and the availability of those nutrients to the plants, running long tendrils of life support for plants under the ground in healthy soil. When you see it on slides it's as pretty as lace. I'd never been taught about it in college and was surprised to find out from Colin how crucial it is not only for plant health, but also that it is killed by superphosphate. The fungi's demise from these manmade fertilisers is the reason our soils crash after a time and, like drug addicts, the plants go on to need higher and higher doses of false fertiliser to prop themselves up. No wonder farmers are slowly going broke! I couldn't afford fertiliser so my land was going cold turkey, and even if I could've paid for it I wouldn't have applied it. I knew enough now that Mother Nature, if given the right conditions, fixes herself, relatively cost-free.

The day before the first oat sowing at my place Pip left the machine on my creek flat overnight. As a joke, the girls from our 'grass routes group' gathered and, giggling, painted his seed box a bright pink. We finished off our machinery masterpiece by placing a giant sticker on the back stating 'Pip's Deep Soil Rooter'. When we drew back the tarp to reveal it to Pip he had to be administered wine to cope with his vandalised, scandalised machinery. It was one of the best moments in my post-divorce life – seeing us all gathered for a common cause. The pink paint wasn't just a joke to us. By creating such eye-catching farmware we were getting everyone's attention in the district. It got people talking and asking questions about 'the pink thing' and how the modified direct drill helped restore soils with minimum disturbance and, unlike ploughing, could help cut costs for farmers, as they didn't have to go over the ground several times, chewing up fuel by ploughing. Also, by maintaining the microbiology in the soil, they were making their land more pro-ductive. Word spread about Colin's methods, and a blushing Pip found himself carting his 'pink plonker' on the back of the truck right through Hobart Town to trial direct-drilled pasture south of Hobart. We named it the 'Deep Soil Rooter' because our soil problems are deep-rooted in Australian culture and, as Col puts it, as a society we're 'rooted' or 'stuffed'. Pasture cropping is one answer to reversing that problem.

I could see how the application of Graeme and Col's principles was making my place come to life ecologically, and that in turn would set it up for some kind of enterprise in the future, when I had more time, and earned more money. I could also see how I could've applied the principles to my former commercially run operation. What was applicable on 20 acres could be so on 2000 acres and in turn on 200 000 acres. All it took to begin was for a farmer to be curious enough to lock up one of the worst-performing paddocks to see what happened. To watch what grew there. To observe Mother Nature. Then to turn all that growth that Mother Nature gave into manure and mulch, and then give the ground time to be rested again. Of course, it's not that simple, but it's a starting point: one paddock on one farm to give you a sense of farming with the seven-point compass of above, below and within.

I now ran the country with Col's mantra: *100 per cent plant ground cover 100 per cent of the time.* Whether it was with three horses or 3000 sheep, the same principle applies. I put my energies into reviving the native grass species by using controlled grazing, and if I spied kangaroo grass seeding, golden and claw-like on the sides of the roads, I'd pull over and gather up great handfuls to scatter later over my ground. After just two years of those methods, I had more grass than the horses could eat and the diversity of species was on the rise, grub attack was non-existent and we seemed to have more variety of insects and birds. We had encouraged young gum saplings to come back, and amidst the trees delicate orchids bloomed, sheltered by silver tussocks. Colin had taught me that for the health of not only the livestock but also the ecology, we needed to get our pastures functioning like the way our grasslands used to function before white man's arrival. Plant diversity is the key to that. Come springtime two years on, with the place flourishing with all manner of plants, I needed to borrow steers from Janice to help me cycle the grass back into the soil. Our Heavenly Hill was singing as if a choir of angels were upon it.

It was no wonder then, when the kids and I were due for a road trip and I saw some cheap flights, we decided to head to Colin's place in Gulgong. We flew to Sydney, hired a car, and with an eight-year-old in charge of Google Maps on my phone, made our way from Sydney airport to the Ten Dollar Town Motel in Gulgong. The next day, we headed to his property, Winona, where Colin farms regeneratively with his son Nick – meaning they build top soil, not degrade it, on their granite soil farm on the Central Tablelands. It was one of the most exciting moments of my life to see the 2000 acres of Winona. We could tell from our drive to the place that it had been a poor season in the district. But this state of affairs only set us up to see that Winona was truly an oasis in a farming desert of overgrazing and tired soils. Seeing is believing, and walking that soil I felt the life. My kids sank down to their knees and sat in wonder in the long grasses, spending their time plucking stems of grasses and watching insects whilst Col and I talked. The kids sensed there was a kind of alchemy on the place . . . one they'd not experienced in the paddocks on their original farm.

Colin's property was selected and set up by his great-grandfather from Prussia, who started growing wheat and merinos in 1868. Nowadays Colin and Nick run 4000 head of

18 micron merinos and crop about 500 acres of wheat, oats and rye. An addition to their business is the sale of native grass seed to people keen to kickstart the profitable, ecologically healthy system Col is enjoying today using the plants that this continent developed Herself over thousands of years. When the seasons are good they delve into cattle trading, and on top of that, run one of the largest kelpie studs in Australia. On our farm tour, my children were even more thrilled to find there were puppies to rumble with.

As we stood in a paddock now studied by the Australian National University and the University of Sydney, and backed by over a decade's worth of data collected by soil scientist Christine Jones, Colin explained, 'We have at least 200 species that grow in the summer and the winter. There are forbs and herbs as well.' Col said on most farms many of Australia's native warm-season grasses have been lost because they've been selectively grazed out over the years. The old-style summer roadside grasses can be transported back onto our properties easily by simply grazing the roads, then letting the animals manure onto the farming ground on the other side of the fence! Now wherever we drive, we three train our eyes to the roadsides to see what the country ought to look like. There's grass gold reserves to be found there.

Part of the beauty of Colin's farm and its story is the direct comparison to conventional farming systems right next door on his brother's property.

'My brother farms the same way I used to, and the way my father used to, so it's an interesting comparison,' Col said. I remembered the images in his lecture that he had flashed on the screen. The photos showed adjacent paddocks in summer. Colin's filled with thigh-high grasses. The other paddock, his brother's, flat stretch of weeds. There were soil profiles too, cored and cut sharply out of the ground with spades from those paddocks. Colin's soil was active and flourishing for a depth of over half a metre; his brother's topsoil only revealing life in the first 5 centimetres. The differing results of plant growth after rainfall were striking.

Colin explained that most of our farms were dominated by annual weeds because over the years farmers had let the stock graze out all the good native grasses, and yet pre-white man, Aboriginals managed diverse grasslands.

'Only the unpalatable, less nutritious native pastures are left and that's what's given native grasses a bad name with farmers. They think they aren't nutritious or palatable for stock. Farming regeneratively also looks messy. Some people can't cope with the look of it. They like order.'

Col said another advantage of running farms this way is to inhibit the savageness of bushfire.

'In midsummer these grasses are green,' Colin said. 'They are warm-season species that grow right through the hot months. There is 200 per cent more moisture in the soil and that soil is cooler than over the fence on my brother's.'

To summarise the incredible success story of Winona, the Seis family has achieved the following:

- Reduced their fertiliser inputs by 70 per cent
- No manmade fertiliser has been used on the pasture for thirty years
- There is improved ecological function thanks to the creation of a healthy microclimate
- Compatible enterprises are vertically stacked so they grow more food and fibre on the same amount of land
- No insecticide has been used for twenty years, yet they don't suffer from insect or fungal attack
- There are 600 per cent more insects and 125 per cent increased diversity in the insect species compared to conventional farms in the district
- No perennial grasses were sown, yet sixty perennial species or more have come back naturally, proving there is plenty of grass seed in the soil
- Carbon has increased by 200 per cent since they first tested the soil
- There is 200 per cent more soil moisture
- Trace elements have increased by 172 per cent because plants have been allowed to drive the nutrient cycling within the soil by having longer root systems
- They are saving over $80 000 per year in input costs
- There are lower vet costs and animal health inputs in the form of drenches, vaccinations, etc., as the stock are so healthy

- Their annual income is higher, running double the number of stock than Col's brother
- Col's crop yields are similar to his brother's, but he is also harvesting native grass seed from the same paddock he'd harvested a grain crop from
- There is a massive reduction in working hours – less time needed on tractors
- An estimated 2000 farmers are now using Col's technique of pasture cropping in Australia, along with further worldwide adoption of the technique, the more Colin travels to other countries
- It is now a practice adopted all over the world.

Colin's take-home tips for farmers are:

- Never, ever plough
- Keep perennial plants alive
- Manage weeds with thick leaf litter and grazing livestock well – 100 per cent ground cover 100 per cent of the time
- Crop so your oats and wheat are emerging from the dormant pastures
- Graze up to the point of sowing and make sure there are perennial grasses left.

Col explained his method was low-risk cropping because if rain did fail to come and the wheat, barley or oat crop didn't emerge, there was still a banquet of perennial pastures waiting to appear, instead of bare ploughed ground that was susceptible to wind and rain erosion.

'All we've done is run it closer to how Mother Nature had it designed in the first place,' Col said.

I left Colin's farm with a song in my heart. It was the start of a friendship and a mentorship that has utterly changed the way I see and manage and love land. My son constantly searches YouTube clips of Colin and even at the age of eleven is now wanting to grow up so he 'can have a farm and run it like Colin Seis'.

Col is not one to stand still on his mission, nor his trial-and-error study of farming, and recently when I caught up with him he told me he is now trialling multi-species pasture cropping using a mix of forage brassica, oats, field peas, vetch and even vegetables sown into native grassland. He's added photos of the trials into his now globally travelled talk, showing crops so high they swamp farm bikes with kelpies perched upon them.

Not surprisingly Colin went on to win the 2014 Bob Hawke Landcare award. During his acceptance speech, this time wearing a suit and standing next to the former prime minister, Col said plainly, 'We have a planet to fix. This planet is totally stuffed. If we as a species are going to survive on this planet, then we better fix it, and quickly.'

Creating Heaven

Whilst outside there were soils to nurture on the Heavenly Hill, on the inside there were other kinds of major restoration works to be done. Like leaking roofs, no insulation and no matter how much wood I threw on that bloody wood heater, I just couldn't get it to burn properly. It was broken. I recall the first week in the house when I stood shivering amidst the tang of paint fumes trying to visualise what the rooms could look like with furniture. All my things, including my grandmother's hand-crocheted rugs, rolling pins, mixing bowls, jugs and furniture, along with my artwork and my books, were still in place at the old farmhouse.

In the corner of the room I had unrolled our swags not too far from the broken wood fire that seemed more like a black icy cave than a heater. I nestled myself into a big floppy beanbag a friend had lent me. Beneath my double-socked feet was a red shag-pile rug. It was Austin Powers-awful. We'd bought it from one of those cheap plastic furniture stores for one of those dreadful party plan 'adult toy' parties my friend had been conned into hosting for the local ladies. Deciding to make the most of the fact she was committed, it turned out to be a riot of a night – country women who normally behaved when the men were about were given the green light to become girlish again. The dance moves of the Levendale ladies on that shag-pile rug was something to behold. I got good mileage out of that rug and the party, finding the first scene to my novel *The Farmer's Wife*. Amusingly, and tragically, that tacky rug was to be the first piece of decor to set down on the floor of the Heavenly Hill. I was yet to be brave enough to venture back to my home to claim my lovely woollen Turkish kilims I'd splurged on when backpacking. The house sat above a steep bank of young wattles to one side of it and I remember thinking, *If this house ever burns down, I won't lose much.* Forever reaching for the positive.

In the first year the kids shared a postage-stamp-sized room filled with bunk beds, and I crammed my clutter of papers, books and clippings into the second slightly larger bedroom, along with my computer and clothes. On the long dark nights that I experienced in that room, with my small people coming to me in the dead of night for reassuring mummy-cuddles, I wondered if I would ever feel at home in that place. As the days rolled into months, I would drive past the farm and see my brother, my nephews and my dad out cutting wood in the paddocks with my ex-husband. On weekends, when the kids visited, I would catch glimpses of my own children in the stockyards with their father and my biological tribe while I rolled on by, alone. It was as if I was a ghost in my own life.

Why, if I'd been such a good girl and good wife, hadn't I found my happily ever after? Childhood memories flashed again. I remember driving out to Runnymede weekly when I was really little. Dad used to point to derelict huts in lonesome paddocks that we passed and say, 'That's going to be your house when you grow up. The little house on the hill.'

I was so young at the time, I had no idea he was simply teasing. I would look in horror to the windowless, haunted dwellings with falling boards, sagging roofs and an air of poverty and desperation, and wonder if what he said was really true. I tried to imagine that I'd fix them up and put flowers at the front door and pretty curtains, make the best of it, but I was internally devastated. Did I really have to live there – in a cold little house on the hill? So now, as an adult, as I bunkered down into another night of numb madness alone on that hill, and I listened to the wind blowing off the powder-snow top of Brown Mountain and its fierce frostiness curling up and under the gap between the bare roof and the ceiling, I saw his prediction had come true. I would hug my knees to my chest and pull the doona over my head, realising in shock that here I was . . . in 'the little house on the hill'. All alone. Had I created this out of my very own fears?

It wasn't until I found another lifesaving stepping stone in the form of Clarissa Pinkola Estés' book *Women Who Run with the Wolves* that I realised the depth of wisdom for women that has been edited out of fairytales. It is via stories that we form our identity and psyche. In my childhood, girls only had the pared back versions of the original women's wisdom held within stories. I'd been raised thinking we had to find a prince so we could live happily ever after. That was until life taught me otherwise and Clarissa Pinkola Estés showed me the depth of meaning in ancient tales aimed at women living a fully realised life.

I was not all alone. As I began to heal, I realised the experiences I was living through were cracking me open to be a better person, and it was my life's mission to stop the patterns of self-destruction, self-denial and fear. I could become a person who no longer had to believe what she'd been told as a child. I didn't even have to believe the biblical quotes from the Testament of John that an in-law had once shouted at me, that 'women were to obey and serve'. I came to see that the greatest challenges we face are our greatest opportunities.

Looking back, I think I understand why houses are so highly rated by our family. When my dad was a boy it was his job to feed his father's hunting and stockwork dogs. Not a big chore for a lad, you would think, but when your father makes his money from sheep work, hunting and the fur trade – particularly rabbits – and there are forty dogs chained up in a row beneath broody pine trees, I can see how it might put you off dogs. Maybe that's why, no matter how much I begged, we were never allowed a dog. I could also see how my dad had been packed into a tiny weatherboard house during the Depression era that was not much bigger than a dog kennel itself. That tumbling family of eight kids, made up of five tear-about boys and three cheeky girls, lived on the chilly, windswept fringes of the township of Campbell Town in the heart of the Tasmanian midlands.

No wonder when he grew up Dad would want a larger house with no boards to paint or dogs to chuck hunks of meat at and lug water to. He didn't see the sea until he was eight years old, so of course he would be a person who wished for sea views from his chosen adult abode. Ours weren't rambling homes suitable for several dogs and many children and a menagerie of pets. They were tidy places of restraint. As kids, we were allowed one cat, Greebly, a long-haired lady marked like a black-and-white border collie. When I was little she was my constant focus. Poor cat. I would pretend she was a dog and try to teach her to walk on a lead and convince her to sit on command. It never worked.

As a very young child, I remember my mother crying with exhaustion at the front door of our first house after hauling our heavy old-fashioned metal pram up the shin-scraping dog-legging treacherously steep steps, the groceries bursting from the bottoms of brown paper bags dumped on the door mat, and us kids and the cat yowling around her legs. It was not an easy house for a new mum of two kids born eighteen months apart. But it was a sensible house, as it was near Dad's work as a part-time law lecturer at the university and was a place to live whilst he climbed the ladder towards partnership in ye olde Hobart law firm. When it came time, he knew the house would sell well and that would bring more security for us.

When I was about eleven my father chose our second house, again for investment reasons. In this house I recall my mum crying about more steep stairs and the repeated drain of energy that they presented. Again she stood at the top of sharp steps, amidst the tearing collapse of plastic shopping bags. On days like this she exposed her longing for a sunny courtyard on flat ground. And I continued my longing for a dog. But Dad was only doing his best for us. I guess for someone like Dad, who was witness to his own stern father being the centre of the family wheel, with everyone else revolving around the man's every want and need, he knew no other way. Mum's job, even though she was a smart cookie, buried under the expectations of the era, was to keep peace and equilibrium, so we were silenced over and over. I sometimes think that's why I became a writer – because I had no voice. I can understand Dad's love – it was shown through money and security, and based on old principles that he was the provider. It came from the right place of guidance on his compass of living. Who was I to question it? I'd never known the hard slog of Depression-era living that my father did. I had been given a life of privilege from a fiscal perspective, so I had the luxury of being more dreamy about future places to live – places that allow you space to share with animals, plants, trees and people.

Around the time I reached my teenage years and we moved from our bush-surrounded weatherboard house near the university to a growing suburb on the steep slopes above the prestigious suburb Sandy Bay, I began at an ivy-covered private all girls' school. It was a shock on all fronts. My childhood imaginary dogs and horses fell away, as did my dream I could live a life like my farming cousins at St Marys. Even when I was as young as six, clambering over the hay bales with my cousins, I knew I belonged on a farm – not in a city. As a sensitive being linked so solidly to the earth beneath me and the trees that were my childhood companions, the move to an even more urban house and an alien school shocked me. I was an esoteric, ethereal child who saw fairies and spoke to beings unseen. At our old house near the uni, the apricot tree where we played was more home for me than the dark bedroom I feared due to its dank, shadowy energy. I was an 'energy' reader even back then.

The way I saw it, Dad had moved us all to a new house with the coldest of energies, which I only saw for the first time after the deal was done. My dreams of living where there were paddocks for horses and room for sheep and cattle and a dog or two was not on my parents' agenda. I can see now that at the time, both of them must have wanted to escape their rural roots and make a better life for themselves in a well-connected suburb. The farm Dad wanted to own one day was to be a gentleman's hobby. Not the hard yakka his father endured as a farm labourer. His heart, as they say, was in the right place and really, at the end of the day, how lucky we were to have a house, even though it was a corpse-grey structure that was 1970s-ugly. Even the blooming roses, which rectangled in straight-edged garden beds around the compact sloping lawn, couldn't make that house look any better to me. It was constructed with bland concrete-tone bricks stacked in a boxy shape and with blank aluminum windows that faced the sweeping Derwent River far below. When opened, the windows would yawn with the ho-hum of the city commuters on their way to work, livened only with the occasional blast from a moaning boat horn on the river.

The wind on that hillside that hit, icy from the domination of the giant Mount Wellington (yet to reclaim its original name of kunanyi), was sometimes terrifying and shook the windows violently. Inside, bright yellow carpet, elaborate silver light fittings and a bidet, in which my brother and I found much amusement, spoke of the previous Italian owners' tastes, as did the sweeping expanse of the concrete driveway, which was perfect for my daggy 1980s hobby of rollerskating. Even when the house was filled with the remnants of my mother's farming origins in the form of antique country furniture from her mother's farmhouses, the place still had a raw unimaginativeness to it. A coldness. I thought the one thing that could make life feel more comfortable in that house was a dog. I could walk him on the stretch of beach that shouldered the moody waters of the Derwent River, or have him sleep at the foot of my bed at night. He would be there to talk to and, above all, like Lassie or Rin Tin Tin, he could rescue me after unhappy days at high school.

But a dog was not to be. As a budding teenager with the

country in my veins and rampant creativity stymied by suburban living and a regimented private-school routine, my refuge was a vacant paddock over the back fence that had baths for water troughs, along with two lethargic bay horses. Ex-pacers or racers, I suspect. Poor ugly angled things with drooping lips, dull eyes and scarred hides. I don't remember the owners ever doing anything with them, but I do remember the paddocks beside the house more than the house itself. We hadn't been there long when the horses were removed. The dozers came, roads were rammed and steamed onto the earth with a finality, and houses were stacked up in rows, and whoever owned the land stashed money in their bank to spend on more soil coverage elsewhere. Where once a family of plovers had raised their chicks and wallabies had grazed was now premium-priced suburbia. Within a few years of our moving, houses soon stretched across the gully below us and climbed up the hill. Dad's prediction about his asset gaining value had been correct. As the land was smothered with concrete, so too was my inner being. Country life was in my blood and I felt trapped and alone, coming alive only when I went to my aunt's farm in school holidays or heading off in the bush at Runnymede every weekend with my friend, the granddaughter of the investor farmer.

In my dreamscape as a child I saw myself in a white farm cottage with an elegantly curved and slightly rusted tin roof, the delicacy of lace-like peeling paint on old boards and rambling roses over lichen-covered lattice amidst the dapple of eucalyptus trees. Team my dream house with paddocks, bushland views and a couple of working dogs dozing on a split-board wooden verandah, a friendly fire pit in the garden, and my life would be complete. It was odd that when I was in my early teens and Dad bought the 800-acre farm, at its heart nestled a little old white cottage that was similar to my dream home. I set my sights on it when I was older, and as a teenager who loved art, painted it in thick oils onto a firm canvas. As I shadowed the verandah uprights with a grey paint and scratched in the limbs of the trees that flanked the house with the wooden end of the paintbrush, I had dreams of living there, with my horse in the adjacent paddock, grazing beneath the poplars.

Later, when I'd done my formal studies in agriculture and journalism, then had wandered overseas, I'd drawn the farm cottage again in my travel journal. I had been in Cork, Ireland at the time, sick with a travel bug, lying on a bunk bed of a backpacker hostel. After I'd sketched the cottage from memory, I'd written to my parents flowingly and emotionally that all I wanted to do was come home to live in that cottage on the farm. I lovingly remembered the hand-split timber boards and the cute little windows that looked like kindly eyes. I didn't mind so much that there were Tassie devils that lived under its lifting floorboards, along with mean-eyed snakes. Nor did I care that there were raucous fighting possums that skittered on the rusted tin roof at night during killer frosts. Or that the septic was not far enough from the back step of the slumping add-on kitchen to render a stench each time you walked out the door. None of that mattered. To me it was my dream house. With my artist's eye I could see that it was one that could be crafted back to life in the most rudimentary, rustic but beautiful way with elbow grease and love. Pressed-tin ceilings with delicate designs and a dormant kitchen woodstove awaited me. I knew it was a wreck that could be lured back to life.

But my father didn't see it that way. The vacant house to him was a costly problem, only ever fit for renters who paid their rent with dole and dope money. The invitation for me to live there never came, and going back to the farm to start my dream of farming was never entertained. At least not until I was married. And even then, Dad steered my new husband and me into buying a solid investment of a brick house and 20 acres next to his farm. A house I made the best of and infused with love. Until I had to leave it.

Now when I see people on the television news crying over burnt or flooded housing, I think *You'll be ok. Stuff really doesn't matter. People and animals do. You have your life. Trust in the process of life and it will get you through.* Such sudden enforced change through crisis can be the making of a person. I now know that for sure.

Not long after moving into the Heavenly Hill the drought of 2009 broke. It rained with such savageness that the floods washed the bridge away to the house. In the darkness of the winter solstice the kids and I found ourselves lugging school bags and shopping while we balanced on one treacherous beam across still gushing waters. We would hike up to the house in the dark pretending we were on an adventure to make the best of the situation. Ironically, without much consultation or dialogue, my dad pulled in his construction crew contacts and paid to have the bridge replaced. I couldn't help wondering whether he was building a metaphorical bridge for me.

Today, as I write in the flystrike-green rental, I have our Heavenly Hill on the market. We three decided together that we can never go back. But for a time we did turn it into heaven. The kids and I laughed there, we hosted friends in the sunny space we created. We fixed the wood heater. We warmed our hearts. I, as a woman, fell apart up there and then pieced myself together again.

I now envision myself in a white house, with a sunny breeze lifting curtains that reveal a view to a sky-blue sea. And in that house is the laughter of my children and the ruckus of dogs. I will be the queen of my domain, and perhaps my fictional king will become a reality and place his strong arms around me to love and protect me. Outside the house the world will be rich with the scent and sensation of Mother Earth thriving. I can see it. I can feel it. I know it is on its way.

The Sheila from Snowy River

It's so alluring – that Aussie image of a man in a Driza-Bone coat and akubra hat astride a work-fit horse, rivulets of mountain mist dampening his steed's sheened, muscled sides. The horse stands in silver waters tumbling over river rocks, with a backdrop swathe of twisting snow gums. Perhaps beyond that is the craggy, expansive blue-tinged mountain range and with a split-log hut on a grassy spur in the near distance. Romantic? Or is it one of our nation's gender-biased, cultural, stereotypical clichés? And if it is, how did we arrive at it?

One of the most influential poems that set me on the path to writing was Banjo Paterson's 'The Man from Snowy River', and of course the famous movie the poem inspired. You know the one . . . where Siggy Thornton and Tom Burlinson had that oh-so-breathtaking kiss on the back of that gorgeous dun-coloured gelding. But even as I watched that film over and over as a teenager, I was concerned by what was embedded within the messages of that movie. Basically it was the guys who got to fang about on horses and chase cattle and brumbies through the scrub, while the chicks waited back at the homestead and played piano in frilly dresses. When the character of Jessica did venture out into the wilds of the mountains, her horse hit a pothole and Jessica ended up screaming on a cliff's edge, and had to be rescued by a bloke. I remember loving the romance and visuals of the film, but mistrusting the unconscious message buried within. Why couldn't Jessica ride the ranges and be a brilliant horsewoman, then go back to the homestead, soak in a goddess oil-scented bath, put her dress back on and make music?

It wasn't until I read *Women Who Run with the Wolves* that I saw the way society's mainstream stories tend to paint women as feeble, evil, or if they are strong, they are emulating the strengths of males . . . not our own strengths that I was learning to acknowledge and embrace as gifts that come with my gender, like nurture and intuition. How many kick-boxing, pump-action shotgun women are out there blasting and karate-chopping their way to domination now in films, taking on traditional male traits? Is it a step in the right direction in empowering women – or is it unbalancing us? In rejecting our feminine traits are we also rejecting good men and peace? I wonder what legend and fairytale expert Clarissa Pinkola Estés would have to say about it.

In the film version of *The Man from Snowy River*, the whole impetus of the movie's plot was from the never-seen-on-screen character of Jessica's mother, a woman meddling with the love of twin brothers – saucy vixen she must've been. The men were not held accountable for their own destructive jealousies. It was all the fault of the woman and her racehorse gift from one of the brothers that had landed them in this pickle. The movie show-cased that women were not to be trusted, and when it came to the great outdoors, they were not strong or smart enough to belong on the rugged mountain beside the men. Don't get me wrong, I love the movie, so much so that I fell for and married a man from the High Country, spent seven bliss-filled years with him in Gippsland riding droving routes to cattlemen huts and through snow country tailing a herd of cattle before we were married, and I now have beautiful children with the snow-gum bush in their blood to show for it. But the movie sat in contrast to what I knew of rural women.

During my years in Gippsland I got to see the beauty and strength of the Treasure women, stemming back to their forebears' matriarch, Emily Treasure. She was the woman who, unbeknownst to her husband, rode all the way (haphazardly, because she wasn't much of a horse rider) with her son to Omeo to secure the High Country lease that the Treasure fam-ily continue to hold a connection to today. Emily became the subject of my novel *The Cattleman's Daughter*, coloured by my own days spent riding behind red hides in snow-gum country with fantastic in-law women like Auntie Christa, Rhonda Treasure and cousin-in-law Lyric Anderson. My time with those gorgeous ladies allowed me to know that I was part of a clan of women who were unlikely to sit about a homestead and wait for a bloke.

It was also here with my in-law ladies that I saw the positive impact grazing could have on a landscape. I was yet to study it in a formal way, but my woman's intuition, guided by the other women who loved their dogs, horses, cattle and landscape as much as me, told me banning grazing from Alpine regions was a political move, rather than an environmental one. The national parks that had been locked up were a disgrace, as far as I could see, overrun with blackberries, ragwort and whatever other single dominant species comes from a lack of nutrient cycling and the required soil disturbance. It's this disturbance that allows a variety of seeds to set, due to the stimulation by grazing animals. The cattle-grazing ban was all about political image, votes and steering attention away from the people with money who truly profited from the Alpine landscape. The government wasn't trying to ban skiing in the posh resorts, which, in summer, when viewed from the Treasures' grazing runs, looked like lumpy brown scars on the mountain's face. Those same wounds were opened up year in, year out, each time the ski runs were dusted with snow, and people rushed to the mountainside hotels, bars and ski lifts. No one saw it. You had to ride to a certain ridge to get a proper view of the degradation, yet all the environmental hoo-ha had been focused on the cattlemen's families. Families that were headed by hardy women, but who were limited in their time and energy to fight political battles that made no sense. I still miss those Treasure women and I still long for their company in their country. I now know why I related to them so much. In Tasmania I had grown up witnessing my maternal grandmother, Joan Wise, shoot a feed of rabbits with a .22-calibre rifle, and hand-fish flathead out of a tumblesome sea in a tiny dinghy that she launched fearlessly through frothing dumpers. She was a strong lady with big, square hands and broad shoulders. There was no outboard motor on her boat, just her fists on the oars and her wide back set to the horizon of the sea beyond Maria Island as she rowed.

Once when I was a young woman, and a few years after my grandmother had died, I ventured far around the rock face of that shore and risked getting caught by tides swallowing the bases of cliffs, but something compelled me to keep going, and there on a rock I found her name carved deeply onto the face of a giant boulder. *Joan*. To this day I've never found the rock and her name carving again, and sometimes I feel I dreamed the whole thing, but I recall sitting on the huge warm seaside slab and running my fingers in the grooves of the letters, imagining what patience she must have had to set her name in stone. And what strength in her hands and heart.

I feel to this day a synergy with her. Like me, she was a farmer and she wrote stories too. I never knew her on the farm. I only remember her life after they'd sold the land – three daughters meant the future of the farm was lost back then. Her 'retirement home' was a vertical-board beach shack in the bush, where we'd sump oil the boards to stop them curling from the drying sea breeze. Inside, bookshelves were packed with Australian titles like *Brumby Jack Saves the Wild Bush Horses*, *Kings in Grass Castles*, *The Magic Pudding*, and *Snugglepot and Cuddlepie*. On the walls were heavy still-life oils painted by my great-uncles, along with a beautiful Mary Durack original painting of an Aboriginal boy (or girl) in a stockman's hat. Granno told me stories of the Dreamtime and showed me layers of meaning behind the Aboriginal artwork that hung on her wall. Great slabs of bark, handpainted with dots showing serpents, rock pools and the sun – art that she'd collected herself on her travels in the 1960s to Aboriginal settlements in remote Western Australia. It was where she must've also gathered her Durack sisters' collection of books and that beautiful stockman painting.

She also had Aboriginal and Papua New Guinean artefacts she'd gathered, which my mum eventually donated to the Tasmanian Museum and Art Gallery. Then there were her own manuscripts on the go, stacked beside her typewriter. The shack in which she lived held a kind of magic for me. At night native cats and quolls caught moths against the windowpane. Possums roamed the roof. Tassie devils squabbled under the floor as if gurgling blood. Magpies, noisy miner and butcherbirds ate the family offerings of chop fat and toast set out on a stump outside the kitchen window. There was the constant backdrop of waves, louder at night, and in summer, ABC cricket on the radio adding to the constant symphony of Australian living.

Some days I was allowed to put the turntable needle on the spinning black records so we could listen to Slim Dusty or Rolf Harris. Australiana in the 1970s flooded that sun-drenched, sea-horizoned room. Anything with an Aussie flavour set my senses alive and Gran brought life to the stories, music, art and Indigenous culture she had all around her. Grandfather Archie, who had Parkinson's disease and had suffered a stroke, would sit at the table in an old wooden swivel chair he had once used in his farm office and watch us. He was unable to speak, but still smiled through his kindly clear blue eyes at his blonde-haired brood of grandkids. With such art and literature placed under my nose at an early age – particularly by Australian women and by my own family members in the setting of a bush shack – the magic of storytelling was lit from within me, along with a deep understanding that another culture that at the time most white Tasmanians denied knew the true stories of the landscape upon which we walked.

Years later, my Auntie Susie gave me a box of Gran's writing. It was a mess of notes, manuscripts, letters, receipts and a dry-cleaning slip. In it I found a story Gran had written about Grandfather Archie and how, after his stroke, he'd disappeared with a gun into the bush, worrying her sick. Her fretting did nothing to bring him back but eventually when he did return he had a rabbit for the pot. She could not be cross with him for long. Love for him was woven into that story, despite the burden of her being his carer for what must have been many years.

I think there's a mistaken belief that women 'in the old days' had less freedom than we do now. But when I piece together the stories about the women in my family, there are no 'Jessicas' waiting in homesteads or on cliffs screaming to be rescued. They are out there in the bush catching game or carving their name in stone and, it seems – if family folklore has it right – claiming the men they wanted.

I don't know if the stories are true, because the aunts can be vague or tight-lipped about the family's couplings, but it was rumoured my great-grannie Lizzie McDowell (my Grandfather Archie's mum) was a good seventeen years older than the bloke she fell for. One can only assume it was such a scandal back then for a woman to take a 'toy boy' that after the lovers married they moved on from the family farm of Logan at Bothwell in the Tasmanian highlands to resettle on the coastal property of Fulhum, at Dunalley near the Tasman Peninsula. My Grandfather Archie was an only child, because Great-Grannie was late into her forties when she had him. Not the done thing back then, but I bet she had a wow of a time falling in love with her young man, who came from the large and prosperous Wise family who owned stone wharf factories in Hobart Town that still stand today. Their pretty white farmhouse overlooking the sea still stands too, and I've driven past it, longing to live there like Great-Grannie and Grandpa Wise did with their little son Archie.

The family story goes that a generation later, Archie and Joan hooked up at the Wellington Ski Club Hut where they both enjoyed, clearly, very social cross-country skiing. Joan was the Hobart-born daughter of Coralie Annie Donnolly – Coralie was a beauty in her day with an 18-inch waist and a good set of lungs. I was told by the aunts she was a brilliant singer who once performed alongside Dame Nellie Melba, and was invited to tour with her, but Coralie's parents wouldn't allow it. Typical of the day. Instead Coralie married well into the large Boyd family, choosing Eric, the son of one of the commandants at Port Arthur, and the result was the birth of two boys and one girl . . . that being Joan. According to my aunts, Joan and Archie had to be quickly married within nine months before my Auntie Elizabeth arrived along with the next snow season. In Elizabeth's album, there's black-and-white photos of groups of the old-style skiers, rugged up in the wintry Tasmanian bush amidst powdery snow. I saw that photo recently at Elizabeth's eightieth birthday gathering, where a collection of photographs was spread out on my cousin's farmhouse kitchen table for all the family to see.

There she was . . . my cradle-snatching great-grannie Lizzie, sitting in their rather rickety-looking wooden fishing boat with a few other long-skirted friends, her handsome young son Archie in their midst. I've been told they spent a lot of time on the water, and used to row sheep out to the tiny Green Island to graze near Dunalley. In the photograph Great-Grannie Lizzie was wearing a ladies' hat, bowed white blouse and the long dark skirts of her day, but it was no stern formal family portrait that one normally sees from that era. What made me smile with wry understanding of my legacy was what she was doing in the picture. She has one hand on the tiller, and in the other she holds a pistol, aiming straight for the camera! Her son, Archie, is perched on the sailing boom, smiling indulgently. Elizabeth's formally attired husband, Norfolk John Wise, stands above her, looking as if he's trying not to be amused. Seated with them all in the boat is a younger woman raising a long-neck bottle of beer or cider. I think it is Joan, Archie's young wife. Her head is turned so I can't see her face, but I sure can recognise those strong hands gripping the corked bottle and enamel mug. They mirror my own hands. There was something powerful and playful about the image of those skylarking women, and remembering it has often given me fuel in my tank to keep being a strident voice for rural women, despite a society that may want to keep me stuck on a cliff edge or in a homestead wearing appropriate length frocks.

It seems the women in our family were always ones for bucking fashion. Outside the corrugated-iron-roofed coastal shack, in the centre of a gravel turning circle, my gran had the most wonderful native garden that was netted to keep the rabbits, possums and pademelons out. She was certainly not 'on-trend' for the time in terms of garden style. Back then, English gardens were all the rage in Tasmania. Roses, daffodils, hawthorn hedges and granny's bonnet filled up most Tasmanian gardens, along with neat lawns and deciduous trees that glowed in autumn when their leaves turned the colour of bronze or liquid honey. But Joan didn't seem to care for such gardens, such was her love for all things native.

Inside the shack on the tables and the fire mantel, kangaroo paws and bottlebrush sat alongside mother-of-pearl-washed half-shells of abalone that she often used as ashtrays.

Gran was an adventurer in the outdoors. She had once braved wild seas, harnessed to a flying fox over cliff-smashing swells, just to get from the boat to Tasman Island to visit the lighthouse there. The result of the experience was a children's book called *Trapped on Tasman*, which she published in 1971. She also ventured to the Sahara Desert to see a lighthouse that once guided the camel trains. Unlike Jessica, she wasn't chasing a bloke. She was wanting to have a look about the place. Also a keen golfer, I can imagine her in her tweed skirt with pin, trudging in her fringed leather lace-ups over Tasmanian golf courses that were alive with diving magpies and snakes in the rough. During crib games, she would eyeball her opponents competitively through a haze of smoke. There were no flies on her.

From what my mother says, Joan wasn't a motherly mother. She sent my mum off to boarding school at six because the war years' petrol rations meant there wasn't enough fuel to get the three girls to and from the local school. Despite my mum's frostiness towards her memory, it seems Joan has been my muse for all my adult writer's life. Since her passing in 1985 when I was just finishing school, I've felt myself drawn into reading her work and contemplating her life. One of her books, *The Silver Fish*, set in the Derwent Valley, shows what life must've been like for her during the hop-harvesting times, when the industry thrived for the local beer-brewing companies. I've read that book to my own kids and it's been wonderful to have her strong voice in their lives via her writing.

One story, which I shall tell now, is a startling reminder to us all that we are connected by unseen threads that take us beyond the time, space and reality we think we know. Roadways don't just take us to physical places in the here and now. These paths of connectivity can take us across the thin quicksilver divide into another realm and across time. This story is not so much eerie as 'otherworldly' about my Granno and me.

I have a clever friend and colleague, Danielle Wood, whom I met in our 'baby journalist' days when she was a reporter for the Hobart *Mercury* and I was a writer for the *Tasmanian Country*. I remember the work pressures and how our editors were getting to us both when one day Danielle cheekily swanned into my office with her impish grin and parked her butt on my desk.

'Some day we won't have to worry about any of this,' she said with a glorious sweep of her hand. 'We are going to be famous novelists.'

As the earth turned and the years passed, Danielle went on to win the prestigious Vogel prize with her novel *The Alphabet of Light and Dark*, set on Bruny Island, not far from Gran's stopover, Tasman Island. Like Granno's book, Danielle's fiction celebrated lighthouses and Tasmanian life. I went on to write *Jillaroo*, which opened the door for other rural women's manuscripts, and built a name for myself in that newly created genre. It seems Danielle's prediction all those years earlier was correct.

But this is where the story gets spectacularly serendipitous. Later, as a university academic, Danielle began to compile a book with Professor Ralph Crane called *Deep South*, which featured Tasmanian writers, past and present. She'd selected a story I'd written called 'The Mysterious Handbag' to go in the collection. I remember I wrote the original version at a writers' workshop in Emerald, Queensland. I was working on 'Planet Downs' cattle station at the time. I had begged our head stockman, Jason, for the day off, travelling a six-hour round trip and staying overnight for a workshop with writer Rowena Lindquist.

As with many stories, I tapped into that vein of creativity I can't explain and wrote a piece that brought to life my childhood pastime of tacking the skins of rabbits and the plague-proportioned brush-tailed possums on the shearing-shed walls to dry and later sell. I loved the task and it must've had something to do with that ol' surly grandfather of mine on Dad's side who once had his forty rabbiting dogs. Back then in my childhood, Tasmania still had a fur trade and an animal hide industry, which ensured all parts of the animals, including the pelts, were used. I was lucky enough to catch the tail end of that era before it died out altogether and skin processing went offshore, and the commercial harvesting of native skins ended. In discovering the story, Danielle liked the feminist voice in the piece and the 'Tasmanian-ness' of my reference to skinning.

Time passed and many months later Danielle called to tell me the collection was nearly done. My story had been set right at the back because she wanted to place it alongside a story written in the 1950s that she said 'complemented it'. She said the story that melded well with mine was set in the highlands of Tasmania and was about a woman fur trapper. Danielle said both had similar strong female voices. Happy that my story had made the final list out of hundreds, and not too concerned about where the story went in the collection, I hung up the phone, my ego feeling privileged I was to be included alongside some great Tasmanian writers. More time passed until one day in the farm office, the phone rang. It was Danielle, delivering astounding news.

I remember my skin pricking with goosebumps and tears coming to my eyes involuntarily when Danielle told me.

'I've just had to be picked up off the floor of the university!' she had said. 'You know that story I mentioned that complemented yours, "The Conquest of Emmie"?'

'Yes,' I said slowly.

'It was written by your grandmother! Joan Wise!'

It was as if the universe swirled around me in that moment and I felt chills of connectivity – there actually were no words for what I felt. We'd had no idea of the connection. A master at digging out literature gold, Danielle in her excavations had uncovered the story in the 1950s *Bulletin* magazine by the relatively unknown writer Joan Wise. She couldn't find any biography on her when she searched archives and online, so when you live in a small city like Hobart, you simply ask around. Danielle set about quizzing her mother's friends. One person at last said,

'Ah, yes. Joan Wise . . . I think one of her daughters married a Hobart lawyer.' When she heard his name, a light flashed in Danielle's head. She knew he was my father, so as the piece of the puzzle fell into place and the picture became complete, her breath was momentarily taken. Against the odds, across time, across space, across life and death, a grandmother and her grand-daughter's stories had come together, to sit side by side together in a collection. Despite the gap of a generation, the bloodline that placed words upon the page connected, as did the strong theme of capable women in the landscape.

I told Danielle about the box of notes and writing Auntie Susie gave me of Gran's work, complete with that dry-cleaning receipt and sprinkling of mouse poo. Once I realised the importance of those creative threads down the family line, the box has since been taken to the University of Tasmania by Danielle to a much more respectful place than under my bed for the dogs to sleep beside and mice to rummage in.

Through Danielle's contacts, an emerging filmmaker called Pauline Marsh secured a grant to turn 'The Conquest of Emmie' into a short film. Danielle converted Gran's story into a screenplay for her and we worked together to finesse it. Pauline was captivated by the tale because it was ahead of its time. It showcases a strong mother of one with another on the way deciding which man to marry – a love triangle about an unwed mother. Again, not the done thing for women to tell stories about in the fifties. Women in the landscape of the

Australian wilds and in our oceans are powerful metaphors and my female forebears were the real deal. Not a single 'Jessica' amongst them.

Joan's daughter, Auntie Susie, still uses the expression 'Go about your traps', meaning go and see what you may have captured in life from the traps you have set for your future. I've set many traps of positivity and know in time my traps will be full of bounty. Imagination is my light that guides me, and in it I see a woman in a long skirt with dead rabbits tied about her waist, standing in high-country boggy marshes with a ruddy face and a strong stance. I see a woman astride a horse in a mountain stream shifting cattle and later boiling a billy outside a log hut. I was happy to say that woman for a time was me, living that clichéd image, with my man by my side. I got to live that dream of high-country life for a good few years with my former husband. Precious years.

After I lost access to that life, and the hope died that we would be together forever like the old fairytales had taught me, I was a woman stripped bare. I had lost all but my children. Even my dignity was holding on by the merest thread. There was not much further for me to fall and I had no place left to go. Except to the place that told me I was a strong woman, capable of standing on my own two feet on this land . . . and that one day I would be ready to stand alongside another, but with my own self complete. To help heal, I sought out the sea. So I went with my horse (whom I'd named Archie, after my grandfather) to the east coast of Tasmania, where my grandmother must have gone when she carved her name in that rock.

Archie came a year or so after the tragic death of my beautiful horse Dreams – the death I am yet to speak of, in an accident that has ugly barbs to people who tangle themselves in a backstory I'm not ready to tackle and prune away just yet. The thorns of those memories would cut me too much. Archie is young and beautiful. Solid. Like Dreams, he's a buckskin. While Dreams was a soft buttery colour, Archie's body is the strong colour of bronze with a mane and tail as dark as night. His legs are brushstroked with the same black, as if he had galloped across a night sky. I had named him Archie after my handsome farming grandfather because, as my mother reported, he was a man who was kind to his farm animals, loved his daughters and gave them a go of the rabbit trap and the rifle. And now here I was, his land-lost granddaughter seeking solace by the sea, with the memories of my grandmother in her dinghy setting off to check cray pots with him. This day, though, I wasn't on Gran's beach, but with my friends, a little further up the coast near the township of Swansea. Today the waves were mild, but gave enough of a crash and a boom to spark a side shy from Archie, but once over the break, a wave surged upwards and suddenly, we were swimming in the sea. Wearing just my bathers and a T-shirt, no shoes and no helmet, like the teenage girl I'd once been, I was swimming with my horse. Above us, the skies were a moody blue, hazed with bushfire smoke, and stretching before us the sea was a sulky grey in the heat of the day.

Even Freycinet Peninsula hulked in the distance like a prehistoric beast, too drowsy from warmth to stand.

With my bare thighs wrapped around the gold-gloss coat of my horse's hide, his thin charcoal-lined ears flickering backward and forward, I felt a rush of gratitude. It was incredible to feel the power of such an animal beneath me. I was washed with joy that I had another chance to experience the absolute privilege of owning a horse like him and of earning his trust and feeling his commitment to keep us safe and swimming. I still recall his playful snorts of pleasure as the water took us and bathed us in a new life and a new way forward. We emerged from the surf, dripping wet, with silver rivulets falling onto white squelching sand.

The glory of the moment has not faded, so when the desolation of my land-less life tries to crowd me again, I think to myself, *I have my horse. And I have the sea. And I have that day, when he and I went swimming. And above all, I have my forebears out there in the stars guiding me and cheering me on as I become that woman in the landscape.*

In my writing endeavours, on the cover of my first novel *Jillaroo* I deliberately asked photographer Bill Bachman to take a shot of a girl riding her work-fit, mountain-bred horse with the beautiful Great Dividing Range in the background. In the photo she was to be looking down to her bloke. He had to walk. For a short time before the covers of women's rural genre fiction reverted back to cliché and images of passive women in the landscape, I got to, in a small way, help alter the psyche of a nation when that cover hit the bookshelves. I know my Granno Joan and Granddad Archie would be proud of me. There are as many sheilas from Snowy River as there are men in our country, and there always have been. Now's our time, girls, to pick up our reins and ride!

The Grassland Goddess

As the sun rose slowly in the sky, the frozen tin on the Lemont shearing shed ticked and banged as it expanded above our heads. The ice fuzz that had covered the corrugated iron during the cracker overnight frost began to melt and drip down onto the ground. Inside, a kettle was chugging steam into the Midlands' chill and the arriving field-day participants were writing their names on silver '1000-mile-an-hour tape' to stick on woollen jumpers and jackets as name tags – farmer style. Today we were going to hear from a range of speakers about the benefits of native grassland in Tasmania's extreme conditions, and how native grasses don't need expensive fertilisers and can be a precious resource to farmers. The speaker line-up included our pasture-cropping guy Colin Seis, grazing guru Graeme Hand and a woman I hadn't heard of, Annabel Walsh, from a large property in New South Wales.

As I chatted with my farming friends, we made our cups of tea, gathered up biscuits and settled in against the morning cold on plastic chairs on the lanolin-soaked wooden floor that faced a whiteboard. Clasping the heat of the cup, I held it to my face, the steam warming my reddened nose. Despite thermal long sleeves, a thick polar fleece and a wool-lined oilskin vest, and my feet encased in Tassie-made woollen socks and my old faithful long-top boots, I was still cold. I shivered. It was the first farmer event I'd been to since I'd moved off my old farm, and I was still finding my way on my new patch of soil and in my heart. With me always, like a shadow, was the shame that I was no longer on my farm. Because of those thoughts that played on a loop in my head, I found myself feeling awkward at social gatherings. The opening line of 'Where are you from?' or 'Do you farm?' sent my internals in a spin. Where to start on that?

One of my main 'shames' was with my ego-based identity that I was no longer a 'farmer'. Not officially. Not commercially. In my head I'd become a busted-arse single mum, rejected by her blood kin, like an ugly featherless chick thrown out of the nest. But something in me stirred and grumbled at this very pathetic portrait of self. Deep within I knew I was on a mission that was bigger than just me, and the layers of belief and bullshit I'd amassed in a lifetime needed to be peeled away if I was to continue on that inner calling. It was a mission to discover more about Mother Earth, Mother Nature – Mother herself – and to put it all into words that others could absorb and enjoy . . . and to use as leverage to change our thinking, our lives and, above all, our land. We get what we focus on, so my intention was to get more people focusing on a new road in agriculture, the topic we were gathered there to talk about on that brisk morning.

I planned on using my newly bought 20 acres to trial what I was learning about resting pasture, managing grazing and watching what happened when the land was given time to heal. I began to see it was actually a blessing in disguise that I was no longer 'farming' back with 'the boys'. Here was a chance to take all pressure off the land to make a dollar from it and see what happened. It was an experiment I could never have undertaken had I been caught in the family systems of my home farm. Today at Lemont I was hoping to put more tools in my tool kit by hearing the speakers and to weave their knowledge into my fictional works. Increasingly I was discovering a deep inner calling to help open people's mindsets about landscape and how it functions (or fails to function) under farming practices. Since I no longer had much of a farm to showcase effective methods of the new agro-ecology methods I was learning, my beloved fiction writing was a place I was still empowered to share those ideas.

As the introductions were made, I shifted in my seat, already looking forward to the part of the field day where we would be warming our bodies by walking pastures and inspecting native grasses, and learning to identify species under the gentle pale sunshine that was emerging from a low-slung sun. I told myself, uncomfortable as I was, it was nice to be with others. It was also lovely to notice that, because of the changes I was making within myself, I was gravitating towards an entirely new crowd of people. People who were open to listening and learning from others, but also listening and learning from the land itself. I noticed too, there was a higher percentage of women in the crowd than previous farmer gatherings I'd been to. I had read from many sources that once you begin to change within, sometimes other people in your life fall away. Since the divorce I was certainly drifting through changes in social groups.

The clock ticked on the pale-blue wall, overseeing the bent steel down tubes of shearing stands, and the day of speaking began. I fell into a spell of awe and admiration when it was Annabel Walsh's turn. Tall, slim and beautiful, and unquestioningly feminine, even in khaki drill shirt, denim jeans and work boots, Annabel was standing in front of us as the chairman of Stipa Native Grasses Association.

Stipa is not an acronym. The association was named after Stipa, the most common genus of grasses, which includes spear grass. It's a plant found all across this continent but few of us could identify it by name. The Stipa Association aims to change attitudes towards native grasses and promote them to make landscapes healthier and farms more profitable. In doing so, with green summer native grasses, it's likely their restoration could reduce the savageness of bushfires in this land. I'd been involved in Australian agriculture all my life and yet I'd not heard of Stipa grasses. I was so conditioned in my farming education to adopt only British thinking and focus, that my knowledge of native grasses was non-existent. I'd also very rarely heard women speak in the way Annabel did. She did not reference a man when she was describing her system of farming. My mind drifted and I wondered why. Was she like me? Single? I hadn't known at the time that she'd suffered an immense personal tragedy that had been the subject of an *Australian Story* episode on the ABC back in 1998. I noticed she spoke with assurance, and she used a different language from men who 'work and manage' land. As a woman she used language that set her up as a caretaker who learns from the land and sees it as her 'teacher'. She also held an energy of love when she talked of her farming landscape. Her presence before me prompted a profound awakening, particularly when framed by the deep questions I'd been asking about the very masculine slant of our world and rural systems that I'd experienced.

I'd been reading a very interesting book, *Farmacology*, by a family physician and nutritionist, Dr Daphne Miller, about her research and enquiry into finding healing for her patients via nutrition grown from fertile soil. In her brilliant book, Dr Miller quotes from the 1970 Nobel Peace Prize winner, Norman Borlaug, who was the man touted as being 'the father of the Green Revolution'. During his prize acceptance speech he said, 'With the help of our Gods and our science, we must not only increase our food supplies, but also insure them against biological and physical catastrophes.'

When I first read this quote I felt a pulse of both amusement and frustration. Gods? Dr Borlaug was asking our 'Gods' to help us with farming, but there are no male gods of agriculture. They are all female goddesses. No wonder our systems since the 1970s, heavily reliant on science and manmade process, are failing us! We need to be seeking help from our goddesses. They are all female when it comes to food production – with the exception of an occasional hermaphrodite. Our yummy-mummy foodie goddesses include Greek goddess Demeter, the goddess of corn, grain and harvest, who blesses grasses and fertile land. There's Fulla, the Norse goddess of our bounty. Chicomecoatl is the Aztec goddess of agriculture and nourishment. Our Native American Corn Mother protects our grain and harvest. Ops is the Roman protector of the harvest. Then there is Ceres, the Roman goddess of agriculture. Set in that classic Egyptian pose, body front on, head turned sideways, is Heqet, the goddess of fertility and germination of the crops. In Australia we have our beautiful goddess Nungeena, who gives us beauty and balance in nature and was responsible for engaging the birds to resolve an insect attack on the land. Little did I know, in that icebox of a shearing shed, I was about to discover a real-life goddess of grasslands. A living, breathing representation of what can happen to land under a woman's stewardship.

Annabel runs an historic 30 000 hectare property called Moorna, which has grazed mainly wool sheep since about 1858. The property is downstream from the town of Wentworth in the south-west corner of New South Wales and fronts the Murray River. The original lease was over 500 000 acres and at shearing time at one point in the property's history 150 000 sheep were dragged across the board of the busy shearing shed. Those sheep would've been run on the productive native grasses that grew year-round and covered the soil, capturing any rain, keeping the ground warm in winter and cool in summer. Annabel said these types of green native grasses at times didn't even need a rain event to retain their vigour because they were able to make the most of the dewy mornings.

However, by the time Annabel arrived at the property twenty-five years ago when she married into the Walsh family, the property could only sustain 10 000 dry sheep equivalent. She said the property's history of continuous grazing that didn't match rainfall, along with rabbits and increased numbers of kangaroos, meant that the vegetation composition had gone into survival mode. Annabel described the environmental degradation and corrosion of ecology as a 'loss of natural capital'. I liked that description. Suddenly here was a term that the more hard-arsed economic, linear-minded amongst us could understand. I find some people switch off when you talk about 'environmental health' but here was Annabel with a great term to switch on the mindsets of the most sceptical.

'Approximately 80 per cent of the natural capital had been lost and many of the properties in the district were becoming unviable even without the wool market slump,' Annabel said.

To add to that, the effects of the Murray–Darling irrigation scheme of expanding the lake systems through damming had created a rising water table beneath the ground at Moorna. It meant that grasslands were becoming salt land before Annabel's eyes. The official government irrigation bodies said the salt land problem would be so bad by 2025 that the land would have to be 'retired', bought up by the government and locked up and left! Faced with a tough choice between selling up or staying put, Annabel saw it would be up to her and her family to increase their knowledge to counter the salt problem.

Whilst other properties were being bought to be locked up by the government, Annabel and her family set about on the most incredible journey of land regeneration. Instead of focusing on enhanced genetics, fertilisers and improved pastures as most grazing managers do, Annabel began to focus on rest and time for the land. The rotational grazing system she developed gives her ground ten months of rest before her large mobs of sheep – sometimes as many as 4000 in one mob – return to the area for two months of grazing. She's been carrying out this style of livestock management since the mid-1990s and as a result of the dramatic changes to the landscape, she now hosts visiting scientists from around the world. The longer rest for the countryside from grazing animals means the ecosystem is now flourishing. In her words, 'Keep your ecosystem complex and your business simple.'

As I sat in that shearing shed and heard her story, I began to feel excited there were women like her, so busy in her passion that she'd long ago left the notion that she had to 'show the boys' or 'prove herself'. She was just getting on with it. So eager was she to encourage native perennial grasses back onto Moorna, she had collected, by hand, great swathes of bottlewash seed from other areas, bagged them up into garbage bags, and had her son hang out the back of her plane casting it over the expansive country whilst she flew. Annabel's goal was to bring her country to life with the grasses that had naturally been there for thousands of years, until we arrived with our domestic animals and selectively grazed them out of the landscape, or cooked them out with rising salty water from artificial lake systems to feed big irrigators downstream.

When she spoke I was absorbed by her grace, humour and fully-fledged, empowered woman presence in what was a male-dominated audience. In my own public speaking gigs, I've been referred to in derisive tones as 'girlie' by farmer fellas who didn't like what I had to say. I began to take note of how Annabel just presented her life's calling with a noble grace. During the break a friend who had been to school with Annabel filled me in about the traumatic event in Annabel's past. She was a Tassie girl originally who had fallen in love with Moorna man Horrie Walsh and married him, moving onto the land with him. But after a single vehicle accident about twenty years ago, Horrie was hospitalised permanently. Rather than sell up, she continued on with the property to restore it, and raised her three young boys into adventurous, successful men. Annabel has since been campaigning for change in grazing methods, with the wonderful perennial native grasses at the heart of her success and mission.

Her passion for plants and a healthy ecology means she has run over 60 kilometres of PVC pipe out and spread watering points to encourage stock to graze more evenly over the hard grey dirt of Moorna. Annabel has been doing away with the already slumping fences and trialling rotating her stock using watering points as a guide for stock to graze. No fences.

As she was a patient woman, I could see her animal behavioural training had great potential to mimic the natural process of grazing and rest of country using animals as a migratory herd from water point to water point. Even with parched earth due to low rainfall, Annabel is still able to coax bottlewash grass out of the salt-affected earth so that it sways gently golden in the breeze, where once there was just baked, capped soil. Dotting the flat landscape also, perennial saltbush and bluebush help to hold the moisture and have enough rest to seed for when rain does arrive. Native perennial mulka grasses and bottlewashes, river couch, bent grass, yam daisies, samphire, pigface and glasswort have rebounded.

'The grasses have been my teachers,' Annabel said.

As she stood before me – a grassland goddess – I knew the wisdom of the ancient feminine was alive and well in Annabel. She also showcased a deep change in perception within myself. Even though she had many thousands of acres, and I had only a few, the outcomes were the same. I was witness to not only the rejuvenation of the landscape I was caring for, but also a healing in my own self.

One of the defining moments when I saw just how much I'd transitioned from my old culture was after I'd been invited to Christmas drinks, where I found myself in a pub with a bunch of land owners I had known from my schooldays. Private boarding-school boys. Post-divorce I'd been in hiding, but now with my regenerative agricultural work under my belt, I felt ready to start networking again. I was nervous to walk into the pub by myself, but excited I was at last confident enough to hang once more with the farmer crowd. Instead, as the evening wore on and my rural colleagues had loosened their grazier-gentlemen personas with beer, I found myself fending off the most abrasive of questions.

'Are you single?'

'Do you date?'

'Have you got a boyfriend?'

And then came the whopper. 'We were wondering if you've had a boob job?'

I was left holding my drink with my mouth hanging open. The comments stung. I ended up jovially punching the fella's arm, saying, 'Sit down, you dirty old dog,' trying to laugh it off, but inside I raged. I turned the anger at myself, lamenting that I should never have come out alone, or been roped back into that world with people who clearly weren't on the road I was travelling. I realised that I no longer fitted into this crowd, if I ever had at all. I looked around the room and saw that almost all of the men there didn't have their wives or partners with them. I felt sorry for these blokes, and at the same time gobsmacked they would even think cosmetic surgery on the bits of my body that had sustained my kids was in any way my thing, just to look good for men?

Had it always been this 'base' in my rural world? Was I just noticing it now because I'd found my power and my path? Had agriculture become such a mechanised, masculine and corporate pursuit that women were excluded unless they rolled with the sexist punches? Was that why there were very few women here? Was it social conditioning? Had I lost my sense of humour? Shouldn't I just lighten up, move on and have another drink? It got my mind racing.

As I stood there, I thought about the old black-and-white pictures of my grandmother, great-grandmother and great-great-grandmother. Hair knotted in buns, with long feminine skirts, but wearing boots and expressions that suggested they meant business. With aprons on and sleeves rolled up for work, these women were present in the efforts on the farm. I saw them in photos with a milking cow. Feeding a litter of partly weaned sheepdog puppies. In the hop field toiling beside the men. My grandmother Joan Wise, who worked so hard, milking cows, folding washing, digging spuds, that her hands failed to function for a time and she had to wear plaster casts on both wrists. In her later years she used those same hands to type out carbon-copy manuscripts on a clunky old typewriter with a cigarette smouldering. Stories woven richly with firsthand experiences about women who defied society's rulings. Women ahead of their time. Women who were naturally a part of farm business – or so I had thought.

As I looked about that busy, beery, buzzy Hobart pub where blue-striped rural shirts formed a wall to the bar, I realised I had been independent for so long and happy in my own groove, that as I scanned these familiar faces I suspected change might be very hard for them. They were the sons of sons of sons of white settlers and they still seemed to have such an assumed right to the land they lived on and a right to be above the women and even the creatures of the ecosystem they 'owned'. Was conquering and dominating nature for profit, to the detriment of all creatures, still their foundation? I don't want generalise about the fellas who were simply enjoying Christmas drinks, and I'm sure there were some good-uns amongst them, but I truly began to ponder the notion that women were not only excluded (or willingly excluded themselves) from their farming domain, but that women were not honoured. They were ultimately, after enough beers, reduced to objects, only worthy of having pissy conversations with about breast size. And these were blokes who'd had the privilege of a 'good' education. Sure, there are more girls out on cattle stations now in charge of stock camps and women are getting a handful of managerial roles on properties, but there is no streamlined way to funnel talented young women into work on the land, to grow pure food – the education system does not support it, and nor does the culture.

Recently I was asked to give a talk at my old school. Think private. Think all girls. Think wooden banisters from the war years and dark oil portraits of former female principals, and uniform hems worn at the 'appropriate length'. Before I arrived, I was a bit like a snorty, nervous horse, not really wanting to go back into a stable after running so free (and feral) in the wild for so many years. But I made myself go, because I wanted to ask the girls this question: 'Who is aiming for a career in agriculture?'

After I asked it, there was an uncomfortable silence and an awkward pause. Only two girls out of 150 senior secondary students tentatively put up their hands, and even then I think it was because they were being polite. My next question was a hopeful one – hopeful for me, because I wanted the girls to see . . . to see within to their inner, ancient womanhood, to see the past, the present, the future, for all of humanity . . . to know what really turns this big old world that we all walk and share. I asked, 'Who here eats food?'

There was a collective chuckle amongst them. Food! Of course every person in the room put up their hand.

'Food,' I repeated. 'It's kind of important. And that's why I'm here.'

Most of the young ladies sitting inside the red-brick walls of the auditorium were being steered towards university pathways such as science, nursing, law, medicine, accounting, computing – areas that are all worthy, but skewed towards economics and science. And, they are all areas that don't produce food.

In our education system there is no formal pathway to teach feminine wisdom. This wisdom was once part of ancient food production knowledge that women held, but has been lost to society around the world since agriculture was hijacked by corporations after World War II. Nowhere in the masculine education systems are there places to teach women about holistic farming. The movement to impart such knowledge is grassroots and organic, and in some third world countries bound by governments that support big seed and chemical companies, such teaching, wisdom sharing and seed sharing is even considered rebellious.

Even the agricultural college I attended in Orange, which at times to me felt more like a dating service for blokes needing good farmer's wives, has closed most of its rural course component. The Orange campus that once offered on-farm practical lessons is now mostly used for studies that are non-agricultural. There are many vibrant, clever young women agronomists, scientists, researchers and administrators who are working in agriculture, but their belief systems and inner ideology are mostly founded on masculine principles and systems, and they are taught in universities that have rigid systems locked into technology as the answer to our global food shortages. Blokey roads of thought, which are great . . . but only when balanced and tempered by feminine wisdom.

In that pub I was surrounded by the result of those slanted educational foundations. I farwelled the boys, and cheerfully headed home to watch the cricket. It was good knowing that I had moved on, that I was travelling towards my own pack . . . men and women who embraced nature, balance, inner truth and desires.

I could feel that chilly morning in the shearing shed, after driving the winding potholed road to the field day, under rural railway bridges and past dying gums, that I had found a cluster of like-minded beings. The audience members weren't blocking the flow by putting up their hands and challenging the ideas of the speakers, like what happens so often at gatherings. Instead they were asking constructive questions about the lessons we were learning. The male speakers too, brave boys like Graeme Hand and Col Seis, were making statements about the need for greater gender balance in farming. Nowadays I look to be around 'gentle men' – not gentlemen in the old-fashioned sense who still used their status to be superior to women while using polite etiquette, but a new breed of male . . . a gentle version. Gentle on self, on land, on women, on livestock, gentle on their own gender but strong within themselves. As an expression of how I'd outgrown my old beliefs, I'd trashed my hero character Charlie Lewis in the sequel to *Jillaroo*, *The Farmer's Wife*. It was an expression to other women to not believe the fairytale. To really dig deep towards men who honour women and the land. Life was bigger, richer and more exhilarating if you didn't waste your time and energy chasing that elusive false dream of 'the one'.

As a maturing writer and a maturing woman, I didn't want to keep hitting the repeat button about our romantic notions about 'the Australian bush' (I cringe at that simplistic term). And I also didn't want to keep us trapped in the confines of old notions of romance between rural men and women. But in getting the message out, we need it to come from the people who hold the power in our world . . . men.

There speaking with Annabel was grazing expert Graeme Hand, a power pack of a man who 'tells it like it is'. He likens our future food shortage and the environmental disaster that's happening all around us to driving off a cliff. He said all government environmental protection policy will do is slow down the vehicle, but we are still heading in the same direction so we will eventually drive off the cliff.

'We actually need to turn the vehicle *around* and drive *away* from the cliff,' Graeme said. He added that many men know they need to change, but they don't change to regenerative farming ways because it can take too long to see the results.

'If the ground takes five years to recover, it's too long for a lot of Y chromosome characters.'

I've heard Graeme have a dig like this in each of his talks. He says it jokingly, but he's deadly serious about jolting men to change their mindsets. Overgrazing is an accepted norm in this country. People who don't know otherwise bang on about 'the cloven hooves' of animals not suited to our 'delicate' Australian environment, saying it's the hooves causing the degradation. But that's a fallacy that has been disproven by people at a grassroots level. The people in the bricks-and-mortar institutions and the ones inside the building in Canberra with the upside-down Hills Hoist on top of it are yet to catch up. As Graeme Hand points out, 'It's not the hooves causing the problem, it's the number of *mouths*.'

He said when he hears people blaming cloven-hoofed animals for the disaster on this continent, he says to them, 'Well, it's lucky rabbits have soft feet.' He makes the point that country that is never rested from grazing is damaged . . . no matter what sort of feet the animal has.

The grazing management on Moorna has revealed that grazing can be used to both destroy a landscape and restore a landscape. It all depends on management. It all depends on the number of mouths and the time the land is given to recover. In that shearing shed, I began to wonder why there weren't more Annabel Walshes on the planet taking care of and restoring vast tracts of degraded land?

My question led me back along a fog-bound road of thought to a time 5000 years ago when the feminine and all her powers were celebrated, respected and revered. I began to read how Mother Earth was our religion, and as a collective society we knew we were governed by her feminine powers. I saw clearly how humanity changed, in particular for women, when our 'modern' forms of religion started to strip away the powers of my gender. Something deep within my very *knowing* linked me to my past sisterhood and those who had been subject to horrors if they didn't tow the Christian line. I began to dream of past burnings, hangings, stoning, beheadings as if I had experienced them myself. I could feel the legacy of those mental and physical tortures as generation after generation of women were forced to give up feminine worship of the seasons or our power of healing using Mother Earth's plants. For several generations girls were taught by their mothers to dull their inner light. If they shone too brightly in the world they were dubbed witches and heretics. Via church-based religions, I saw how we became the property of men who owned us for their own wealth gathering, for procreation to produce a line of males, and how we were in service to them.

In my mind, it has never been more important for humanity to restore respect for the feminine and to create holistic systems that encourage women and children back onto the land. Globally women need to be involved not only in re-visioning our food systems, but also contributing feminine design of the landscape and housing in which we live. Even in politics, we women are limited by male language and systems. I believe if we are to survive as a species, women need to be encouraged to share their vision of how the world can look and be heard by the blokes, and supported by gentle men and awakened women. We are the givers of life. Western agriculture needs the feminine balance returned, and feminine wisdom needs to be restored to our society. In that shearing shed I saw clearly my need to be fearless and to declare that it's time to put the feminine back into farming.

Les, Dolly and Life's Lyrics

I've often said, 'When I grow up I want to be a cross between American country singer Dolly Parton and Australian poet Les Murray.' People laugh, but I'm serious. To me, music is poetry and poetry is music, and those two people are amazing in their chosen fields. I've often imagined what would happen if I could combine the two. Over the years I've written a few poems but I'd always wanted to write songs. Aussie songs. Country songs.

When I was about seven or eight, my friend Luella and I would set the needle on the record player and crank up Slim Dusty's hit single, 'I Love to Have a Beer with Duncan'. We'd sit behind her granddad's bar on stools, chugging empty pewter beer mugs together, singing our guts out to his song over and over, while the adults, who were half-cut on beer, laughed at us. A few short years later, I was shoved into an all-girls school, away from my bestie Luella. I must've spoken so much like an Aussie bush pig that the teachers had to give me speech lessons. I blame it on bloody Slim! Or was it those early years of Rolf Harris? Or was it the beer-drinking uncles of mine who called me 'girt' or 'cobber' or, when I was being cheeky, a 'rum'un'? There was no denying it, I revelled in country-rough and was shocked that the school and my parents seemed to think I had to somehow 'improve' myself.

At recess in the first week I was dragged, perplexed and ashamed, into the drama room with another farm girl from Campania, so they could sandpaper the rough edges from our ocker Tasmanian tongues. Over time, the speech-and-drama teacher, with her ivory clasp in her elegant scrolled hair and her blue eyes that expressed such patience, set about turning my words 'crick' into 'creek', 'I seen it' to 'I saw it', 'we done that' into 'we did that', 'youse' into 'you' and 'arks' into 'ask'. I had no idea why, of all the girls, we were singled out from the herd of first-year intakes. Despite the teacher's kindness, it made me feel like a wormy tail-ender in a mob of sheep. It was devastating, but also, in hindsight, thrillingly convenient, because it gave me something to rail and push against. It was this abrasive start to my teenage years that forged me into someone who never wanted to fit into social norms and systems that were on offer for Sandy Bay-schooled children of Hobart professionals or Tasmanian blueblood graziers. As far as I was concerned they could stick that kind of life up their tweed skirts and pleated trousers!

The dedicated school staff certainly had their work cut out for them, trying to get me to bend to the school's formalities of dress, speech and conduct. To me the building was like an alien mothership, transported straight out of Scotland with grand steps, a bland, austere brick face, rose gardens and the sound of orchestral music flooding its gloomy rooms. Like many of our British-style dwellings, it was pretending to be something that belonged here . . . but to me it was a trespasser on the foothills of the noble wilderness mountain. That giant bush-covered mountain, kunanyi, which overshadows the city of Hobart, is so rugged, wild and imposing, it haunts us all, reminding us of the people who lived here, before the uniformed man brought his pomp to these shores and named the dolerite-faced mountain after a Duke in Wellington, then plonked buildings like my school at the mountain's feet. Why was everything in this place named after a dead white dude, I often wondered as a young woman. And why did we have to wear boater hats in summer and tartan berets, complete with brown pom-pom, in winter? We were 'Straylian', for chrissakes, not bloody Poms.

At home, my mum had given her best shot at steering me towards more compliant ladylike ways, but the problem was I was a deep-thinking tomboy, who loved all things Australiana – and the grubbier, the better! I was happier in the world of my farming or tradie cousins, and saw no reason why I ought to insert a plum in my mouth so I could join the Hobart who's who. I had graduated from Slim Dusty on the old cassette recorder to a rougher musical adventure by learning every single Kevin Bloody Wilson song off by heart or quoting the jokes of Rodney Rude. Throw in a bit of John Williamson, some Paul Hogan and a dash of Jeannie Little, and my nasal twang training was complete. Doubling my unwillingness to be converted to a 'townie', I also had a passion for all things cowgirl. It stemmed from when I was really little and adored a Little Golden Book featuring a beautiful dreamy horse in western gear. My fascination with the cowgirl was cemented when at eleven years of age my parents took me on a tour of the USA to watch Luella's mother, Lindy Goggin, play golf for Australia.

The tour took us to North and South Carolina, San Diego, Kentucky and Los Angeles. I recall a party in a country club after one golf tournament, complete with dinosaur-sized barbecue spare ribs, red-chequered tablecloths, the hoedown and collectively stomping boots to a lively fiddle. Happy people with a rich southern drawl were all about me under lantern party lights. It explains why these days I have a 'thing' for the cowgirl look and feel, particularly boots, turquoise, cut-off shorts, silver jewellery and country music. I love to combine American cowgirl culture with my own Aussie culture. Even my dream of being a cross between Les Murray and Dolly Parton is expressed in my horse, Archie. He is a half Australian stock horse and half American quarter horse. (There's some confusing maths in that sentence if you read it the wrong way!) But during that brief trip to the States, I fell even more in love with American country music. Dolly Parton, I idolised. I loved seeing her on the telly in her short skirts, with thin waist, towering blonde hair, cowgirl boots and straight-shootin' mouth. After reading her autobiography

I discovered more than ever there's a businesswoman's brain beneath that big hair, and her devotion to giving books to children is something that floats my boat. She tells it like it is. She has unshakeable faith. Behind the sequins there's a steady class of commitment to being a lady who walks her own path and talks her own way. No wonder I want to be like her.

The trip to the States also gave me a glimpse of a wider world, and I saw firsthand amazing women from all around the world playing golf at a high international standard. At the time Luella's mum Lindy played off a plus-four handicap, which was the lowest handicap in the world. I was shocked when my mum explained Lindy was an amateur golfer, but even the women who turned professional still had less of a pay packet than their male counterparts. I was stunned that these amazing women, at the top of their sport, were equally as talented and committed as the men to golf, but doubly poor for their efforts in terms of prize money. I couldn't figure out why, in the late 1970s, Lindy Goggin's incredible winning blitz of the golfing world didn't make the papers as much as men's golf. The gender divide bit hard and early in my life as I watched Lindy's skill with her teammates bring Australia home in second place by a whisker behind the Americans in the tour. I flew back to Australia with my long blonde hair tinged green at the ends from swimming in so many turquoise-coloured motel pools, and my mind racing with uncertainty about my place in the world as a female. We were lesser. Society was showing me that. Yet, I puzzled, how could that be when

I didn't feel less, when women like those golfers didn't seem less?

When I started high school, I didn't know it intellectually, but I could feel the school was culturally layered with social expectations for my gender. Correct hem lengths. The right sort of knickers: beige. Sitting in position that was 'ladylike'. There was also an unspoken expectation to marry well socially, or go to university and conquer the upper echelons of academic society, squeezing into a man's domain if you were clever enough, and before you had children. Boring! I wasn't having a bar of it. No sir-ee! I was happiest in jeans with holes in the knees, a pony tangle rather than a ponytail, and lanolin-covered, thistle-pricked hands from work in a shearing shed, or to be out in the bush bareback on my little dun-and-white patched pony, Tristan, with my cracker friends Luella and Manty.

Heading back to the city after those pony-filled weekends brought a sense of devastation, and I called that time 'the brown years'. I didn't realise the privilege of my education until much later in my life. If it weren't for the teachers at that school, I may never have been given such a foundation in English or had a love for story and novels fostered so well. I may never have become a businesswoman running a company from my writing, and I certainly wouldn't have got a job on ABC radio as a rural reporter. It was there the speech lessons with the drama teacher paid off! Can you imagine it?

'Youse are all listening to Ay, Be, Cee raydio.' I still have a dreadful rising inflection on the ends of my sentences, and a voice that is as light as a pavlova, but thank goodness I can speak half-way correctly if I put my mind to it. Despite my determination to remain 'unbroken' at that school, the days passed into terms and the terms into years. I began to sink in my despair and try to unsuccessfully reach my parents with self-harm cuts on my hands and wrists, along with stormy silences or tantrums behind slammed bedroom doors. But no matter what I did, I was forced to remain at the school.

For my parents the school's location was convenient because I could walk to and from there, they didn't have to drive me. My father had never had such educational opportunities so maybe in his eyes, I ought not to have been such an ungrateful, dramatic, troublesome teenage girl. 'Put up and shut up' is our unspoken family rule and I knew the school was costing him a lot of money. The school also came with a social calling card for my parents, who obviously wanted the best for me, but the more unheard I felt, the more I began to be swallowed and crushed by that school. At home in town, without my $150 saviour pony Tristan, who my Auntie Susie had found for me, I sought refuge in the only animals we had – an obese pet mouse called Soot, an elderly cat called Greebly, and a baby hare, Lenny the Leveret, who Luella's granddad found on a golf course.

During those angst-ridden teen years, I turned into a dreamer to survive. I believe the poor fit of that school and urban life was what transformed me into an artist and a seeker. I spent the slow ticking minutes of my school years escaping by sitting in assembly creating alternative farming worlds in my mind's eye, like a film running in my head. In the classroom I gazed out the rain-streaked window, imagining a life beyond tartan kilts and brown school ties . . . a life in denim, flannelette and boots in the bushland I'd come to love so well, riding out on my horse. A creative life, a free life, where you didn't give a shit what other people thought . . . like Les. Like Dolly.

One day, the universe, as though tired of hearing my misery, answered my prayers. When I was in Year 10 I was given a glimpse of the possibility of freedom on the other side of my all-girls school prison. I shall never forget the moment when the school bus dropped a cluster of us off at the public Rosny College on the opposite shore of the Derwent River, the eastern shore – the 'less affluent shore', according to those from the riverside suburbs on the western river bank.

Like a flock of canaries in our summer yellow uniforms we chirruped our way into a lecture theatre and the teachers sat us down in our flesh-coloured tights and brown shoes to listen to poet Les Murray. It was a wake-up moment for me in life. I saw Les saunter onto stage and was in awe of him. Not because of what he said – he hadn't opened his mouth yet – but what he wore. The way he looked, walked, stood . . . the way he was.

In my memory I have him in a flannie shirt with a giant home-knitted woollen jumper, threadbare at the elbows and holes in the tummy. I picture him with bare feet, but I know he must've been wearing shoes, but I like to think he had bare feet. He was so utterly ordinary and true to himself. He hadn't dressed the part of a poet as you'd expect, nor did he address the crowd as if he really cared to impress. But impress he did. When he spoke his poetry, oh my Lord, did his words speak to me! As I sat in that audience and soaked up his beautiful word paintings about the Australian way of life and landscape with all its complexities, beauty and conflicted, sometimes tragic, identities, I knew then I had found my path forward for my own self. I knew that there was freedom on the other side of this school life, and that when I grew up I too would be like him. Unaffected by faux society rules. And painting with words.

Years later, fate, the universe or divine trust led me to Sydney literary agent Margaret Connolly. With an offer from Penguin Australia already in my hand for my manuscript *Jillaroo*, I called Margaret out of a word-of-mouth recommendation to ask if she would represent me. It turned out she also represented my dear treasured Les Murray, and for me, that was a sign from above to follow my new publishing road with Margaret. I've been with her ever since 2002 and even though I've not met Les personally, I've channelled his rebellious true-to-self, bugger-the-academics spirit in all that I do. In my quest to merge my idols of Dolly and Les, I began to find little stepping stones to lead me on the path.

One year at Agfest, Tasmania's three-day rural exhibition, I had a mutual fan moment with Tania Kernaghan, who came to see me when I was demonstrating working-dog handling and selling books. The next year, two gorgeous girls with long blonde hair and big black hats stopped by to say hi. It was Celeste and Sophie Clabburn of The Sunny Cowgirls. Musicians were dropping into my space. But not just any old music. *Country music*. The stuff that kept me rolling forward in life. A little while later Celeste got in touch to see if I had a kelpie pup to sell. Without a litter at that time, I sent her in the direction of Ian O'Connell.

Celeste not only got her pup Suey from Ian, but went on to combine her musical talents with farm management and ended up living in a cottage on Ian and Kay's farm for many years. It's the cottage where I recently stayed, putting down the finishing touches to this book. Celeste even wrote a beautiful, drifting song called 'Kelpie', about the breed's origin, based on a poem by local fencing contractor Peter Dowsley. It was the same poem that gave me the framework for my tribute to the kelpie in novel form, *The Stockmen*. Again here was poetry combining with music, and I was more transfixed with the idea than ever about songwriting. I just didn't know where to start. I had limited musical knowledge but I decided that shouldn't be a block. Trusting I would one day write song lyrics, emerging from the same stream of trust that I knew I would one day write novels, I set off in life, waiting for the next stepping stone on my path.

That came in 2010, when my Dolly wish was about to come true in a small way . . . I was going to get the chance to write songs. But not just songs . . . country rock songs! With an invitation to open the Bushy Park Show, I loaded up with books and a couple of kelpies and a crazily creative colleague called Helen, and we headed off in my old red ute, winding along the blacktop ribbon road that follows the bends of the increasingly narrowing Derwent River. As I journeyed upstream away from Hobart, past tall fluffy poplars and the remnants of the hop industry, I was eager to experience the tiny little Tasmanian show. It was where my aunties and my Granno Wise used to show their ponies in the forties. We turned off the Derwent River Highway onto a small leafy road, dipped over a narrow bridge and there we were . . . at the Bushy Park Show. We pulled up and looked for someone to steer us towards the area where we needed to go. Lauren, the bright-faced organiser, a country girl with a tonne of heart and enthusiasm, came over to say hello, her giant woolly pet sheep in tow.

'I hope you don't mind, but you'll be sharing a table and a marquee with the band.'

She nodded her head towards a blue-and-white tent that had been begged and borrowed from Roberts Ltd, the livestock agents. Beyond that there was a big truck with the sides rolled up, and on its checker-plate surface were some blokes setting up drum kits, mike stands and lugging big black amps.

'No worries,' I said. I was slightly sheepish as I had no idea who 'the band' were.

Even when they strung up their black-and-white banner reading 'The Wolfe Brothers' I had to admit I hadn't heard of them. For the past few years, I'd been buried under farm work and raising babies so I hadn't been part of the Tassie country pub-and-party scene, but judging by the excitement from those arriving at the show, and clustering near, these boys were loved by many. It was a meaningful meeting when, for the first time, I shook the hands of brothers Tom and Nick Wolfe, and their childhood buddies, band members Brodie Rainbird and Casey Kostiuk. Right from the outset, it was like meeting my own clan. They were country boys with creativity in their veins, a rural heritage similar to mine and they were on a road like mine . . . one that has roots in a small place like Tasmania but our artistic branches spreading out across all of Australia and bearing fruit both here and internationally.

We clicked straight away. Once I heard them rock their first song, I was sold on them. It was country rock that had a class to it I'd never heard in this state. I'd been to many interstate events that had brilliant country artists that filled up the dome of the night sky with heart-thumping country music from the back of a truck. From The Sunny Cowgirls at the Deni Ute Muster, to Steve Forde at the Mountain Cattlemen's Annual Get Together near Cobungra Station, and Lee Kernaghan himself in Omeo, I'd seen my fair share and loved every paddock-stomping moment of our Australian artists. As the Wolfe Brothers ripped through their set, I had to do a double take. Here I was in my home state, watching homegrown talent that matched the best I'd seen on the mainland, their sound even transcending Australian waters to that of the latest music I was listening to out of the USA. Offstage, they were 'Tassie-as', and when I offered to look after their merchandise for them when they were onstage, I found they spoke the same lingo. They had an easy grace to them, not to mention the humour that was in tune with my own. As they came offstage and thanked us, Helen said casually, 'Hey, you should write a song together.'

It was no surprise we kept in touch, became mates, and then, with my Dolly wishes fulfilled, the chance to write songs arrived.

The first song I co-wrote with Nick Wolfe emerged when I bumped into Tom Wolfe for the second time in a row on the same street corner outside the same pockmarked sandstone face of a convict-built pub in Hobart's Salamanca where I had seen him the previous week.

'If you're gunna stalk someone,' I said jokingly, 'it's best not to wear high-vis, Tom.' I indicated his vibrant, eye-smackingly orange shirt he was still wearing due to his day job as a builder. He laughed and invited me into the dimly lit Irish pub to say hi to the boys. There was Nick, also in his green-yellow postman's high-vis top, unwinding leads and smiling at me. Looking at them, busy with their pre-gig setup, I said, 'We oughta write a song about hi-vis.' And that was that. Soon I found myself at Nick's kitchen table, with a cup of tea and an open Bundy can chaser, a black crazy kitten climbing the screen door, a sheepdog sleeping on the mat outside and Nick's dad's tractor trundling along the steep face of a hill outside. In this environment, I began my first lesson in the basics of lyric writing. Nick with his guitar and me with my love for playing with words, together we soon channelled a 'Hi-Vis Anthem' into the world. The song's lyrics reflect exactly my journey from all those days ago at my private school, and with Nick's working-class spin we wrote a fun first-time song: 'I'll never have a law degree, that'll never bother me. I'm working hard and sleeping well at night. You can keep your tie and shirt, I'll keep my hands down in the dirt. I'd rather wear high-vis to work. Clear and bright. It's a real good sign.'

Since that first songwriting session, Nick and I joined up again. I was so 'rock-chick mother' as I sat in my house sampling a bit of his family tradition home-brew moonshine as we wrote, 'Got nothing to do and all day to do it' before downing tools because the kids had arrived at the bottom of the farm road from the school bus. I'd only had one nip, but the fuel of that smooth hard liquor helped the song arrive, if only to settle my nerves at working beside a musician with such talent. In the time I collaborated with Nick I could tell he was as much a muso as he was a poet. Not so much a Les–Dolly cross, but maybe a Les–Johnny Cash cross?

Fresh back from Nashville working on the band's latest album, Nick held his own with the US greats in songwriting. It's no surprise they've been booked for over thirty American gigs this year. It was on the cards a few years ago when they won second place on television show *Australia's Got Talent*, were picked up by Stephen White Management and began touring the country with Lee Kernaghan. On Lee's 'Spirit of the Anzacs' tour, the Wolfe Brothers got to sing songs of real-life Tassie war heroes while behind them on the big screen flashed images of their own grandfather, handsome and young in his navy uniform in World War II. It's been a privilege to share a small part in the boys' journey, and as artists they have helped me embrace my Tasmanian-ness.

Time has brought me full circle. Luella and I, with our kids a similar age as we were when clanking beer mugs to Slim, discovered a definite 'edge' to our kids' speech. There was a 'living out the back of whoop-whoop' slant to their words and diction. For fun and in a bid to raise our kids' awareness of how to speak 'correctly', we decided to create 'Manners Monday' each week. Here, after school, we got out Luella's grandmother's Wedgwood china tea set with delicate cups, set down on the table by our chunky work-worn hands, encouraged the children to 'take tea' and enunciate and articulate properly, with little pinkies out and backs straight. Never mind the horse-manure-smeared dog under the table and the little black dots of flies stuck to the strip of sticky paper above the tea table.

'Gawd, Mum!' came the ocker protest. 'Do we hafta?' But the kids joined in. Manners Mondays didn't last long, but at least Luella and I gave it our best shot. These days I'm unapologetic about my twang . . . in words and my taste in music and clothing, despite what they tried to teach me during the 'brown years'. My kids will grow up proud to be 'Straylian' and know that country's where it's at.

The Grass Is Always Greener

The other day Auntie Susie offered me a rabbit. Not the cute, floppy-eared kind you put in a hutch. No! It was a skun carcass, still bloody in a plastic bag, wrapped like a gift in brown paper and nestled in a cardboard wine box, along with some home-grown garlic and onions. Apparently the retirees in Auntie Susie's seaside village like to 'pop' a few bunnies on the lawn from their verandahs – with silencers so they don't disturb the neighbours. Courteous bunch. I can only hope that in my mentioning this, the local cops turn a blind eye. Those who understand our island culture know we rural Tasmanians like our guns for food harvesting. They used to be everyday items until some crazy bugger went bonkers with one at Port Arthur a couple of decades ago and ripped apart people's lives for generations to come. After that dreadful, heartbreaking, peace-shattering day, our gun laws understandably and thankfully changed.

But as a Tassie kid I grew up with gunpowder in my nostrils and unlocked guns racked on the wall. Instead of Saturday morning cartoons at Granno's beach shack we got to shoot Cascade tinnies from the flat surface of stumps, shrieking when we hit one, watching them dance and flip into the crisp seaside air, a bullet hole punctured in their side. In our family it was stock-standard practice to teach your kids to handle a gun, set a trap or a snare, bait a line or a cray pot, start a fire and cook with it, sow and grow a seed. I think it was a legacy of convict white folk trying to survive, find a meal and build a life in a new but stolen, and oftentimes scary, land.

So here I was, rinsing this little bunny under the kitchen tap, its raw fleshy body unlocking thoughts in me as I began to ponder what it is to be a mother cooking for her children, making food choices for them. I had found myself struggling with the knowledge that the feminists in the 1970s fought hard to 'free women from the kitchens', yet I sensed within me a constant niggling feeling that I wanted to spend time there. On other days, when I didn't want to, I knew that I had to for the health and wellbeing of my family. The inner conflict annoyed me. Something about my gender seemed to lock me into cooking for my little darlings no matter what – even with no men in the house hovering saying, 'What are we having for dinner?' as if it was always my responsibility. There was also the compulsion to lure the children into the kitchen with me to teach them the basics – ahead of doing homework. Somehow, to me, learning about food seemed more important than spelling or maths.

Even with our severed little family of just three, most nights on the Heavenly Hill and now in the flystrike house, the kids and I sit up at the table for meals. Our shared dinners are a place for cultivating conversations, gently pointing out manners, allowing much laughter and a load of silliness, along with a chance to discuss the food we have before us. How it is grown. How it is precious, and how there is a compelling need to be grateful for it, and to bless it as it enters our bodies. Even in the early days of setting up a new home on the Heavenly Hill, when my nerves were stretched to capacity and my heart still felt so cracked it might shatter onto my plate with a crash, I kept our family ritual of peaceful mealtimes sacred. As I set down our meals, I tried to steer my focus away from the laminate plastic-fantastic table that had been bought hastily out of necessity. It felt soulless and tainted with factory toxins and was a poor echo of the massive old wooden kitchen table that remained in my former home that was imbued with age, memories and nature's warmth.

No matter how much writing work I had due, or how rugged the road had been in our uprooted lives, I stuck to my kitchen commitment even when the kitchen was cold with unfamiliarity and I barely had a pot. I remember my darling friends Rod and Leanne gifting me a spud masher and a set of kitchen scales and me crying from their act of kindness. It was such a symbolic gesture of caring. All my familiar beautiful cooking items, some held by my grandmother's and great-grandmother's hands, were still in my old world. I now found myself in the 'refuge house' where the oven door had to be jammed shut with the back of a chair and only two of the four hotplates worked. For a year or so, all I could do was cook lopsided cakes and smoke the kitchen out with roasts, but still I cooked, and even when the recipe didn't require salty tears, they still ended up in our dishes. When the chickens came into the house to poop on the ugly brown linoleum I would gather up my gratitude and think to myself there were plenty worse off and more war-torn than me. It was up to me to find all the funny parts in this fog of change. If I ran it as a comedy, life was so much easier.

Now at another stranger's sink in our new rental, as I tugged the little bits of remaining fur from the rabbit's legs and plucked a few blobs of red bits from it, I wondered why I was doing this. Sure, I had to be very careful with money on my stop-start author income, but I hated rabbit. However, I was raised to be frugal and never to refuse free food. In my childhood household, if you didn't eat what was put in front of you, the crime of turning your nose up at good food was met with harsh punishment. Broad beans made me vomit, yet still I was made to eat them, with old-style punishments that many children of the era endured. Leather belts and wooden spoons hold so much more meaning to kids of my generation beyond their actual purpose of keeping trousers up or stirring cake mix.

In my own parenting, I've never laid a hand on my kids. We are a cultured, egalitarian lot, and maybe I've raised them to be too soft . . . time will tell, but for a sensitive child like me, such mealtime dominations were often too much for me to handle. It became ingrained in me that rabbits in the pot also came with physical shock and dinnertime drama. No wonder I didn't like rabbit. But I was raised not to waste food, and a rabbit offered was not to be turned down, plus it was a chance for my kids to give it a go. No harm in that. I didn't want my children being limited by my own childhood beliefs and experiences.

I remember the first time I saw Dad skin a rabbit on the back step of that shadowy solemn house near the university, when I was about four or five. I puked then from the smell, the death stare of that glassy eye and the incomprehensible tragedy that the soft gentle creature had been turned inside out – its pelt now pink slime instead of pretty mottled soft grey fur. But with time I got used to it. It was food.

Dad always kept a gun under the seat of our Ford Falcon station wagon and he'd drag out that handy .22 on any road, anywhere, any time, if it meant getting a bunny for the pot, or nabbing a pesky lamb's-eyeball-pecking crow that was bothering a farmer's flock. Dad was into eating the guts of things too. A legacy of his own raising. I once saw him sawing a pig's head in half on the kitchen bench to get to the brains. No, he wasn't a sociopath, he was just raised in an era where nothing was wasted. Feeding eight kids on labourer's wages meant rabbit and rhubarb were often on the menu for his clan. Dad, the uncles and aunties still speak of wearing undies and singlets stitched from old flour bags by their pint-sized, gracious but tough little mother, my Nanna.

As a kid, I witnessed my mother cooking whatever Dad brought home from the farm. She was masterful at it, even though she juggled that kitchen craft with her own education studies and teaching work. As a result of the Depression-era fare, I was raised on sheeps' kidneys and livers in stews. Offal that made me retch. However, over my little blondie-girl head loomed that belt or spoon, so I would eat it, crying and slobbering. I can understand Dad's rationale and strict ways, and I can forgive it and be thankful for it: it taught me to eat in season, cook from scratch, and eat simply and healthily – most of the time.

Few in this country nowadays have ever known real hunger. We get to have our strong platforms of belief on diets: vegan versus vego, versus paleo versus keto, and some hardcore people feel the need to slam meat-eaters, leather- or fur-wearers – all because most of us have never known the ache of hunger or the bite of cold. We have never had to watch our children starve or freeze in front of us. We are raised with full bellies and warmth, so we have time and energy to pontificate and judge others' diet choices or animal-by-product clothing.

In the postwar years of the forties my Granno would make butter from the cows she milked and swap the butter for petrol rations to get her three girls to school. Anything else that could be produced from the farm would be swapped for other foodstuffs or cloth. Out-of-work vagrants would walk the long drive up to my Grandma's Kinvarra homestead kitchen door, knocking in search of work. My Granno Joan and Grandfather Archie couldn't give them work, but instead sent them on their way with bread and dripping to fill their bellies. All three of their girls set about at an early age roaming the farm for rabbits with guns, and wearing itchy woollen blanket-stitch dresses Joan had sewn herself. I often chuckle when I see big business now clutching for market share in a commercial version of the newly styled and marketed trend for 'environmentally conscious living' – because it is pretty much how we have always lived down here in Tassie and you don't need to consume product to achieve that kind of lifestyle. Life is basic. Life is good. Not a scrap of food is wasted in my kitchen. If it doesn't reach our mouths, it goes to the dogs, the chooks or the worm farm. None of it, not even a grain, goes in the general rubbish. This is not a brag about my state of waste-free living . . . far from it. Sometimes I wish I could scrape whole plates into the rubbish and unplug from the rigid programming that says 'Waste not'.

Because we have a good vegie garden, freerange eggs and loving friends who give us fresh-caught salmon, wild venison, home-slaughtered pork, kitchen-created sausages and spare sides of lamb, we eat like kings and queens whether the unreliable royalty train arrives or not. I am blessed to have those hunter-gatherer friends, and blessed that after losing all my money in the divorce, I have the capacity to believe I can live on love, laughter, fresh air and trust that all will be well. I'm so grateful to the wise women in my family for teaching me how to make a meal from next to nothing. For a time, when we first moved into the house on the hill and I went to ground, I relied on what was packaged into Aussie Helpers drought-donation food boxes that Janice had urged me to help myself to from the local hall. I still cringe a little in shame at the plight I was in – accepting charity sat at odds with my own identity. I was a bestselling author, living on food donations. I still laugh at the random contents of those boxes. I could never work out why, amidst the tins of corn and peas, there were packets and packets of Mylanta. Why supply farmer charity boxes with indigestion tablets? Maybe the charity providers thought sometimes farming was hard to stomach?

In the cheap little house on our rugged 20 acres, I committed myself to starting a small vegetable garden whilst still grieving the large and loved one I had left behind. I stuck to my guns on the preparation of fresh food from scratch in that tiny, tatty kitchen as if it were a matter of life and death. And, as it turns out, I discovered it is a matter of life and death.

My compulsion as a mother to give my children good food and protect them from danger was presented and explained to me from a scientific perspective by the grooviest and loveliest of professors I've ever met. In truth, I've not met many professors, but if Fred Provenza from Utah State University is anything to go by, I'd love to meet more like him. As a behavioural scientist, Fred has given me the insight to help my 'chained to the kitchen sink' battles that I was having within. Through Fred's work,

I learned to be at peace with and even proud of my culinary commitment to my kids. After living through the era that encouraged women to shatter the glass ceiling in business and politics and turn their backs on home duties, Fred's science helps explain the torn feeling I had. I realised I had been spanning myself across the divide of the feminine energy of home life, and the masculine energy of work life. It was a constant, confusing juggle without the knowledge to reground myself.

The first time I saw Fred speak, I travelled into Hobart with my bunch of regenerative agriculture devotees from Levendale to his lecture at the University of Tasmania. I remember the trip well because my soils-regeneration friends, all in their sixties but as immature as teenagers, were being side-splittingly funny, acting like eejits as we drove down the sweeping bends of Black Charlie's Opening mountainside. We were talking about 'Janice's flaps', because my beautiful neighbour had given me the flaps from a batch of home-killed sheep to cook. They're the bit of skin and selvedge that lines the ribs of a sheep and encases the guts, and it normally goes to the dogs at Janice's place.

On hearing this I had said to Janice, 'No – don't waste them on the dogs! They are really yummy if you cook them right!'

Rolled, stuffed and seasoned and tied with string, flaps make a great roast – a little on the fatty side, depending on the sheep, but once in a while they're a great change from a stock-standard leg of lamb. I best liked them from older mutton, boned with the ribs and cooked slowly in a white sauce, with clutches of parsley thrown on top. My mother had taught me the recipe as she was often left to deal with entire sides of lamb we brought her home, quartered into beer boxes and carted in fresh from the farm. She would cook the flaps dish a day ahead, cool it to set the fat, then dish it up with fresh-dug spud, mashed with drooling dollops of butter. Because of my family's legacy of making a meal out of what's on hand, I was determined to show Janice that flaps were worth more than dog tucker. Like with the rabbit, I was up for the challenge of proving my food point.

So during that trip, it was decided with many snorts of childish laughter that we would have a 'flaps party', where my friends would come to my house and 'eat Janice's flaps'. That statement alone prompted wheezing hysterics, so by the time we rolled into the rather serious atmosphere of the university lecture theatre, we had to tone down our redneck energies amidst the seemingly more sensible young agricultural science students. We picked a row at the front, played a bit with the fascinating swivel desks that university lecture theatres offer, and settled in for some serious science on the topic of 'Linking Soil and Plants with Herbivores and People'. I wasn't sure what we were going to get in terms of information, but I sat with an open mind and a hopeful heart that we weren't going to be blinded by science and bored to death by the American speaker.

Instead, quite the opposite occurred! When I first saw Fred Provenza I did a double take. The fit-looking guy was wearing Wrangler jeans and lace-up rodeo boots as if he had jumped the cattle-yard rails to get here. As soon I heard Fred's voice, with his super-cool American accent, I detected a deep level of humility and humour. Wise, profound and often funny words were spoken through a handsome, bushy salt-'n'-pepper beard. When he began to talk about our interconnectedness within what he termed 'the web of life', and then spoke about the instinctive nutritional wisdom held within mothers, I knew I'd stumbled on yet another key to my own self-awareness. I had also found more information I could weave into my novels to help other women understand their deep biological female function, which the modern world seems to steer us away from. The theme of farming and the feminine had serendipitously landed in my lap yet again. Here I was being given the keys to a greater understanding of how societal change had left many women like me straddling two worlds of work and home life, and feeling depleted and confused by their dissatisfaction despite, apparently, 'having it all'.

Fred is a member of BEHAVE – a research and outreach program that seeks to understand the principles of animal behaviour. Established in 2001, BEHAVE stands for Behavioural Education for Human, Animal, Vegetation and Ecosystem Management. Based at Utah State University, its work has extended across many ranches, farms and national parks and into science labs and lecture theatres around the world. Its projects don't just work with sheep and cattle, but concern behaviour in many animals including elk, bison and even bears. Most importantly for me, Fred and his colleagues have studied how leaving animals on their mothers longer leads to greater productivity and greater nutritional wisdom for their young. It was his work on mothers and nutrition that really drew me in and helped me on the home front to leave my boots at the door, computer idle for a time, and plant my bare feet proudly in the kitchen as a woman passing on 'nutritional wisdom' to her children.

As the years have passed, Fred and I have become email buddies and he would bless my inbox with thought-provoking gems from some of his 250 publications, or gift me with his keynote slides and other papers he has written. A couple of years ago, Fred bestowed upon me the honour of asking me to read the manuscript of a book he was editing, *The Art and Science of Shepherding: Tapping the Wisdom of French Herders*, and to give him a support quote for it. Edited by Dr Michel Meuret and Fred, the book seemed to encapsulate all I was learning on my hill about moveable fences and varied diets for livestock. I was fascinated to learn that Fred's colleague Michel was a Brussels University graduate who researched the value of livestock grazing for improving wildlife habitat and bio-diversity conservation. This was the exact same practical process I'd been part of on the Dargo High Plains with periodic grazing in Alpine regions with the mountain cattlemen, and what I was aiming for on my own 20 acres. Michel and Fred's book was again a reflection of what I knew to be true, that the synergy and complexity between human, beast, dog and landscape are not simple archaic systems – so often dismissed by many urban dwellers as 'quaint' – but instead provide the key to unlocking better societies and better health for all through improved soil and healthy animal grazing systems.

After reading that book, I began to think . . . Southern France . . . Southern Tasmania . . . similar in a way. Surely it was possible to bring some of those French shepherding practices here? Grazing our roadways strategically with community meat or fibre producing animals could reduce the amount of chemicals we needed to spray to manage roadside 'weeds' and give retired or unemployed people a valuable role in the animals' care. Imagine one reformed druggie girl and her goat, or a former alcoholic old man and his sheep. In my utopian world I could see a landscape sprinkled with happy herders and their animals managing vegetation working seamlessly.

My daughter's tubby pony, Gemma, is a classic example of the benefits a tethered animal brings to vegetation control. Gemma is my chief gardener in the hard-to-mow areas and is often borrowed by neighbours on 'contract' gardening jobs to eat grass they can't be bothered mowing or in places that are too steep or boggy. Currently I'm using Gemma to teach my kids when to move stock on from pastures. We are grazing her between two moveable fences and, in our real-life classroom, we trundle about, heads bowed, inspecting vegetation and manure, watching Gemma closely and the pattern in which she grazes on fresh ground, selecting plants in a set sequence. After reading Michel and Fred's book, I saw how it would be possible to create a stock route in Tasmania that served the community in many ways on the road where I used to live.

Agricultural systems globally need to be re-envisioned if we are to survive in the future. By utilising our roadsides to convert plants into protein or fibre by droving sheep or cattle systematically along public roads, we could teach young students the science of animal and human behavior. What better classroom to learn herbivores' relationship with plants and palatability, along with teaching the complex and artful vocation of low-stress dogmanship, horsemanship, stockmanship and land care through grazing. In other words, the art and science of forage grazing, animal handling and environmental observation.

This community grazing enterprise would also provide a much-needed tourist attraction that could reconnect us to the 'slow' ways that have been lost to us since our obsession with the car and technology in our society. Imagine a droving vista where motorists stop and get out of their cars to see this living synergy that sustains us all. It would give many a new perspective that can't be achieved by roaring down a terrifying four-lane highway or simply stopping to read an information sign as many enthusiastic tourists do.

I was well familiar with the poetry and spectacle caused by the drift of a herd of cattle along a road after the years I spent working with the Treasure family in the High Country of Victoria on the Dargo Road. From the back of my horse I would witness the delight that we drovers and our dogs, horses and cattle sparked in travellers. We were representatives of a slower time that people now crave. I could see that if droving grazing animals to control roadside vegetation could be applied here in southern Tasmania, replicating southern France, it would be a win-win-win for rural education, environmental enhancement and tourism, and yet when I suggested it to a mob of council fellas, all they could talk about was occupational health and safety, insurance costs and the legal cases that would arise should a motorist run into shepherded stock on the road.

'People are in too much of a hurry to put up with stock on the road,' one councilman said as he sat at the community hall table.

'You'd never get the insurance to cover it,' another said.

'The legalities would be a minefield,' came as the final full stop to my idea from a third man.

I knew this fledgling idea could benefit so many, and get those kids out of science labs and classrooms and learning in the real world. Even though the fenced-in human mindset dismissed the idea immediately, and a road block of thought put up several barriers to it, one day it could just happen. It's an idea waiting to flourish and I gift it to some clever person reading this book now! Perhaps it would boost a community near where you live? And you'll be able to say, as you sit on your horse on a spray-free road, teaching the next generation of animal handlers and ecologists while posing for a photo, 'I got the idea from a book I read once.'

It's these unfenced ideas that will save humanity. Fred says the only constant in life is change and it's our guiding principle.

'When Mother Earth gives us drought, tsunamis, flood and earthquakes, hurricanes, eruptions, we see it as nature behaving badly – kind of like a geological tantrum, but that soon our old planet will regain its balance, its sameness. But the truth is it's only our short tenure on earth that deludes us. Our time here is too short to see continents crash together, then tear apart, mountains rise and fall. Plant and animal species coming and going like a kaleidoscope. Any species, if it's going to survive, has got to be able to co-create with changing environments.'

Can you get the sense of how poetic this scientist is? Fred says animals and people adapt to change through what's called 'the wisdom of the body'. All creatures, including you and me, have body wisdom. But it's more than a matter of taste. We eat to feed cells. These cells are communicating with our tastebuds to tell our brain what our body needs. Because we alter human food so drastically in processing, adding sugars, salts and fats, and eat so much on the run, our wisdom bodies are out of whack and obesity and diseases are on the rise. We can no longer self-medicate using food, and now rely on drug companies and health supplements. Double that with plant varieties and production practices that produce food with fewer nutrients in it, and we're on a downhill slide.

What he was saying made sense to me, as I'd intuitively swerved my supermarket trolley away from formulas and infant baby mush encased in jars and tins. Instead I stewed my own local apples, mushed homegrown spuds and pumpkins and boiled my own chicken stock, along with garden-fresh celery or anything else I could grow or find from other people's gardens to introduce my children to. It seemed I naturally knew their palates would be altered for the worse if, as babies, I gave them high doses of sugars in white breads and cordials, or salt and sweeteners in baby foods. I wasn't trying to win an award for Mother of the Year, or wear a halo for being some kind of food purist, but there was an inbuilt wisdom in me – one Fred was naming up now scientifically! I also somehow knew to let my kids crawl on shearing-shed floors, through garden beds and rumble on the back lawn with border collie pups in the chook poop, because I also knew instinctively that there was 'good' bacteria there – and even exposure to the 'bad' bacteria helped my kids' immunity. I knew how to clean a house without toxic chemicals. It was cheaper to use water and white vinegar and bicarb soda or vanilla essence anyway. My kids had been raised around the raw facts of life and death and animal guts. They were healthier for it.

When the professional dog-food shooters came our way, I used to beg a batch of dead possums from them or pick up what I could from roadkill. Waste not, want not. Brush-tailed possums were plentiful before the tree plantation companies wiped out their populations with poison. On an old stump, I would axe the claws from the carcasses and singe the fur on a fire out in the house paddock. There was something calming and ritualistic about that act. Modern people who have never been poor or hungry might see my actions as barbaric, but for me it was a natural act. Possum meat is terrific for hard-working farm dogs. The dogs love a bit of fur and gut, along with the vegetable matter found in the possum's stomach. My babies would be rugged up in their prams, watching the flames, the imprint of the fire and singed possum hair in their nostrils. It was an ancient act. A quiet act. One where I blessed each possum that men with guns had shot.

Because of our lifestyle on the farm, my kids were also weaned onto roo patties. I made the mince into burgers and then cooked them in a gravy. I innately knew the healthy native meat, grazed on a variety of plants grown on a variety of soils, would be better for my children than that of domestic animals grazed on limited pastures and soils. I knew somehow, without needing to obtain a PhD on the subject, that the microbiology of soil and our guts were inextricably linked, and that modern processed food played havoc with what I now know as 'the wisdom body'.

To help me get over my agony of eating meat when I am an animal lover, Fred also explained that eating food is simply, scientifically 'energy transfer'. Whether it's a carrot or a cow, when you eat it, it is transferring its energy system into your energy system and that is simply how the world turns in all natural cycles. When an eagle eats a mouse, it is energy transfer. When a cow eats a plant, it's energy transfer. When a human eats a fish, it's energy transfer.

Fred's work supported all I was discovering on my farm about the benefits of multi-species pastures that were not just made up of a few introduced grasses, but were a blend of native ones alongside shrubs, forbs and herbs and the British species. By understanding how palatability works in livestock Fred has been able to train animals to avoid eating certain plants or encourage them to eat others. It's meant primary producers can now train stock to graze in areas where animals once may have destroyed certain crops. For example stock can be trained to forage in forest plantations without harming the trees. He's taught wine makers how to train sheep so they can graze in vineyards yet they won't touch the vines. Fewer sprays mean a more diverse insect population and that means fewer pests. The act of grazing also feeds the soil with manures and urines, so the produce grown in those soils is more nutrient-dense. Sheep now mow grasses in citrus groves without ringbarking trees. Dr Fred's work has even helped people train horses to avoid eating local toxic plants. His method has worked on cattle too, so they can graze in areas where poisonous plants used to be a problem. Excitingly, animals can be trained to eat particular weeds, even invasive species like thistles. Fred's training techniques have also been used in wild populations of herbivores to stop overgrazing in riparian areas, or to protect rare plants. Cattle and sheep become low-cost alternatives to herbicides and mechanical means.

Apply this to humans, and how we now have young mothers with no food education, and an entire generation that has sadly lost their food wisdom due to processed food. Fred showed some pretty confronting slides on obesity, and how it alters gene expression, meaning the babies born to overweight mothers are much more likely to be obese.

In his talk, Fred began to speak of the grassroots movement that was underway around the world. I knew he was referring to people like Colin Seis, who were inspiring people who all wanted to be part of that sweep of change to a better, more profitable and more environmentally balanced form of farming.

'Productivity doesn't equal profitability,' Dr Fred said. I had seen myself the rise of the 'bigger is better' mentality within farming since the 1980s. Fred said that because we've developed this style of modern larger, genetically enhanced livestock, we can no longer survive on what nature provided. These 'super' creatures need higher inputs at higher costs. The old-timers may have had smaller animals, but they had smaller input costs and so therefore were more productive. We are duped into believing in constantly 'improving' animals from genetics outside the local region, and as a result our animals have lost their inherited wisdom to survive on nature's local banquet. These 'enhanced' breeds then need expensive introduced plants that have to be bought from multinational seed companies for them to achieve the desired weight gain. It's like the animals only know how to dine on manufactured 'fast food' and this in turn limits a farmer's profits.

After Fred's talk, my neighbour and I mobbed him as if we were groupies gushing over a rock star. His information was so practical and profound, and his delivery of such complex science, made easy for rough-nut farmers like us, lit us with excitement, particularly as women who cared so much for our land, animals and the food we ate and dished up to our kids. When I returned to my kitchen, I did so with a new awareness. If I was offered free-range food like rabbit I ought to take it, and teach my kids to cook it and to eat it. A bunny grown in the wild is nutritionally worth more than a giant pumped-up chicken from the supermarket. I knew it contained some lovely natural nutrients for my kiddies.

'Would you like to try some rabbit?' I asked the kids as I picked up the kitchen scissors and cut the carcass into pieces and began to coat it in stone-ground flour and salt and pepper.

They looked up at me, momentarily taken from the universe of their Lego building, and pondered the question. It would be good to let them eat rabbit. It was, after all, the animal that our forebears made their living from.

'I'll cook a chicken casserole too in case you don't like it,' I reassured. 'No pressure.'

'Okay,' came their answer, 'we'll try it.' They went back to their Lego.

I didn't need a recipe book to cook it. I had my mother and my auntie's nutritional wisdom built into me, so I knew to fry it first in butter, then put bacon and barley and onion in with it along with some chicken stock powder. The kids ate it with no fuss. As I tentatively joined them, I decided it was delicious. The next night, with the leftover gravy, I made rabbit rice balls, fried up and eaten again with no complaint. Just gratitude for the rabbit and the wise auntie who gave it to us.

From Bundy To Buddha

Some of the earliest memories I have are gazing up at Dad's dad, Grandfather Smith, sitting in a halo of pipe smoke on a brown vinyl couch, with a backdrop of Nan's pristine white lace curtains lit by sunshine. He would perch beside his silver smoking stand, braces stretched taut over lean workman's shoulders, heaving air like Darth Vader on one good lung. On the sunny porch beside some potted succulents a budgie called Pretty Boy, who was possibly not a boy, chirruped. It was here at a very young age that my uncles and my grandfather taught me three of life's major lessons: how to shake hands firmly, how to pour a beer properly, and to never smoke (this third lesson I absorbed more than was taught). Granddad was the living – or half-living – result of it.

Despite Granddad's shuffling and wheezing, the house was always a riot of fun when the Smith siblings got together, with my tiny gracious Nana egging them on with the slightest of disapproving smiles that held no serious threat of reproach. The uncles would stand over me jovially and coach me on, tilting the beer glass sideways to get the right amount of froth. What an Aussie thing to teach a kid! When I was first learning to talk, my brother would lead me about and make me say 'bottle of beer' to the adults in my wonky baby speak. I sounded like a ventriloquist's dummy so the adults would roar with laughter, and raise their beers in cheer.

Beer was a central feature of our lives. Cartons would arrive home in the back of the Ford Falcon station wagon, and they would be the first thing put away in the fridge, moving aside all manner of more healthy dietary choices, to the constant quiet grumble of my mother: 'The beer takes up too much room!'

Looking back, what an apt thing to say! Life revolved around beer. If we were caught washing Dad's or Granddad's pewter mug with dishwashing liquid, we'd be in trouble. It flattened the beer, apparently. I grew up thinking that men on weekends had a can of beer permanently attached to their hands, only to be set down for a short time if there was a lawn to mow, sheep carcass to cut up or spuds to dig. I saw barbecues were great for men, because the beer could remain in one hand whilst tongs were held in the other to turn a chop or a sausage on a hotplate. It made them look busy and useful in front of the women, as they sizzled and sipped, standing beside a halved 44-gallon drum that housed spitting flames. My chief routine to impress a male adult was to toddle to the fridge to get another coldie and hand it to them when their other beer was done. Or to remind Dad there was a longneck in the freezer and he needed to take it out before it shattered into brown splinters amidst the ice. I learned there were rewards for honouring men's beer . . . it meant I got positive attention, ahead of disciplinary actions.

As life moved us to more sophisticated circles, those boxes of beer were replaced by wine club orders, and the Ford Falcon that we used to cart sheep shit in for Nana's roses was replaced with a Saab. My mechanic uncle had become Tasmania's only Saab dealer and he'd had to upgrade his showroom to match his new clientele. As I grew older, heavy reds, rich with the weight of importance and with labels that leveraged one up in society, entered our life, as did European cars with seat heating, but thanks to the grounding of those cheeky uncles, who hadn't chased a university education like my father, the ocker seed had already been sown within me.

Now, as an adult with square farming-woman hands, I tend to hold a stubbie like a shearer and shake hands like a truck driver. Not such a good thing when I'm at author events trying to clutch a slim-stemmed champagne glass. Or the error I feel when I'm crushing some clever soft-handed Sydney or Melbourne publishing fella with my 'I can crutch sheep' handshake. Amidst that mainland city swank I sometimes feel like a woman who has more balls than a billiard table standing next to those perfumed, preened, but extremely lovely and gorgeous men.

With such childhood shaping, it's also no wonder that as a

teenager I kept on with the family tradition of boozing mind-lessly, without any thought of the culture that lay beneath it, let alone the harm it did me. Alcohol went hand in hand with my search for male love – in all the wrong places, like pubs and the rural rumbles of Bachelor and Spinster Balls. Starting relation-ships on such liquid foundations only led to more lessons in life on how not to live it and how not to choose partners. It was a time of binge-drinking gone bonkers, leaving me vulnerable to male predators. In my generation date rape wasn't 'date rape' – it was our own female fault for getting so trashed. Booze saturates our culture and impacts women dreadfully. It comes from a long history that takes a lot of personal unpacking to see it clearly, like an old forgotten trunk stowed away on a First Fleet voyage.

My forebears lived in a time when Hobart ran on rum currency and beer was better than water. Rough days, tough days. A place where arriving ships filled with female convicts were ambushed by convicts and soldiers alike and a frenzy of rape occurred. The men then were probably mostly drunk, as rum was standard ration for all. During the early years of white set-tlement, there used to be a drink called 'Blow ye skull-off rum' in Hobart. I know, after tasting the homemade moonshine that my muso friends create, that the legacy of rebellious Tasmanian pride in 'brew your own' continues. The homemade liquid fire is the kinda stuff that warms your guts, but it tastes oh so smoooooooth and it lubricates song lyrics like you wouldn't believe.

After divorce I discovered, as a mother at home alone with

her children in a remote area, using alcohol as a prop to counter loneliness was not really an option. If I ever had to drive the kids in an emergency and I was schnozzled, I would never have forgiven myself. When the children weren't with me, I soon learned alcohol didn't drown the sadness I was wading through, but instead preserved it. I was pickling those inner self-damning patterns from the past like interesting gizzards in formaldehyde sealed in a jar. With each sip I was beginning to sense a conflict in me. Teamed with booze, I knew I would keep repeating the same mistakes with men, disastrously.

It wasn't until after my one and only failed volatile relationship post-divorce, with a man who loved the bottle more than me, that I was prompted to read a few books by British author Allan Carr on addiction, to help me understand the alcohol trap. I realised how weird it is that in our culture we celebrate and use alcohol as a kind of lubrication to courtship, and that alcohol is the same stuff we use to swab wounds and kill germs. No matter how much advertising using sexy ladies or uber-chic bars to enhance the glamour of our fancy wine or spirits, at its core, the stuff of alcohol ruins lives and, bottom line, is a poison. And yet here I am with my stubbie-holder collection, looking forward to a hot Friday arvo where I can share a beer with a buddy or drink a wine with a friend by the fire after a winter's ride on my horse. Drinking together is part of the weft and weave that gives rural living its richness. When there's bushfire, the pain of the flames is doused with beer. When there's floods, it's the dry space of the pub where folks gather. When there's a drought, there may be no water in your stock dams, but the community club fridge always holds a liquid refreshment for those parched spirits and a place to whet your whistle. Every single big 'woo-hoo!' moment in my life, be it a Tim McGraw country music concert with my wild country gal pals to a bush wedding, has been framed by alcohol. It brings joy. It brings devastation. It is part of life.

In the village where I now live, there's always Friday-night happy hour. The volunteer firemen gather for a beer and pass the helmet around for a few gold coins in exchange for a ticket in a meat tray or chook raffle. It's traditional Aussie local community volunteer activity like this that makes my heart sing as I chuck my coins into the mix. But here in our town, more and more, the hills are planted out with rows of vines and we can look upon them romantically as if we exist in a transplanted version of France or Italy. How sophisticated! Or is it a waste of food-producing resources like land and water? Shouldn't we grow vegies instead on such ground, or do we keep expanding our posh poison plots in the same way we are growing more and more sugar in the north of Australia in giant irrigation schemes just when the world is waking up to the fact that we don't need more of that kind of foodstuff?

In our town, vegies are less glamorous than growing grapes for boutique wine and so is left to the local hardworking Hmong community to sell at the Saturday market, or greens are grown commercially on great swathes of exposed, pummelled soil for the big players like Coles and Woolies. Wine growing is oft times reserved for the sophisticates and the ones who can afford the land on tourist trails. Don't get me wrong, I like the occasional stop-off at a vineyard on a sunny day, but it sits at odds with me due to my upbringing and the unstable ground I set beneath my feet from toasting both joy and misery in my life with a glass.

Even my author image is founded on 'Bundy Chick' and I have the stickers on my ute to prove it. That's a drink that adds caffeine and sugar to alcohol. Yet in my younger days I worshipped 'the square bear' and had a giant cardboard cut-out of him, which moved house with me each time I found another place to adventure to. Nowadays I've noticed beer and cider are climbing the ladder into the sophisticates' world. Labelled 'craft', boutique beer and cider are all the rage in Hobart Town, along with whiskey and gin distilleries – history repeats. Recently when I was writing in a coffee shop, again waiting for the school pick-up, I found myself 'mature-lady perving' on the good-looking young men with trendy beards and carrying computer man-bags. They were out and about promoting their artisan brewing and looking so eye-catchingly cool. Surely boutique beer – although in my book a little bit wanky as well as swanky – is a healthier option than that which is produced by giant beer companies that pump out amber fluid like petrol to be sold by the carton beside service stations? Isn't celebrating crafted-and-cared-for booze a good thing? And surely carefully created whiskey is a better option, ahead of the lolly-water laced with rocket fuel sold at chain-store liquor outlets to kiddies? Isn't it? I don't know. I'm asking you.

We identify ourselves and our class by what we drink, and given that my upbringing had one boot on workman's ground on Dad's family's side and the other lady shoe on grazier grasses from my mum's farming side, I never know what to drink, or even if I want to drink at all.

Trying to avoid our culture of booze and betting is tricky. It's all around us. My son, heavily into sport, was as young as six when he began clicking onto the web to find the footy scores. There, flashing live and large were bottles of beer and ads for betting. I started his education about advertising then and there! All around us, advertisers program our children to see it as normal to drink, bet, consume and not question. I was influenced as a child too, back when cigarettes were chic. I remember being eleven years old and having a crush on the Marlborough Man. Who wouldn't love a cowboy, even if he had a stinky habit like smoking, so long as he had a horse and a range to ride?

Recently I took myself off to The Falls music festival on the rolling seaside hills of Marion Bay to see how that kind of crowd rolls there compared to the paddock festivals I know and love so well at rural events, like ute musters and cattlemen's get-togethers. Back when I was going to Bachelor and Spinster Balls in the late eighties and nineties, if the partygoers caught someone smoking marijuana or taking drugs, there was a rumble of disquiet, often a fight, followed by an undignified eviction of the drug takers.

It was a country law not imposed by security or police, but by the rural party people themselves. Rural folk having good clean fun on rum. You could get soaked from the inside of your liver out to your boots on booze and you'd be a living legend, but if you took illegal drugs, you were an outcast and labelled a loser.

Now 'doof doof' drugs that go with 'doof doof' music have spread to regional areas. They are rife in our culture. As I sat in the traffic jam in the paddock lined with gumtree-log lanes at the entrance to Falls, I hoped I would be proved wrong about drugs and music festivals. I noticed most of the crowd were arriving in sedans. I was used to paddock line-ups of utes. The crowd felt foreign to me. A policewoman walked past. I suddenly remembered the large bag of clover hay I had in the back of the ute. My plan was to drop it into my horse, Archie, on my way home the following day. Fresh cut from an irrigated paddock on the red soils of northern Tasmania, the hay looked green and lush, even in dried form. Would it be mistaken for something I could sell or smoke? Would I be apprehended for having the biggest bag of clover hooch ever taken into a Falls party? I never found out.

I think, given the backlog of cars to search and my age, I was simply waved through and I never found out if my horses' hay would be treated as a suspicious illegal substance. I mustn't have looked like the drug-taking type . . . middle-aged mother that I am. No matter my age, I've never been one for drugs. The only two substances of my undoing have been lost love and liquor. Having an imagination like mine meant I've never needed mind-altering experiences. My mind, if let loose to wander, is constantly in an altered state, lost in the depths of my creative daydreaming and philosophising, when I'm supposed to be watching the clock and getting kids to school.

At the festival, as I 'set up camp', which involved the very simple act of rolling out my swag in the back of the ute, I passed a car, all four doors flung open and cops all over it. A sniffer dog, looking proud of itself, sat beside the car, wagging its beagle tail, hoping for another drug-bust treat. I looked at the young man talking to the policewoman and I wondered why people risked getting arrested in a bid to get high. With tablets that may result in death? I couldn't understand it. To me, with nature all around, the sea vista along with a sea of summer grasses and bush-covered hills, surely this place was enough to get high on? Marion Bay is spectacular. The festival village is set above a white crescent beach, and today a perfect turquoise and azure sea was greeting us. Just looking at it told me that life, if you let it, is spectacular. How greedy we humans are. We want more and more of everything when what is about us and within us is really *enough*.

After heading into the crowd and hearing some of the bands I thought I might need some drugs after all to help me cope with the music. Surely it must've been assaulting the wildlife around me too? Discord and doof. *Each to their own*, I thought, as I watched privileged teens walking over paddocks in their cool-dude get-ups. Did they notice the docked lambs' tails that lay in the paddocks? Or the cow dung on grazed pastures over which they walked? Did they spare a second of thought for what goes on here eleven months of the year? I wondered if there were feminine struggles and self-esteem issues present in the girls of fourteen who sauntered along the path to the beach. What was it like to be female in this day and age for them? These young, fortunate festival-goers were generally people who had never known what it's like to lack food or experience life without technology.

At the food section of the festival, there weren't just burgers, hot chips and dagwood dogs on offer. This crowd was far too sophisticated for that. Instead there were food choices for the educated and the ethical. I ordered thyme-roasted vegie haloumi salad with chimichurri and cumin yoghurt on cyprus pita. Really! In the middle of a paddock that had now been cultivated as lawn! I was used to farmer-clearing-sale fare of sausage in bread. Tomato sauce if you were lucky and onions if you wanted to be flash. At the bar I discovered, gobsmacked, there was no Bundy. Were country-person beverages really that uncool? As I sat on the watered lawn amidst bushland to eat my fancy food, and drink my cappuccino, I realised few of the fly-ins would know that there was a drought in Tasmania, and that recently the township of Dunalley not far along the coast from the festival site had been razed by bushfires. For the next couple of days, the biggest crisis for the festival-goers would be having to walk a long way to get your mobile phone charged at the Telstra stations, or walking hungover to the beach.

When I went in search of the waves I heard complaints about the time it took to get to the beach. As I travelled over beautiful saline wetlands, on boarded pathways in a conga line of people, I studied the plants and the story of the management the landscape told me. I caught snippets of conversations, saw people by the thousands. Beside the dunes I watched girls drain tanks of fresh drinking water just to rinse their hair and wash the sand from their pretty feet.

This was a cushy, cushy festival for people who led cushy, cushy lives. Myself included. Since leaving the farm, I've never known life to be this empty of hard labour . . . so physically easy. Mentally for me it's been hard, but I feel myself and even my physical body softening with every pass of a full moon into a person I am not. I love bush life and hard labour. My body likes it. It must be in my DNA. Without hills to walk and livestock to check, I was turning into a blob. The festival found me missing my farm and the connection to the deep realities of life's cycles with an ache. I would rather have been riding a horse or moving sheep over the paddocks than sitting on a lawn in the midst of the bush drinking a cappuccino and eating a thyme-roasted vegie haloumi salad with chimichurri and cumin yoghurt on cyprus pita. At this pristine, beautiful festival realities were masked. Which, I guess, is the point.

Even the long-drop toilets were something palatial, with tubs to wash one's hands in with hand-pump soaps! I was supremely impressed, after years of going to the Tassie Mountain Cattleman's where you did your biz in a bottomless bucket above a shovel-dug pit, behind a wall of tin with a sheet of black plastic weighed down with a length of wood as a door so you got a bit of privacy. We bushies at our bush events take a bit of pride in roughing it. Not so at the doof doof festivals. It was luxury all round. But good on them. You would need good dunnies with the amount of dhal and lentils that were on offer, washed down with elegant wines.

I noticed the elaborate tents and camping setups too. 'Glamping', as my friends call it, in reference to glamour and camping. There was not a single fat aerial in sight on a big bull-barred ute, nor a blue singlet or akubra. Not one of Lee Kernaghan's dirt-road songs was blaring from ute speakers, like they do in a country crowd. There was an absence of Aussie-as whip-cracking by keen girls and boys, and no proud dads in black hats, who had done the prams up as trucks or utes with grinning country kids in them. The bush culture was absent from the bush at this Falls festival, with city imports landing on paddocks and looking like Dr Who had vortexed them here from the inner bars of cities. As a rural person, it was a culture I didn't recognise, but at least there was colour here. In dress, in music, in dance. As the sun sank and I met some local farmer friends who were volunteer firefighters, we settled in to people-watch and enjoy the slow turn of the earth to music that began to at last wrap me in a desire to dance. The Falls Festival was a peaceful celebration of life, of creativity and the beautiful landscape in which we live, and by day two, like a culture-shocked tourist, I'd adjusted. I found things to love about it.

In contrast, on my last book tour I got to see the homogenised, concreted, oh-so-bland version of Australia. I spent the bulk of my travels heading to shopping centres and the bookstores buried within major retail chains. It got to the point I could barely tell which town I was in. Give me a sophisticated Falls crowd any day ahead of hypnotised shoppers and globalised selling centres. A shopping mall in regional Victoria was very similar to the ones in Western Australia, which were similar to the ones in South Australia, which were similar to the ones in my home state. When I enter those places, I find myself cowering from the weird lighting and mind-numbing consumer rush. As I make rare mad dashes into those sorts of stores to grab mundane things like school socks for my children I find myself saying to them too loudly, 'How can the world sustain this? This is a nightmare! Are people mad? Look at them all shopping, like it's the new religion! Do people realise they've been brainwashed and we don't need all this *stuff*?' Poor kids. They just needed socks and were probably hoping their mother would stay long enough to get them a Boost Juice.

Another unravelling and homogenising of Aussie culture has been the beautiful country and inner-city pubs that have been undone with pokies money. Horrible carpets, awful lighting and dreadful energies. At least at the Deni Ute Muster you can drink your beer and toast a sunset, even if you have to lift your eyes beyond the XXXX girls who stand about in their skimpy clothes promoting beer and misogyny. The blokes there certainly don't notice the sunset. In my days of early motherhood, when my body was not my own and my husband's attentions had gone AWOL, I remember bitterly calling the scantily clad Bundy promotional girls at a cattlemen's event 'prostitutes without the fuck'. I was not so much offended by their choice to get paid for looking bare and beautiful, but angry with society and the leering men around them, who most likely had wives, mothers of their own children, or girlfriends who deserved honouring. I was drunk at the time and not proud of myself for the outburst. Poor Bundy girls. But something comes undone in a woman when she has gifted her body to a man to bear his children, only to find he is hungry for the manufactured image of women, and not the reality of the one standing before him, who is battle-scarred and bloodied by birth. It seemed to me society made mothers invisible and irrelevant, while marketers steered our culture towards celebrating mindless, young and sexy.

A turning point for me came when I found Buddha. Literally. Well, at least I found *a* Buddha. He was at Agfest, our three-day Tasmanian rural festival of which I was patron of at the time. I'd been going to Agfest every year for almost a decade, at first as a support to my dog education friend Paul Macphail, then later with my own pups to demo and sell, then later still, with novels to my name. The year I found Buddha, our tent was next to a garden ornament site. You know the sort . . . concrete bird baths, griffins, cast iron archways, tinkling stone fountains. Over the three mornings that I'd been arriving at Agfest, I'd look into the garden ornament stall, and give my greeting to a little grey concrete Buddha, sitting cross-legged and smiling with his eyes shut. Palms pressed together. A serene little bloke.

'Good morning, Buddha,' I would call to him, before setting up shop.

On the last day, I saw the Buddha again. Suddenly I had an overwhelming feeling that he had to come home with me. On a limited budget in divorce-recovery mode, I couldn't justify buying a useless ornament, but something in me had to take my little friend home. I sat the Buddha on the front seat of my ute, putting his seatbelt on. I laughed at the idea. Buddha riding shotgun home with me. Inside I felt at the time I needed Divine protection. It was dusk and I had a three-hour drive home, with some winding dirt and kangaroo-lined roads to get through. After three full days of giving my all to my lovely readers who come to say hello at Agfest, but nursing a broken heart, I needed a buddy. As I went to drive off I saw some funny clown had put a can of Bundy and Cola on Buddha's lap. So there I was sitting with this irony beside me.

It made me think of a stopover in Bangkok where the kids and I found the teachings of Buddha in a book in the bedside drawer of our hotel. In the front of it, printed on the crackling thin pages, were instructions on 'How to become a Buddhist'. As my young children wallowed in their bath, I sat on the edge and read them the dot points on what we had to do to become Buddhist. I could do kindness, I could do forgiveness, but one of the other undertakings was to give up alcohol. I remember pausing, wrestling with something within, then shutting the book and thinking, *Mummy's in trouble there, kids*. Culturally, letting go of alcohol was something I struggled with. But I did not want my kids growing up like me, thinking that each dinner had to be hosted by the biggest star of the family . . . the bottle of wine on the table.

My little stone Buddha friend from Agfest now sits in a sun-filled bedroom below the wooden cut-out letters that spell WRITE. He still has his hands pressed together in prayer, but my little man no longer holds rum cans for me. That part of my life is over now. The manmade religion of idolising booze and instilling the obedience of women has no place under my roof. And the stars of the show at dinner time are my children, home-grown food and our gratitude for life. I have set down the long-held generational tradition of the bottle and now have both hands free in which to hold my children.

The Merino Mother

Vividly I remember how the world around me swirled as we drove from the hospital, my tiny daughter, still hued with golden jaundice skin, in the car capsule behind me. We arrived home to the back step of boots and barking dogs, me feeling as if I'd had an out-of-body experience. I think the truth was, I had. No one had prepared me for the stormy seas of a traumatic birth . . . where I felt myself and my baby hovering between the thin veil of the living and the dead. The labour was long, the baby was trying to arrive bum first and both our energies were running low. For hour upon hour I battled to birth. I could feel myself fading, surrendering my life in a stupor of exhaustion and extreme pain, but my daughter was far more resilient than I. All of a sudden, she turned herself and was born naturally, right when I was about to be wheeled away to emergency theatre.

With my newborn, I stepped into my home, was handed a

cup of tea and gingerly propped on the couch, sitting on a rubber ring the hospital had loaned me to stop the many stitches tugging. The expression 'ripped from arsehole to breakfast time' took on a whole new meaning after childbirth. As I thought back to the birthing, I wondered how on earth I hadn't seen that one coming. On the farm I'd faced birth over and over, with its bloody brutality. I'd pulled lambs from cast ewes, saving the lamb but too late for the mother. I'd seen the way crows feasted on dark placentas in paddocks and how cows strained in a futile attempt to calve a tail-first baby. Why then had I been so shocked at the blood that kept coming from my body, and the milk that arrived in such painful quantities for a baby that was too dozy from birthing drugs to drink?

Little did I know I was on a whole new journey of understanding about what it is to be female, and animal. Someone had once said to me about babies, 'Start how you mean to go on,' so with determination that first day home, I had that cup of tea, then with the help of my step-mother-in-law, I strapped my tiny baby to my body in a front pack and called my working dogs to heel. It took us a while to move that mob. I was stiff, sore and bleeding and soon learned that I could no longer slip through a six-strand plain wire fence with a child strapped to me, so waddling to the gates made the job slower.

Looking back, I wish I hadn't been so stoic. I wish I'd nestled myself into a cocoon with my baby and had others serve me, but I had been raised so much to emulate the masculine traits of being human, I had no idea how to proceed in life embracing my feminine qualities. I'd no idea how to proceed as 'mother', such was the silence in our family culture on matters such as women, birthing and rearing children. I had other tough women modelling similar behaviour, so on I plodded as a new mother. Lost.

It was years later that Fred Provenza, through his studies, helped me understand my base animal journey as 'mother' in feeding and teaching my young. He explained that the 'mother' of almost all species has a lifelong influence on both diet selection and behaviour of her offspring.

'It starts in utero,' Fred said. 'Flavours in mother's amniotic fluids influence the flavours chosen after birth. Flavours that are in mother's milk influence food choices. Also, there's mother as a model. All are hugely important.'

Fred went on to talk about a field of study that I've been fascinated in for a number of years after discovering the work of stem cell biologist Dr Bruce Lipton. The area of science is called epigenetics, where scientists discovered gene codes are not fixed as previously thought, but can be modified.

'What we're learning,' Fred said, 'is that genes are being switched on and off early in life to create new relationships with changing environments.'

Fred's conclusion is that it's not nature versus nurture. It's both those things all the time.

As a farmer I had watched merino mothers closely and saw how different they were within the group. Some mums would stomp the ground and defend their newborn lambs with a brave defiance. Others would turn, in a sea of hormonal upheaval, and no matter how gentle and respectful I kept my arced distant passing of them in the paddock, with my dog close and my eyes averted, the mother would abandon her lamb and take off, tail-end bloody, placenta dragging. She would momentarily scram from her lamb in a fog of panic.

I saw the variation in the behaviour of cows too. Some were attentive mothers; others were not. Those crazy cows were often culled from the herd, because they would often produce crazy calves.

In all the species, though, there was a clear pattern that the young would watch and mimic the adults. When the cattle found their way unexpectedly over a fence, compliments of a fallen tree, I would observe how the mothers would browse excitedly on the banquet of varied vegetation that was not available in the paddock. With gentle patience they ensured their calves were at their flanks, watching their every move, despite their excitement of their newfound browsing freedoms. When the sheep got in my garden I would leave them there awhile and watch the way they went from plant to plant, tree to tree, bush to bush. A nibble here, a nibble there, the lambs at foot watching, imitating, following.

When we were breeding horses I would make sure I put the mare and her foal in the bush runs for a while, so the mare could teach her baby to cross creeks without panic and snatch up tussocks, a few wattle leaves and native grasses. The foal, behind his mother, would navigate his way over uneven ground, low wattles dragging on their backs – all familiarisation for when the babies were ridden out in the bush later in life, and for developing a palate for rougher sorts of plants. So often horses are fed luxury feed mixes and sweet hay, ahead of what they really need, which is bulky dry matter and natural variety. Instinctively, too, I knew the mothers needed a broader environment than just the bland square manmade paddock to teach their young about the environment they would have to one day navigate under saddle.

After observing so many mothers of other species, when my first child arrived I saw how the natural instinct of motherhood fundamentally changed me forever. It was my turn to become that defiant mother, stomping her front hoof, turning to face dangers. Once, on a misty early morning back at the family farm, I was breastfeeding my baby on the couch. I saw out the front window of our lounge room a four-wheel drive pull up in the white haze. A man got out and, carrying a gun, climbed through the roadside fence. At the time, we had a big herd of wild deer that grazed above our house and I knew he was out to stalk one. It wasn't deer season, he had no permission from us, and yet there he was in my front paddock. My nostrils flared. My foot stomped. Without thinking and with a growl in my throat, I bundled up my baby, put her in the ute's baby capsule and revved my still-cold diesel engine hard around the road to warn the stranger away.

'Excuse me,' I said, as I braked beside him and got out, 'what do you think you're doing?' My voice had a she-wolf tone.

I must've looked terrifying, or at least mad – hair askew in a sleep-ravaged ponytail, polar fleece over flannel pyjamas, feet shoved into dogger boots, breasts most likely still leaking milk beneath my clothing. He turned in surprise and began to walk towards me, his gun pointing down to the frosted ground, the sun, screened by mist, turning him into a shadow on a white back-ground so I couldn't see the expression on his face.

'I spotted a few deer,' he said, his voice a little fumbly.

From the back of the twin-cab ute my little baby girl mewed.

'I know there are deer there,' I said as frostily as the road surface beneath my boots. 'They are there most mornings. That's my house, and I was feeding my baby.' My words were nonsensical, and I don't know what compelled me to roar out of my house with my baby to tell a stranger with a gun to clear out and get off my paddocks. I wasn't angry, but I was ridiculously territorial. When I look back I realise I was gripped with what I termed 'merino mother madness'. I was totally fearless, and in hindsight stupid, but in that moment I was bulletproof and stomping my hoof and snorting. I also now realise I didn't call on my then-husband to protect me or the baby. It never occurred to me. He was still snoring in bed. Instead I had instinctively rushed to defend my nest and my young. Thankfully the dumbstruck man simply apologised and left.

As I came away from that experience and watched myself in a fog of post-birth weirdness, I wanted more understanding about motherhood and Mother Nature. I paralleled my own behaviour with animals, and started to see our farming systems were far too harsh on mothers and their young. As was our society. I wanted to find ways of weaning our animals later, giving more richness and diversity not just to the animals' pastures but to the environment our animals lived in. I had heard about a study that one of my friends had conducted. He had given one mob of feedlot lambs toys and equipment to play on, whilst a second mob had no entertainment. The lambs who had more stimulation and played more – in other words, who were happier – showed greater weight gains than the lambs with no toys. To me that study and its results were no surprise, yet most people must 'see the science' before they adapt their own management of animals, rather than go with their gut instinct and, dare I say it, give *love* to the animals we are essentially raising for meat.

Fred Provenza specialises in understanding behaviour and it's why I'm enthralled in his work. 'Behaviour is what everything does,' he says. 'From microbes to humans, we all behave. So understanding behaviour is crucial in understanding how to work within systems.'

Fred's philosophical thinking is nothing like what I expected. I'd stereotyped scientists as being very narrow in their mindsets and very fixed in the 'realities' of time and space. While Fred had his foundation as a young man working on ranches before heading into the academic world, his far-reaching mind sat alongside my own stargazing and earth-watching tendencies.

This style of mid-paddock philosophising led me to wonder

how society had come so far away from educating women about their bodies, birth and their wisdom within. I remembered my prepubescent self going to Sunday school to study the Bible. I wasn't interested in religion, but I was keen to spend as much time as I could with one of my best friends, Libby, and to be witness to her loving family. Her gentle kindly dad was a shipping pilot, and as we drove to the Anglican church in the Kombi van, he would shout, 'Clear to port!' or 'Clear to starboard!', depending on whether there was traffic on our left or right. That Kombi was a kid's dream taxi of the most fun kind, as we clambered into it in our cord flares with our iron-on peace signs on back pockets, quoting The Goodies, or singing The Irish Rovers' songs.

On Sundays, dressed a little more formally in cardigans and daggy dresses, when we arrived at the church for lessons followed by a service, I recall the thin paper of the Bibles that were laid out on the pews and being perplexed at the capitalisation of Him and He printed within. To me, it highlighted, so obviously, the fact there was no capitalised Her within. As we worked our way through learning about the book, I saw all the chapters in the Bible were written by men. Where were the women writers, I wondered? I remember the devastation of feeling that I was a 'her' and not a Him. Was I really second-class to men? With the lean of the storytelling towards the masculine, I saw that my gender was again, somehow lesser. Because of this, my place of worship became a blue-sky cathedral and my religion centred around Mother Nature, for she was a deity who gave fair and equal value to both genders.

With my own daughter now at that same age facing woman-hood, I've been giving a lot of thought to how to educate, and, most of all, empower her, particularly as her own body becomes that of a menstruating woman. We are still only a short way along the road of waking society up about such topics and learning to bask in our heavenly femaleness. The blood of woman is still taboo and continues to carry a weight of shame. In our society too, a woman's inner desires are buried deeply, so much so that some of us can't recognise what they actually are. I was never taught to wrap myself in pleasure by doing things I loved the most. I was taught to put others first every time. It wasn't until I discovered a woman called Mama Gena, who runs the New York School of Womanly Arts, that I began to learn about the mass awakening of Western woman, sweeping through society. I began to ask, What do I really want as a woman? What do I really want to teach both my son and my daughter about what it is to be female and mother?

I thought why not create a culture where we celebrate our daughters' very first journey into womanhood like our ances-tral women did, by running warm baths of oil-softened waters sprinkled with blood-red petals of roses for them? Why not light candles for them and read them passages from insightful books like *The Red Tent*? This novel, given to me by my art teacher, brings to light the life of biblical women that has been lost to history by the chronicles of men. Here I learned that young girls would 'marry the earth' with their first blood.

That notion struck a chord with me. Again, I was being shown a deep link between the feminine and farming. Women and soils are as connected as our cycles are to the moon, but in my very masculine culture of conventional farming, to speak of such things would taint me as 'out there'.

Instead women are taught to mistrust our bodies, silence ourselves about the gory business of birth and we are sold 'feminine hygiene' products as if we are unclean. This wording alone suggests our cycles are not only something that is dirty, but that we need to be protected from them as a form of illness. Very few of us have the courage to find a voice to express our inner views on the matter, yet in farming we routinely discuss animal cycles. In my rural work I've palpitated ram's testicles, slid my arm up the bum of a cow and cupped her uterus through the bowel wall, while injecting semen into her. I've written articles for the dairy industry on cows' udders and retained placentas. In the racing game I've seen prize thoroughbred mares have their vulvas stitched up to prevent infection. I've assisted vets to pull out hormonal implants from the vaginas of ewes, and in college we were taught about gestations of the female and the function of the penis in the male of each domestic livestock species. All without a hint of a snigger. It's all part of the business of farming. But when it comes to human women and their biz . . . we censor ourselves.

I want my daughter and all those who come after her to know womanhood that is not shrouded in silence and shame but set by a new tradition; that she is not 'cursed', as I was taught by other girls in school, but rather it's a rite of passage into a sisterhood that courses beyond stars, beyond time itself. It's a power. Because we live in such a masculine-focused world of economics, rigid education and patriarchal power, we have forgotten motherhood and womanhood is the truth of mankind – birth via a woman is the one thing that is common to us all. I miss my role as midwife to my animals on the farm but I'm grateful for the education I gained from those wonderful female creatures. In our role as farmer, we get to see the miracle and gift of life and death, birth and blood, up close, right before our eyes.

Stars Above

The day came when I knew we had to leave the Heavenly Hill. During the previous year, my children had changed schools after the little Levendale Primary School had finally closed, convulsing with a last gasp of defeat against shortsighted city-based bureaucratic and political systems. With one final sponge cake hurrah and big pot of tea, we shut up the school for good. But even as we closed the gate, I knew our Janice was forging plans to convert the ground to something new for the community in the future, but I had little time or stamina left to help her. My fire had gone out for community-giving. I had turned into a taxi driver for my kids to get them to their new schools and it was the unravelling of me. It wasn't the travel that bothered me. Nor the fact I was running a writing business from an office in a V8 ute. When I was farming I'd always worked with that flexibility and flow.

The problem was that to get out to the main highway, I had to pass the paddocks that didn't just contain my former beloved sheep and cattle, but also hundreds of memories. The children's new schools were a two-hour round trip, sometimes involving leaving in frost-filled darkness and inching slowly down treacherous mountain bends, then crawling, even slower, in city traffic to make it to school drop-off in time. It soon became apparent I couldn't keep it up because the emotional pain of seeing that old farm daily was excruciating and it kept tracking me down that same old road of thought.

I'd glance into a paddock and remember an autumn when I once ran over that place, gathering up perfect umbrella-shaped field mushrooms. Or I'd glimpse the tricky gate, eased with a length of wire, that I would open from the back of my sturdy mare Jess to let a mob of freshly crutched crossbred ewes drift through. Up would bubble the memory of when the ute was bogged by the blokes and I had to haul two little kids, splashing and laughing, over wet paddocks layered with silver water, the dogs dancing droplets into the air as we went off to find a tractor to pull the men out. That same journey repeated in the summer when the earth was baked, with the kids dinking on little Blossom, the mini pony, and the dogs trailing us, dodging dry thistles, their tongues pink in bright sunlight.

On days when I saw cars outside the shearing shed, with freshly shorn sheep dotting the holding paddock with their dazzling white skins, I wondered why it wasn't me treading those beloved boards within, classing the wool inside with the shearing men I had grown up with and idolised. Why wasn't I out the back in the yards, classing the sheep in the old wooden drafting race, as I had done for years for Dad? I would see the spot where I used to tie a keen-eyed young pup to the tank stand, a legend-in-waiting as he received his patient but time-consuming initiation into the world of the fully grown working dog.

Along with the memories that invaded my morning drive came observations on the current farm management that I witnessed as I passed. Although not as mind-scarringly awful as the wasteland that other land managers create in Tasmania from overgrazing, I could see that my former sheep needed lice treatment, or crutching, or moving so they had fresh tucker, and with my grassland-goddess awareness, I could see that the paddocks needed more time and rest. Glancing over fencelines, I could still feel how the environment and the livestock craved a different way. The pasture was that same short, manmade version of 'grass' that had been sown since seed companies and marketers hijacked the system of agriculture. I would hear Col Seis say, 'Ecologically functioning farms should not look like parklands. To conventional farmers, they appear messy.' I thought of the paddocks I had on the new place that were, with each turn of the earth, filling up with a rampant, wild and outrageous flourishing of plant life, dishing up a biodiverse banquet for my animals – all created by time-controlled grazing, natural manures and my very own love. Insects, birds, snakes, wallabies, kangaroos, wombats and a bounty of minuscule creatures too that I couldn't see, but I could feel, thriving both above and beneath the soil.

I couldn't help myself, constantly wishing to be custodian of that land again, on the old farm, creating the same life and abundance. A richness that was not measured in money, but in a farming system that spent less, and made more and gave more to the world, like Colin's.

On some mornings driving past, when the sun flickered in shafts through the tree canopies, I would spot my Hereford girls grazing amidst the bush runs, and feel a swamping of grief. Worse was when I would glimpse my old border collie, Diamond, wandering, doddery and almost blind, in the garden of my old house. She was my best dog, a gentle New Zealand bloodline short-hair collie who calmed sheep, cast wide and moved mobs steadily enough you could virtually sit back and have a cup of tea while she worked. She was a sweetheart, and losing her to the farm partnership (which had also claimed my ute, trailer, shed, cattle, sheep and horse yards and self-esteem) was one of the hardest parts of the divorce. There's a story about Diamond and how she came back to 'we three' briefly before she died because of a bushfire. It's too raw to tell here, but that dog was one in a million, and leaving her behind was as big a rip as losing a child to the other parent, never to be held again.

When I saw my Diamond girl amidst the first flush of yellow from the bulbs I had once planted years ago with a baby in my belly, I would clutch the steering wheel of the ute and suck in a ragged breath. Unable to stem quiet tears, I would hope the children hadn't seen my emotion, so would resolutely turn up my Pistol Annies country music tunes louder to stop the noise of pain that ran in my head. I would try to put imaginary blinkers on so I could no longer see the lost lifestyle that slid past silently on either side of my ute windows. But I never fooled those kids. I would feel a small hand reach over and rest on my arm comfortingly. Those children can read me like an open book and we were all suffering far, far too long.

As I reached the intersection and clicked the indicator to turn right onto the highway, I found myself with the same questions running in my mind. It was always the same rant about my situation. If I was to run this sort of narrative in my head over and over, it would destroy me and hurt my children more than it already had. But where was I to go? How was I to transcend the story?

I recently learned from a lecture by neuroscience expert Dr Joe Dispenza that of the thousands of thoughts we have per day – around 50 000 to 70 000 of them – 90 per cent are the same thoughts from the day before. I would find myself being triggered into travelling down those same rutted mental pathways. I'd reach the intersection and realise I'd been on that thought-road again. It was time to stop thinking in the same way and to reshape my perception of what had happened. To rewrite the narrative of my journey.

I began to remember how Dad had always said, 'If I leave you this farm when I cark it, you'll have to promise to keep it tidy.'

It dawned on me that a whole new story could be constructed. Maybe my situation was a blessing in disguise? Maybe I was being sent on a bigger mission than working just one farm? Maybe my experience was something I could learn from, and in the healing of it, I could write about finding new ways of thinking and living?

I realised if I had stayed to manage the farm, I would've broken my dear dad's promise. If I'd had my way, the farm wouldn't look like the parkland he so desperately cultivated by slashing ferns, pin rushes, spraying weeds, burning and clearing trees. I would've betrayed his wishes. My version of the farm would look like a tumbling version of the Garden of Eden – a tangle of fecund life, with moveable fences contoured over the place, kids and adults teeming on it, selling a multilayered, mishmash offering of farm produce sourced from creative flow rather than planning. But as the biblical story teaches, a woman in Eden is a dangerous thing. She can't be trusted. Maybe this notion had infiltrated our cultural thinking so much that that's why the men in my life took my Garden of Eden away from me. Or maybe, as the new story goes, I was on a path to create a new Eden, and maybe even find a new Adam, but how could I do that if every day those curved bushland hillsides and sweeping green paddocks triggered those old neural roadways of thought?

One day those clever kids said boldly and matter-of-factly, 'We think we'd better move, Mummy, so you can stop crying about the farm.'

I was resistant at first. This farming district was my home.

Plus I now knew I could create a farming enterprise on the newly lush Heavenly Hill. But the question was did I want to do it alone any more? The property now had soil that sang, and at the little farm's heart we had created a sunny, love-drenched, artful home, thanks to a series of blow-in builders who saw my plight and pitched in to help. Along with it came my determination to make our space beautiful. We had created a home there. It was filled with love and laughter. And I knew I could create a farming enterprise . . . but the location of the farm was now the problem. I suddenly realised I had to get out. I had to leave. I was in a stalemate with my family and ex-husband. They weren't going to change anything. It was costing the children dearly emotionally, so we started to look for houses.

It was my son who suggested we look around a pretty historic village for somewhere to live – not far from Hobart, but with a definite rural feel to it. As we moved into our spacious sun-filled cottage on the dirt cul-de-sac, we began to adjust. The kids did so quickly. They got their dose of farming life fortnightly when they visited their dad, but it took me longer to assimilate. On damp days, when the kids were away and I ached for them and, in particular, being with them 'out there' on the farm, I would stand on the front porch and look to the yet-to-be developed paddocks that had sheep grazing in them. I would inhale their scent like perfume.

Next to our house, over what was once a creek before it was dug out and cleared to look like a drain, is a vacant block. The generosity of our landladies meant we could keep our dogs and chooks and even run our tubby, patchy pony Gemma there. Having the animals was our anchor, and village living had great gifts I was yet to unwrap and accept. After school, even until dark, reaching my ears and my heart was the sound of my kids laughing outside, and the repeated scudding of bike tyres on gravel as they practised their skids. More children from other houses came and one evening I counted eleven kids, a cheerful golden retriever and our escaped poodle all enjoying life in a community that held rural values at its core.

When it rains the same gang of kids plays in the mud in the creek that runs right through our yard and beneath a warped fence bowed by past flooding. The creek continues on between two cul-de-sacs and it was here, outside our yard, I would graze Gemma on a tether near some fledgling blackwoods. Some days passing Asian tourists capture her cute-as-a-cartoon image on their smart phones as if she is a local monument of note. With my eye for agricultural hydrology, I could see that our rental house was in a flood plain. Not beside one – *in one*. Local gossip told me it was an old hydroelectric-scheme house from Poatina Power Station that had been plonked here before anyone had time to notice – the paperwork had been snuck through in the busy run-up to Christmas holidays. From my upstairs window I witnessed a new house getting built in a spot where I would put a farm dam. I was perplexed.

Once when hanging washing, I got to talking to my neighbour Jean. Now in her nineties, Jean had lived in her house for sixty years and could point out the very shed that used to be the local slaughterhouse, or where they would milk cows in the dairy. She told me the story of how she and her husband could've bought the land once – all of it – for £50 back in the day, and now she wished they had. Real estate is premium in this convict-created village that, two blocks away from us, swarms with tourists tumbling off big buses, or Hobartians wanting to take their elderly parents out for an easy lunch. As Jean and I talked through the fence beneath a pepper tree whilst the chooks scratched at her feet, she told me about the day the water flooded right up to the back fence where I was standing. It was a level well above our lounge-room floor. Jean shook her head when I told her the block next door had sold and the watercourse was earmarked for 'residential development'. I wondered at the logic of the decision-makers. There's money to be made from flood plains apparently.

Where once Aboriginals used to live amidst nature, we whities have to plonk ourselves upon it and own it for ourselves. Smother the soil with concrete. Raze everything on which to build ugly houses and place our barren roads that displace people, animals, plants and even water. A condition of the vacant block's sale that was made on paper in 2009 was that the developers had to connect the road that was severed by the creek. It had been this way since the early 1800s and the locals said the old-timers had never joined the roads for good reason, due to the water flow. Suddenly we discovered our dirt cul-de-sac of laughing children would be lost. The creek in which I'm told the rare species of green and gold bell frog used to live will now for certain be doomed. I'd invited a councillor to come and see the area to ask if during the development the road could remain disconnected and the creek free-running. I could see that a small patch of native habitat could be regenerated and those happy tourists and dog walkers could find a glimpse of Mother Nature in an increasingly urban environment. Instead giant concrete pipes would be needed beneath a dangerous big-dipper road that would catapult cars into a busy intersection at the primary school. The councillor advised that the 2009 'approval' meant the decision was set in stone in the minds of the council and the developers. She told me nothing could be done.

I noticed, lovely as she was, she used 'man speak', a bureaucratic, rigid language I never wanted to embrace. In my career as a journalist, I'd witnessed many brilliant women like her, who were bravely getting into politics and governance, masking or even denying their feminine side in those realms in order to soldier on as a man would. I wondered if the people who make these decisions knew in any way, from the intuitive feminine sides of themselves, that they are part of one web. A web of life that interconnects us to everything and everyone. Or were they tangled in their surface-only human egos, where salary and titles and people-politics shouted so much white noise they couldn't hear the earth sigh or their own universe of truth within their bodies? My frequent visits to the city to drop my daughter at school provided me daily with eye-witness accounts of how humans are a plague upon the earth. The roads are getting bigger, smoother, wider; the cars are getting more plentiful, faster, bigger. Roadkill on four-lane highways in Hobart is a symbol of how much we layer our Mother Earth with our self-focused crap without consideration for other life forms. Our political agenda is so skewed to growth and development of capitalist pursuits that the value of nature holds no place on national financial balance sheets. Sometimes on our drives to school, my daughter and I design the city the way we would want it. We narrate a feminine utopia vastly different to the masculine one we see before us, choked with traffic.

Once when arriving home from school drop-off on a cold-snap day in summer, I could hear the musk lorikeets shrieking and crying. I looked up and there they were, circling in a morbidly grey sky, their bright-green wings outstretched. All their flowering gums that had lined our road had been cut down. No warning to the people who lived here. No warning for the birds. These beautiful little fern-green creatures, with a vibrant splash of red that was painted beside intelligent eyes, seemed to be in shock and chaos. It was feeding time on the flowers, and nesting time. Prior to the angry bite of chainsaws, they had dangled happily upside-down sipping nectar from frothy red-gum flowers. I'd seen how their antics and beauty had attracted bird enthusiasts who came to our road, and spent time photographing them with that intense human joy that comes when one is immersed in the mystery and beauty of nature. But today, on an ordinary weekday, the trees were suddenly gone. And so too went the lorikeets.

I had kept telling myself if I had to move to a town, it might as well be one as beautiful as this one. But the town is changing and changing fast, making it harder to adjust to town living, while right outside my door was human bureaucracy gone mad, building a road where one wasn't needed nor welcomed by most of the locals. For months after first moving, I had displacement dreams. Without the familiarity of the natural surrounds that I'd worshipped and gazed upon with love each day, I was at first unhinged. It was that dirt road, along with the occasional visits from black cockies during rough weather, and the lively lorikeets and warbling comical magpies, that kept me comforted and helped me to reground myself. The move to an urbanish landscape began to creep into my art and my expression. The next time my musician friend Nick Wolfe rolled up to my door and got his guitar out of his ute for a songwriting session, I couldn't help but suffer a weight of shame welcoming him into my urban rental. Everything about me was country. I felt I was living a lie. It was little wonder when we came together creatively that we wrote about a girl displaced. Out came the line, 'Growing up is hard with city lights, when you use the stars above you as your guide.'

That shame is easing now as I begin to see this house as just a stop-off point for healing and learning before moving to a new place. But I still find the streetlights invasive and confronting. For the first time in decades, I have to shut the blinds to the sweep of my beloved moon, because not only can neighbours see in, but because I cannot bear the artificial lights that burn all night. The dogs have had to adjust too, hearing cars and other voices strange to them. When we walked out the front door, the kelpies at first would sniff the wind and look to the sheep in the paddock. They would glance at me and ask the question, 'Can we?' Each time I would say no, I watched their disappointment. They soon learned the sheep were ones never to be moved, and so they have given up asking me the question. They just slink by, blinkers on.

Not since Dubbo in 1990 had I lived in an urban environment and even then I only lasted a few months before seeking out a place to stay amidst paddocks. At the time, I'd recently left Orange Agricultural College where I'd failed one subject – typing. As part of my Rural Business Administration course it was a mandatory requirement. Stubborn me, I'd reacted to the sexist notion that women were to be limited by our typing skills. It smacked of sexism and old-fashioned ethos. I'd witnessed the way Dad's beautifully groomed and perfumed legal secretaries were always in service to men. Typing was the last thing on my agenda. To reach the required typing speed and accuracy, I had to go to Dubbo TAFE for a summer course, otherwise my Rural Business Admin bit of paper was not mine to have! I now know it was the clever universe giving me a giant flat stone foundation that would provide the sure footing I needed to type as fast as my thoughts when I became my future author self.

So there I was in Dubbo, when all my college mates were out and about harvesting, or waterskiing on farm dams having fun, and I was traipsing to typing so I could join them at graduation. After I'd passed my exam, I didn't last long in the share house that was set on the road to Gilgandra in New South Wales. I tried, but I couldn't find any kind of stillness there. I couldn't bear it. The neat path. The door in the middle that led into a hallway with small rooms either side. The smell of ordinariness and sprinkled perfumed carpet cleaner. Not to mention the huge phone bill that came in because one housemate had been making too many phone-sex calls, and hadn't realised they had charged him and listed the number on the bill for his fellow housemates to see! I soon hot-footed it out of there and found a house out of town between Dubbo and Narromine. A place with paddocks, trees, birds, the sweep of the sky and the rhythm of the day uninterrupted by human busyness.

Now here I am nearly a quarter of a century later living in a town again. I've used this time as the perfect way to research urban living for my vocation as a writer and use the experience to compare it to my rural one. To start with, I've stacked on the kilos. Food is so accessible from shops! I've got myself addicted to coffee. One cup a day. My physical labour is limited to getting in the odd load of wood, so I sense my body weakening, softening, and I feel I have to counter it by running the tubby pony up and down over the bike hillocks at the skate park, trailing after my son on his bike, so the pony and I get some exercise in.

I am also witness to 'mind viruses', as Dr Wayne Dyer calls them in his writing, which are messages we catch from society and believe to be true. Like the fact we think we need bigger, better roadways – when in fact we really need new systems of transport. Or that we need bigger, better shopping centres, hardware stores or housing areas, when really we need to reconsider consumerism and environmentally compatible living.

The first few weekends I spent in the village I would wake early and head out to do my chores of the chooks and vegie garden. The township was so silent, I thought there'd been some kind of alien invasion in the night that had removed every living human from their houses and taken them to a parallel universe! So quiet was the place I wondered if I'd missed something in the night. But then, come 10 o'clock, a symphony of lawnmowers would start up and dog walkers bound for the coffee shop would begin strolling past the house. I realised I was adjusting to a new urban time schedule. What baffled me more was how each household exported their soil nutrients from their gardens by putting all their garden clippings into big wheelie bins to be carted away, instead of reusing them as ground cover, worm food or compost.

Every Monday morning when the garbage truck came at 6 a.m. I saw how people had been programmed to put their colour-coded bins out. Yellow lid for recycling material, green lid for garden waste. I would reach to the book beside my bed, Kristin Ohlson's *The Soil Will Save Us*, and start to apply some of her discoveries in her home country of America to my own urban experience here in Australia. She begins her book by telling us that 80 billion tonnes of carbon has been lost from the world's soils from farming, ranching and land practices – especially from modern industrial agriculture. As I read this, and looked out my window at my urban surrounds, where the council gardeners clearly had it in for large trees and long grasses, I wondered why such reported environmental travesties rested entirely on the shoulders of country people and those in rural industry. What about those in towns? People in energy-hungry housing?

In Tasmania we have an army of people protecting 'Wilderness' areas and yet I believe every area, every inch of this planet, is sacred. It's not just the breathtaking forests that are important, it's also the vacant block, the strip beside the highway, the area of land on which your house sits. We fence these places in, and in doing so we fence off our minds. To many 'nature' is a drive away, reached it only when we take annual leave and pack the camping gear into the car. But nature is the everyday. From the bird that alights on your roof, the spider that is carrying out its life purpose under your sink, to the millions of living creatures in the soil that have been smothered by your hosed-down path. Every one of us is already in the natural world, and people in urban areas have as much power as farmers to change the outcomes of our planet.

Ohlson's book begins by her theorising about soils and humans when she stopped raking her leaves on her lawn so that the nutrients within them could cover the ground and feed the microbes beneath. She, like me, watched the gardening habits of neighbours. In her case, they were hard at it, clawing leaves into great piles. Leaving the soil bare, removing the very thing that would keep the soil breathing and breeding. 'Tidy' is a human construct. I too puzzled at the illogical practice of exporting vegetable matter from one's land. I've heard it quoted in various places, but apparently one teaspoon full of healthy soil – from anywhere, city or country – contains approximately 6–7 billion organisms made up of teeny-weeny little fungi, tiny worms and a multitude of microorganisms that science is still catching up on naming.

Given that a huge proportion of people own lawns in Australia, isn't there potential right there to make massive environmental change? According to Kristin, lawns make up the largest irrigated crop in the US, taking up three times as much space as corn. What we do with our urban green matters, whether it's in our yards and our parks, or even our highway median strips. She cites studies that support Colin Seis's theory that if famers improved their community of soil microorganisms by increasing biomass (soil thrumming with life), the amount of carbon sequestered in the soil would offset all our current emissions of carbon dioxide.

Well, what are we waiting for?

We don't need a Legoland lawn of one plastic species. What I would like to see is a trend for multispecies lawns and a change in mindset so that lawns can be seen as 'community carbon collection areas'. A longer, more interesting lawn with wildlife-supporting species of plants would come to symbolise a caring citizen, rather than a lazy gardener. In the same way bare paddocks or bald hillsides ought to be rethought of as being as offensive as smoking over a baby's cot. When people see a hillside that wavers in the wind with the green of Mother Nature's blanket covering it, we should sing our praises to the land manager who helped our earth create it. We can try to change people by enforcing laws, but social pressures and positive leadership is the fastest way to inspire change, rather than impose change.

Have you noticed there is a 'collective consciousness' in humans and our awareness of our oneness with nature is gaining momentum? Have you noticed how fast holistic ideas are spreading due to the internet? Human thoughts are contagious. A person only has to walk into a room to influence the people in it, without uttering a word. How we act, think and exist in the world impacts on others. Any stockman who works livestock for a living understands how mob dynamics are communicated as if through the ethers. One 'bad egg' in a mob can spread that behaviour like wildfire – would the animal break through a fence or split from the herd, taking followers with it? A calm leader can impart wisdom and order to a mob, herd or pack. Even schoolteachers know there are group dynamics in children. When you next walk out in your world, be aware of the mind viruses that infiltrate us all and know you are in control of your own mood and future.

It can be a difficult thing to do because marketers are everywhere. Billboards and buses tell us that we need a new car, a new watch, a new body. News is flashed on big screens and small screens in our palms – most of it mindlessly negative. Like urban living, agriculture is rampant with negative mind viruses too . . . that there's no future, that to be a farmer is to struggle. We have a belief in 'the Aussie battler' doing it hard. But can we be like Joel Salatin and think of it another way? What if we told ourselves a new story about farming? That these are vibrant places of life that sustain many people. That the soil is so healthy that even if rainfall fails to arrive, there is still enough moisture that the plants are sustained? Creating a vibrant new life in agriculture starts in our mindsets.

My way of settling myself into a stillness and strong faith in my world is to meditate daily. Even if it's just for ten minutes, it centres me again to be committed to a world I want to create.

Nowadays, I have come to be very selective about what I focus on. I no longer watch the news or read the paper. I no longer watch television with advertising about how our bodies let us down and are to be tested and medicated. Not because I don't care . . . but because I do care. I don't want to add to those mind viruses and feed my life's energy into those negative areas.

As our neighbours and I are in the midst of pleading with council about the joining of the road, I had hoped I could write a happy ending to this chapter, to say the decision-makers had heard us and our No Through Road safely remains. But we are all left hanging on an answer with the road half dug up, providing the kids mounds of dirt to jump bikes over. In the meantime, I've committed myself to village living for the moment, and am congratulating myself that I've lasted longer here than Dubbo. I'm still practising altering those 70 000 daily thoughts of mine to become thoughts of gratitude, love, forgiveness, joy and hope. Less and less frequently do the thoughts arrive that take me back down that woeful old track I no longer need to go. I began to broaden my horizons to include more self-care: leisurely walks, not just to get fit, bubble baths, not just to get clean, and time to just sit and pat my dogs, not just to train them, but to love them. In this village, I came to see sometimes I am moving and changing the most when I am sitting still.

Cricket Crazy

I must have looked like an Aussie cliché from the 1970s. A typical ocker child wearing a floppy terry-towelling hat with dead-straight wheat-blonde hair emerging beneath it, white zinc smeared across my freckled nose, a red V-neck T-shirt and too-short navy terry-towelling shorts that I was growing out of, fast. I had worn, old thongs that would bust periodically. I'd clumsily tried to sticky-tape them back together from the underside. There I was on the hill at the cricket, dodgy thongs cast aside, sitting under the hot sun on a tasselled, scratchy towel, while Dad, wearing something equally as ocker, sank tinnies out of an esky sloshing with melting ice.

Back then, the main cricket matches in Hobart were played at the old Tasmanian Cricket Association ground on the Queens Domain. A slice of England amidst the bush, with the cream picket fence encircling the ground and an elegant members' stand with a curved tin roof complete with wrought iron and pretty finial touches. The plebs were kept separate on the hill. Around the ground was Tasmanian wilderness. The bush-covered hill that overlooks the heart of the city and the River Derwent remains pretty much unchanged since then and although ringed with human activity, the area gives us a postage-stamp-size remnant of what Hobart's grassland was like. I still run my dogs up there on the reserve whilst waiting for school pick-up time, just so I can inhale the scent of bushland soil and drift my fingertips over the remaining native grasses and listen to the thrum of insects in the dappled shade and honour those quieter communities we have displaced with concrete and consumerism. I soak in all the sounds and scents that echo the legacy of the past, before British buildings, bullshit and the sport of cricket was brought to this land.

I can't look at the sloping hill of the old TCA without thinking of Dad and the bunch of Paul Hogan lookalike yobs who used to cheer on the cricketers. During the hours it took to battle it out over a Sheffield Shield, to pass the time my brother and I invented a game of stacking empty beer cans up into a tall, wavering pyramid. The tins were artfully colour-coded between draught or bitter. Then, when the last can was carefully placed at the top of the stack, the blokes above us on the hill, in between overs, would throw more cans and other objects at it, toppling it and letting out a great cheer when it clattered to the ground. We would repeat the process, making our towers larger and larger as the empty beer-can supplies increased and the overs were bowled and batsmen came and went. There were no recycling wheelie bins back then. The quantity of discarded cans grew and grew, as did the day, into long shadows on the grass. Cricket takes time. And it clearly took a lot of beer.

I'm not sure what my mother would have made of this activity. I don't remember her being at the cricket with us back then much, even though she is more of a cricket fan than my dad, but maybe in those days the hill wasn't the place for wives. I do remember the wobbly-booted 'full as googs' blokes. It has given me a lifelong unhealthy barometer of accepting men who simultaneously drink beer and stare at sport as normal. Heck . . . I used to find it endearing. Little primary-school me was snuck into that male domain, and being a sponge to the world, I soaked it all in, good and bad.

Once, on a close-played Sheffield Shield final where Tassie stood a chance of victory, the crowd was in a frenzy. My brother and I had the cans stacked high – we were almost to the top. Our structure was so tall we had to ask an adult to place the remaining few. But a group of blokes sauntered past and kicked the cans over before we had finished the stack. Like a tsunami, a sudden wave of aggression flowed forward as the men on the hill swarmed, leaping over their eskies, all of them set on punching the lights out of the offenders. I watched with wide-eyed amazement as I felt the surge of male aggro, fuelled with booze. Within seconds, police came. They busted up the fight. There were bloody noses, bad language and back-slapping from the blokes who came out on top. It was all normal at the time. It was the 1970s! As the scuffle died down, my dad called us kids to heel. It was time to simply sit and watch the cricket.

Despite the male focus of the era, I remember the day I discovered cricket wasn't just a male sport. I recall almost falling into a photograph with fascination and surprise. The old black-and-white image was of a woman in long skirts wielding a bat. And another showed women in white sitting amidst the men in a team line-up. After seeing these photographs, I couldn't understand where the women had gone from the game since the 1800s. Like tennis, cricket had started as a mixed-gender sport. Why, then, did it seem so dominated by males at the state and international level? I knew as a kid it was a sport I could play with my brother and succeed in bowling him out, or tonking him over the fence. I was fast, competitive, and honed my catching and throwing to be as good as the boys. I was determined to not be left behind by them. But aside from backyard cricket, there was little support for aspiring female cricketers.

Despite having two country cricket teams in my old farming district of Levendale and Runnymede, women were kept to the sidelines. They sat in the car or on blankets watching the kids. Their job was to provide the sandwiches, maybe keep score if they were short of men to do it, and heat the sausage rolls. There were a few hardcore Jim Beam-kinda gals who made the distance in the clubrooms afterwards, but women actually on the field was something I've never seen in those two clubs. I knew the clubs themselves were a good thing for the district, bringing social life to the area, but women's sport in my rural region was limited to netball, a sport I never warmed to.

Still, the cricket clubs were good, fun places, even if just socially. Once when the kids were younger I went for a ride on my old Dargo droving horse, Jess. She's a palomino who was bought cheaply from the sale yard in Sale, Victoria, years ago, and she comes with an unknown history. Jess was the pony that got me back in the saddle after having my babies and she's been my comfort ever since. Nowadays she's loaned out to Riding for the Disabled (also known as Riding Develops Ability), where my daughter rides her each week. Jess gets to work her golden pony magic on other children too, even taking one vision-impaired rider to a State Championship dressage victory, along with my daughter in reserve place. But back in the early days of motherhood, Jess and I would head off down the road to meet my human friend Jess. There we were on the Woodsdale Road, Jess the horse, and Jess the person riding her horse Fergus. Fergus behaved as if he belonged in a Pantene shampoo commercial. He was so convinced he was the most beautiful grey in all the land that he would spend his time tossing his head and long locks accordingly. It was on this summer evening ride that we discovered in the cluster of roadside mail boxes at the end of the road that the new phone books had been delivered. Judging from the pale sky and the dampness of the air, I knew it was going to be a dewy night so I opted to tuck the phone book under my arm and keep riding.

Jess is like a couch – Jess the horse, that is – round and comfortable to ride, with a terrific drover's horse fast, steady walking pace. You can manoeuvre her with your legs or the press of a rein on her neck, so she's been dubbed the perfect 'drinking horse' because there's always a hand free to hold a can. On Dad's farm, I once lugged a heavy old sick wether slung over her shoulders out of the bush as I sat in the saddle. Even though she'd never carried a sheep before, she stood steady as a rock as I lobbed him over her, then climbed aboard myself. As Jess and Jess, Fergus and I rode past hawthorn hedges that lined the road, we soon spotted cars ringing the cricket ground. The clubrooms were abuzz with post-cricket victory chatter and the bar was open. We rode right up to the windows and proceeded to settle in on the backs of our horses as the cricket boys put our drinks on the tab and brought them to us from the bar. Now with phone book and Bundy rum in hand upon a horse at the cricket club, life was looking pretty good that afternoon . . . unique, in fact.

According to our old laws, it's still illegal to be drunk and ride a horse, so by the time the sun began to sink, it was decided our horse keys ought to be confiscated and we should park our horses in the neighbour's sheep yards overnight. Cars tend not to slow for horses much these days and riding on dusk, with a phone book in hand and a belly full of Bundy rum, was not a good thing. I opted for a lift home instead and was pleased I'd have a reason to ride Jess home again the following day. I was delivered back to my farmhouse into the shadows of disapproval.

It seemed on days like that one, I was 'too much' for those around me, rather than 'not enough', but that rare day of equine freedom from the boundaries of farm and family still makes me smile. It was an 'Aussie-as' outing.

Like horses, my love of cricket was put on hold when the kids were really little. For a time, cricket was merely a background noise whilst I raised the babies into toddlers. The local finals were simply a place to drink socially with the local community, but as my son grew and I became a single mum, it was up to me to bowl to him. Through my son, my love for playing the game was reignited. My skills were rusty, and it took me a while to get my eye and arm in, but I mustn't have been too rusty. One day we were at my daughter's therapy sports day, organised by St Giles – a non-government group that has helped us with my daughter's development for many years – and my son and I were getting a little competitive and raucous playing cricket in a giant basketball stadium amidst the St Giles clients. The Tasmanian Roar girls hosting a cricket activity at the event spotted my action and afterwards asked me for my number. A few weeks later, I got a call from the New Town Cricket Club coach inviting me, as a forty-something-year-old, to play for their club! Overcommitted to supporting my kids and animals, I didn't rise to the challenge. But in some ways I wish I had given myself the time. I'd always dreamed of playing competitively.

When I was about eleven or twelve I did have a brief stint playing with Sandy Bay Cricket Club women's team. Here I received coaching from the men, and began to practise in earnest with my straight bat, and line and length with my bowling. But once my friend Libby quit cricket, my option of lifts to training and games dried up. Because I was just starting out at the all-girls school at the time, unlike at co-ed state primary school, there was no cricket on offer, so my desire for playing the sport competitively had a lid firmly shut on it.

Throughout my teenage years, every day after high school I played in our bricked carport with my brother, converting cricket into our own version of a kind of cricket–squash. In that house in the up-and-coming suburb, many a tennis ball bore the brunt of my teenage frustrations and longing to be out on the farm with my horse as I bowled full pelt over and over at chalked stumps on a brick wall. My life lifted during school holidays, when we had more space to play, in paddocks at the farm or on beaches, particularly on Christmas Day with a cluster of once-a-year cousins and beery-cheery uncles who would not put down their stubbies for love nor money, even when fielding. It could just be the memory of it, a blaze of glory-days nostalgia, but in recent years, watching the skill level in my son develop as he bowls, fields and bats, I can see the fire in the belly I used to have for cricket. I can't help but think that if there had been a clearer path forward for young girls in schools, I may have played at club or state level in women's cricket . . . and if I'd worked hard enough, even beyond. Who's to say? The days are gone, but my love of cricket hasn't.

As I faced my second summer in the flystrike-green rental, I braced myself for the long haul of holidays when the kids go to stay with their dad. It's here when the agony within would rise up in me again – a choking sensation. I knew I would be missing my favourite summertime activities on the farm – shearing, haymaking, barbecues with the rellies in a paddock cooking on a plough disc hot plate, swimming the dogs in the dam at sunset. But it wasn't so much that – it was that I wasn't there by my children's side to impart to them all I had learned and loved about working human, dog and beast within a healthy landscape.

Thankfully the universe delivered me a brilliant distraction at that moment and I was offered a dream job through December and January promoting limited-over cricket to women and children for the Hobart Hurricanes, who play in the raucous, fast-paced Big Bash League of 20-over cricket. It was also the very first year the Hurricanes were introducing a women's side to play alongside the men's in the same purple colours. For the first match I went to as their writer, Hobart couldn't have turned it on better. The frequently chill winds blown over kunanyi and up the River Derwent from the Antarctic were blissfully still. The night was warm and a Christmas moon shaped like the belly of Santa, promising fullness in a few days, was rising in a lavender sky beside the looming light towers of Blundstone Arena.

I'd been asked to invite 'cricket virgins' to attend the matches with me, to spread via word of mouth the thrilling experience of the game in this format. I settled my guests in with a seafood box, a Bundy and a beer, and instructed them on how to use their 'four' and 'six' signs, and with purple Hurricanes Santa hats on, we were ready to roll. My inner-yobbo child from those seventies days was ready to come out to play. I love cricket in all forms of the game. Whether it's at Lord's with players in Test whites or on a bracken-fern-covered bush block beside a caravan, with me wearing board shorts and Crocs, and with a garbage bin as wicket, cricket is heaven to me no matter when, where or how.

It runs in the family too. My mum is a volunteer at the Blundstone Arena Cricket Museum and gives tours to the people who drift through there to gaze at bats and hats behind glass. On match days she sits in the members' area with her friend Lindsay, covered in sunscreen or blankets or both, for the first ball delivery of a five-day Test match, depending on the fickle Hobart weather. Test matches are the style of cricket that showcases the refinement of gentlemen in white and long-held traditions that are clutched close to purists' hearts. While I love the buzz of BBL, Test cricket is my sound of summer. It's the commentary and consistency over days that kept me going during harvest time in western New South Wales or skirting fleeces in the shed until the last sheep was shorn on a sweltering day. In the ute in after-school traffic, it keeps me calm. But because society has changed, with flashing screens and three-second sound grabs, if we are to lure children away from their electrified, buzzy, virtual and far-too-often sedentary worlds, the limited-over style of cricket is the way to do it. BBL is the hook to catch the next generation of cricket fans – particularly girls – with its colour and zing and quick pace. Once the administrators and marketers of Test cricket embrace women into the sport, I believe Test cricket is less likely to die a slow, painful death. The contrast couldn't be greater between Mum's friend Lindsay, doing her crosswords or crochet with her glasses elegantly sitting on the end of her nose whilst watching a Test, and the BBL buzz of firestacks fizzing, thumping music and a 15 000-strong crowd of roaring fans. In BBL, the stadium takes on the quality of a big-league baseball match. White balls tonked over heads against a blue sky, zinger bails sparking and there are catches, fumbles, tumbles, swings, misses, leaps and dives. My guests didn't understand it all, but they didn't need to. They were caught up in the atmosphere of purple passion.

I don't think it was an accident that the very year I was asked to work for the Hobart Hurricanes was the same time the women were being given a crack, albeit with reduced televised matches and salaries that were only a fraction of the men's earnings. The women players had to cram their matches into weekends as most of them were working full-time jobs – unlike many of their male cricketing counterparts, who were paid to play. Again I reiterate if we diminish one half of our community we diminish us all, so thankfully we are on the cusp of sweeping change where we are enjoying a feminine awakening . . . which is vastly different to a feminist uprising. The movement is coming from the core place of a woman . . . a place of peace, love and power, and it is also coming from the feminine awakening within men. I was discovering some wonderful male administrators within the sport who were championing the cause for both-gender cricket competitions, as they knew it would further the sport and bring benefits to families as a whole. It was exciting to be meeting our new brotherhood of gentle men in high-level sports administration.

In the midst of the buzz I spotted a living goddess in the crowd – West Indian heroine Hayley Matthews – fresh from her 77 runs during a 51-ball knock for the Canes.

'That's the future!' I said to my guests. 'Soon we'll get to see women like that paid and celebrated as much as the men! Just like the tennis stars.'

As my ten-year-old son leant over the fence hoping for Ms Matthews' autograph, my mates were beginning to see the bigger picture. Sport feeds our nation's psyche, and yes, the BBL offers rip-roaring entertainment, but it also offers a celebration of life and the freedom of Aussie larrikinism away from daily pressures and a level of intellectualism that keeps us so serious. And it also offers us a chance for women to find inspiration in others, so we have the belief we can claim our right to share the turf on the sports field as well as on our farmland.

The next match I hosted guests was kicked off on New Year's Day, when the women's Hurricanes team claimed their place on the Blundstone Arena paddock as a first in history. *Move aside, bulls*, I thought gleefully, *we have jumped the fence!* My cricket wingmen hailed from the Derwent Valley, Huon region, Orielton and even as distant as Coleraine in far western Victoria. Throw into the mix a few cricket crazy kids and a couple of vet friends, and we thunder-sticked our way into a night that was more sparkly than a Sydney skyline putting on a fireworks show.

My longtime stockman buddy George, who was taking rare time off from his business as a livestock contractor on the mainland, had never been to a BBL event, and being a dyed-in-the-wool country lad, set about comparing human behaviour with livestock flow. We were, after all, a group of friends fascinated with animal psychology. In our minds, the main entrance to Blundstone Arena turnstiles became drafting gates, the curved walls of the stadium became bugle yards to help livestock flow, the inflatable thunder sticks became 'sheep shifters', even though in George's stock camp low-stress stock handling would never see them used.

My working-dog trainer friend Sandra noticed how, like sheep, we followed leaders with an unseen synergy. Like a big mob, we take on a mob mentality when we gather in our human herd, and that's what I loved so much about that year's BBL. The organisers were giving the women a crack at being as big-time as the blokes and I could see that what that does to human mob mentality is invaluable to us as a society, in terms of restoring masculine–feminine balance in our psyche. What that does to mob mentality is invaluable to us as a society.

As a 'Hurricanes ambassador', I'd been offered a place for my guests in the Chairman's room, but my country crowd was too happy with the rest of the herd to be yarded like that. They wanted to remain in the main mob in our informal denim dress with our offspring by our sides, preferring to run with the Hurricanes herd in general admission – and run we did. As we watched the awesome women cricketers become national heroes before our very eyes, my heart sang when my son excitedly cried out, 'Veronica's bowling!' His former Milo Cricket coach from little east coast town Orford, Veronica Pyke promptly went on to take three Brisbane Heat wickets in several goosebump-filled moments.

My boy then said, 'Mummy, in a few years' time, this stadium will be packed when people realise the women are this good!' To educate a young bull like my son in his formative years about the power and place of women is invaluable to me as a mother. I heard my friend Maria sigh, 'It's just so nice to see women out there.' Both of us are mums who met through our daughters' participation at Riding for the Disabled, Kingborough. Here at the cricket we not only got to spend 'mum time' with our beautiful sons, who set aside many of their own needs for the sake of their siblings, but we also got to reevaluate our own self-worth in society. We were proudly witness to the next generation of women and their right to stand alongside the men on the cricket pitch. Under a sky that we all swore had purple hues in the clouded sunset, we cheered the girls to victory, and deep within me I knew that the little cricket-crazy girl on the hill in the seventies would be doing cartwheels in excitement, knowing how the world has turned!

Holidaying with My Horse

It was like a scene out of a rural romance novel that morphed into a comedy, or at least that's how it ran in my creative writer's head. There I was on a hot, windswept, dry, summer-ravaged hill on my buckskin horse, the view of farmland and mountains sweeping around me for 360 degrees with two wedge-tailed eagles to the west soaring in the hazy blue sky. Beside me an Argentine cowboy in a Wrangler shirt, blue jeans and dusty boots was sitting astride a chunky bay horse, looking as if they both belonged in a Harlequin outback romance novel. As I turned my face to the winds I'd said in passing that my lips had blistered, and there he was, swivelling in his saddle, reaching his long tanned fingertips into his jeans pocket and taking out his ChapStick. In his knee-wobbling Latino accent, I heard him say, 'Would you like some, Rachael?', stretching out his arm and waving the small tube of lip balm at me. My imagined heroine looked at his handsome face beneath his broad-brimmed hat, his hazel eyes catching the sunlight, and I found her saying in a husky soap-opera voice, 'Why, yes, Carlos, I would like some. Why don't you apply it to your lips first and then simply kiss me?'

My imagined novelist scenes rarely, if ever, play out in real life for me, and the truth was I was on that hill with a bunch of other women, all gaining insight and skills from one of the most mindful and respected teachers I've ever had the honour of knowing, Carlos Tabernaberri. Instead, in my ocker fashion, I replied, 'Thanks, mate,' as I took the tube from Carlos. 'That'd be great. My lips are caning.'

This kind of 'head play', where I construct scenes for possible future stories, happens often to me at any given time and it was truly novelist gold riding out with a bloke like Carlos Tabernaberri and my new posse of horsey women. Much like my truffle girls, they were strong, vibrant, brilliant women. And oh so funny, not to mention beautiful. They were the kind of women who, when standing in the yards, provided me with classic comedy dialogue like, 'I'm going to look like an adolescent boy by the end of the day cos this bloody dust is sticking to my mo.'

Despite the fun I was having, the reality was I was so challenged by what I was learning from this extremely clever and philosophical horseman that I was using all kinds of self-diversion tactics. Humour was my way of dealing with the gravity of what I had been uncovering during my five-day clinic with him about my very shutdown, self-doubting self and the impact it had had on my horse, Archie. As I sat upon my horse on that hill, I wondered if the other women were going through the same self-esteem wobblies like I was. I had come to the realisation that when I entered my horse's paddock I was not only putting my saddle on his back, but also saddling him up with my life's grief, disappointment and loss, and, most of all, the deep psychological belief in my disempowerment as a woman, and the inner doubt that I was not a fit or worthy leader.

Here it was being clearly reflected back at me during the first few days of the clinic via my very shutdown horse. Horses are such a strong reflection of where you are at with your energy. I'd not risen to the task of taking on Archie's leadership as I was so unsteady in my confidence. Instead I'd leant on others to take him on for me, but I knew I needed to take the reins in my own life. Over the years I'd already reached out to a few trainers to help me with building my horsemanship skills, which seemed stuck in gear from childhood. I didn't just want instruction, I wanted mindfulness and horsemanship that, like my dog training, was all about using the creature's language and bypassing human ego. Our animals are a reflection of ourselves. I've seen it over and over. Good self-esteem in the handler, and the animals reflect it. Loving heart, and the animal reflects it. Calmness – again, that animal mirror shows us the truth of what's within us. I had lost my belief in myself and with it I had not been able to be the best leader to my horse that I wanted to be . . . until Carlos came can- tering into my life as a mentor. I'd been to other trainers – all with important lessons, all mindful, but never had I set five whole days aside for myself and my horse. I'd always given and given to those around me and put myself last. To step out of my routine of children and work to just be with myself and my horse was terrifying, but I knew I would be in good hands and in good company. Carlos is a man who has changed lives – many of them human, many of them horses. In his line of work, he has to be therapist for both equine and human souls. Not an easy thing when modern living leaves us so frazzled and detached and, for me, time-poor with horses.

It was the first time off I'd had to myself in over twelve years, away from my kids and my work commitments. Instead of booking a beach holiday like a normal person would, I of course chose a trip that would include my 'fur kids' . . . my dogs and horses. It felt odd that I didn't have to wake up and focus on what school uniforms were needed for the day and what could be packed into the school lunches, and how many emails I needed to respond to. I'd felt more than a huge twinge of guilt that I'd set aside these five days right on the Australia Day long weekend and had turned down rural community requests for appearances. It felt terrible shutting the door to everyone else, but I needed to just go and be with my horse.

Little did I know it would be a life-changing experience, hanging out with the funniest bunch of women I'd ever met, all taking the mickey out of each other, ourselves and our Latino teacher – who, yes, could be a 'love interest' in a rural romance, but who is also incredibly professional and committed to the welfare and wellbeing of the horse. It's his life calling and he's fallen on his sword many times in his career to defend the rights of horses.

I'd met Carlos several years earlier and had a couple of one-hour sessions with him and completed a one-day clinic with my beloved, gentle but cheeky Dreams. Not long after, she was tragically killed in a road accident during a time of turmoil for Tasmania, when bushfires razed the Peninsula. I hadn't grieved or healed enough for my next horse, so I hadn't yet found the heart or the courage to bond with Archie, let alone be the leader he needed me to be. I'd put my all into being a leader for my children, so with Archie I needed outside help. But the right *kind* of help. Help that was gentle, slow and empathetic. Not harsh or cruel, neither to me nor the horse. It took all my bravery to face that horse as his leader, and face myself for the stillness of five full days of just me and him. The first night I checked into the historic Man O' Ross Hotel in Midlands Tasmania with my two kelpie dogs, Rousie and Connie, I was giddy from nerves after a health scare with my daughter that day. She was okay in the end, but it almost stopped me from leaving, and after a day of doctors and scans, and then finally getting the all-clear that her spleen wasn't rupturing, I realised as I rolled into Ross with the float that I hadn't eaten all day. Just on dusk I'd unloaded Archie and his little pony mate Gemma, whom I'd brought along for the ride, as without Archie she escapes out of any kind of fence to find company or fresher food. I left them to sniff and whinny at the other horses that would be joining us on the course and said a quick hello to Carlos and the girls. They were enjoying the la-di-da comforts of one of the participants who had borrowed the Taj Mahal of trailers from her dad, sitting on an outdoor furniture setting on a patterned mat beneath an awning. They were a riot of humour already, but I was exhausted and being the introvert I am, made worse by writing isolation and 'solo mumdom', I beat a retreat.

At the hotel, behind the bar, Suzie the publican checked me in. On the phone prior, she'd already told me they had a 'pub kelpie' and my two dogs would be more than welcome with him.

'Rosco's upstairs,' Suzie said of her Casterton-bred black-and-tan ten-month-old. 'He refuses to go into his pen, so your dogs can have it.'

After she led me through a pretty beer garden at the back of the hotel, Suzie showed me the tall wire fence and convenient two kennels on offer. Fancy. I promptly shut 'the kids' in, promising I'd be back to feed and water them soon. It was dark and late, so I quickly unpacked my ute, taking bags up the rickety stairs to my room. They were stairs on which my daughter, a few years back, had seen the ghost of a little girl sitting. As I went back downstairs I said hello to the ghost as I passed and went to ferret out the food for the kelpies. My ute was parked out the front of the classic two-storey sandstone hotel, and as I gathered up dog food and bowls and set off around the corner, in the darkness I realised I was being followed by two black dogs. I thought to myself it was a bit irresponsible to have dogs on the loose this time of night, but it was a country town and folks were permitted to be more casual here than in larger towns. From beneath the dim glow of one solitary street lamp I saw an overexcited tail wagging and thought that was a bit of an excessive way to greet a stranger . . . Then I realised *they were my dogs!*

Apparently Connie had dug under the gate and Rousie had made the most of his clever mate's great escape. When I went back into the bar Suzie told me Connie had ventured in and made herself at home, saying hi to the blokes playing Eight Ball. Upstairs Rosco had been so excited to see his own mirrored kind in the shape of two black-and-tan kelpies like him out on the street below that he had squeezed through the fire escape stair railing and climbed onto the pub roof to get a better look! If the first night was anything to go by, I was in for one hell of a perfect holiday. A five-night package tour of Bali couldn't even come close to this! It was my kind of adventure.

The next day I discovered the rodeo yards were a convoluted maze of old wooden railing with few gates, so the wonderful physical exercise of climbing high fences was now included on my holiday package – gym in the form of heavy water buckets and high top rails. My horses whickered to me when I showed up bright and early for day one of the clinic. I spent my time meeting the other girls, shovelling horse poop and dishing out breakfast for Archie and little Gemma.

As I looked up to the rodeo commentator's stand, empty and silent for now, it seemed ironic and poignant to be holding

Carlos's clinic in a rodeo ground. Carlos is the ultimate in speaking up for kindness to horses. While I've loved my fair share of rodeos in my youth, as I travel further down the road of life, my empathy dial has turned itself up so many notches that what I could stomach in my younger days I simply can't now. I'd found myself 'gentling' lately and not being able to watch horseracing or rodeo without a cringe and a twinge of remorse for the animals amongst them who don't enjoy it. Trust me, I've been to Calgary Stampede in my early twenties and seen the broncs bred to buck, ears forward, pumped up and loving it. I've been to the bull-riding beer garden at the Great Western Hotel in Rockhampton and cheered the bulls on to a blaring Garth Brooks soundtrack. I saw they were bulls who were well trained and comfortable in their role, so I'm not going to go all-out 'animal libber' on you. I've led proud racehorses in the mounting yard at race meets for my lifelong best friend and felt the energy of horses that wanted to be there and those that didn't. I've been in stock camps with branding fires and irons in coals. But motherhood and my farm eviction has utterly changed me, and I think finding Carlos as an instructor was all part of this new path to more nurturing ways.

My goal for the five days was to learn how to transition to be a bitless rider – something Carlos specialises in. In fact, as I discovered, all the women there rode their horses bitless. No metal in mouths for these happy horses! Carlos Tabernaberri has to be charming – he's bucking the system of the horse industry across all disciplines, including dressage, western, show and pleasure.

He has a life commitment to freeing horses from the chains of human misunderstanding and he needs all that Latino charm and a dash of masculine steel to get him past the closed mindsets of humans . . . especially competitive ones where prestige, ego and money are tangled up in the horses they own. I found him to be a very smart man and, above all, kind. Plus he sounds really cool, with his Spanish roll to his words. Even after five days I was not tired of listening to him. And we women weren't tired of ribbing him for his inflections. He bore our Aussie piss-taking with such good grace.

'Don't let the looks fool you,' he says to top-end dressage people who may judge him for his cowboy attire. They are seeking answers from him to address for high-energy glossy Grand Prix horses who can't walk from the stables to the arena without a major mental meltdown. His horse language and his willingness to speak it plainly, and impart it to others, means he's hired by the jodhpur-wearing best all around the world. The stories that unfolded from his full, sunscreen-protected lips over those five days were incredible to hear.

We'd be riding along and someone would mention the summer heat.

'Oh, this is not as hot as when I was riding for a week in the Pakistan desert,' Carlos would chip in casually.

Next he would incidentally mention how he would be heading to England soon to help out some friends of the Queen with their horses. Or he would suddenly tell goosebump-raising stories about the Native American women who had seen him on one of their vision quests and had tracked him down, inviting him to the Apache Indian Reservation to help the Native Americans reconnect with their horses the natural way. Then during the course of his instruction he'd throw in a casual reference to the healing and rehabilitation horse clinics he offered for the inmates of an Idaho prison with whom he had once worked. There he spoke of men who had been stripped of their identity and their hope. The former racing thoroughbreds that they retrained were reflecting the very same plight of the hardcore criminals who were essentially deeply frightened, lonely men – like the horses – locked in a system with no escape. Carlos also did brilliant *Little Britain* impersonations from the hilarious TV show, so he wasn't one to be 'on show' as a cool horseman. He was also a wag.

For me, having lived for a time astride horses daily, married into a family of Gippsland mountain cattlemen, I learned that no matter how many hours I had done in the saddle, it didn't make me a better horsewoman. I wanted to delve deeper and work on not just my horse, but myself as a rider and a person. Not to gain ribbons or climb social ladders, but simply because I love my animals like I love my own children.

Carlos Tabernaberri weaves wisdom from author Kahlil Gibran and philosophies of Buddhism into training. In his beaut book *Through the Eyes of the Horse*, he says, 'Having success with horses doesn't depend on how long you've been around them – horses don't read resumes. I may be a fourth-generation horseman, but all I could learn from the generations before, if I wanted, was the traditional way of doing things. I knew I wanted to do things differently – to let the horses teach me. I learn from every horse I work with, and I never stop learning.' It was with this quote that I found myself gaining more and more confidence in myself and my horse. The more I unravel what is false about myself, the stronger I become and the clearer I am with Archie.

By the end of day one of the clinic we were all riding around the rodeo ground amidst summertime dust and the haze of bush-fires on our horses bareback in just halters. By day two, we rode out, not one single bit or whip between us, and off we went down the leafy, busy main street of the pretty historic village of Ross in peak tourist season. We pulled up outside the pub and Suzie and her partner Scott brought us drinks. It was wonderful to see all the horses calm after we'd worked on them that morning to create trust. Rosco the pub dog came out to meet his first ever horse. My beautiful boy Archie calmly dipped his head and let the dog sniff his muzzle. Then one by one we took turns using the old sand-stone mounting block outside the old hall that probably hadn't been used in decades to elegantly help a lady rider upon her horse, or a drunken gentleman. People stopped and took photos. People smiled. People chatted to us and each other. Horses in modern society are great for the soul.

That night, the horses yarded, that same pub became the meeting place for the whole bunch of us in the beer garden, laugh-ing our heads off like cackling hens, Carlos laughing with us. At our feet the three kelpies romped and at one stage Rosco made off with someone's cap and raced into the bar. By day four, we were cantering on loose reins and forming friendships with each other that I knew would last for a lot longer than just the clinic. By day five we were all out there on that summer-hazed hill with Carlos.

I still have a long road to go towards being a better human for my horse, and my days crammed with raising kids and writing work means it's rare I find time to ride, but at least Carlos has given me the tools to set myself straight before I go near my horse. If we live by letting go, it gives us greater freedom to really fly high. People hang on to horses' reins and pull on the bits in their mouths because we are the ones with the control issues.

As I sat looking out from that hill, seeing the overgrazed dry land of Ross, I realised I had work to do, but for now, I needed to stop and rest from my quest in changing the mindsets of farmers. On that horse, I looked within. There was a sensation I'd been avoiding. One that was so unfamiliar that it felt scary to face. I realised in that moment, riding my horse bitless and blissful across a paddock with a bunch of newfound mates . . . I was happy and relaxed. Truly the happiest I'd been in a long, long time. I had let go. And in doing so I had found likeminded women who were all ready to support me and each other in being the best we could be as humans, for our horses and ourselves. My sun-blistered lips, unkissed as they remain, have been smiling ever since at what is ahead of me in the future as a horsewoman.

The Diamond Crunch
of Crisis

On our most recent road trip from south to north to catch the ferry, the kids and I drove through a drought-gripped Tasmania. It was a landscape in crisis. As we travelled up the winding 'Mud Walls' road, the ute was sideswiped by savage dust storms – yes, dust storms in Tasmania! People think of our island as green. Back in the day when Indigenous people held the land's honour in their hearts and respected it, it probably was green, but today the landscape is corpse-yellow and scabby brown. There were giant curtains of topsoil eddying away in the sky to the east. Mobs of scraggly maiden ewes were staggering through open gates on bare brown earth looking as if they would topple over with another strong gust. In their midst tottered an even skinnier ram looking as far from virile as any ram could get.

'I can't look at it, Mum,' my son said, averting his eyes away from the landscape. 'I wish more people understood you can do it another way.'

My stomach turned too for the animals and the land. I knew the horror of the forced pregnancies those emaciated young sheep would endure over a harsh Tasmanian winter, when rain would bring a tinge of feeble green, incapable of sustaining stock. It would be a miracle if the poor ram and his maidens could reproduce at all under such conditions. Why put a ram like that out with the girls onto such exhausted soils in the first place? Was it greed for the next drop of lambs? Was it ignorance? Was it just because we keep doing the same things over and over, because we think the same programmed thoughts daily over and over? The management of most of our farms and urban landscapes is clearly not working but we keep doing the same thing and hope for a different result.

In my lifetime, I've been witness to the slow demise of our state's farmland. People blame it on lack of rain, but I hope now you will see it's not a lack of precipitation. It's a lack of awareness, and an inability to see with unblinkered eyes. The Australian landscape wasn't always this way. It's been caused by the land management of people over five or six generations who were doing their best, and doing what they thought was right. I am one of many people around the world who are speaking on behalf of the life of the soil, that ought to be nurtured by natural manures and tended to by caretakers, instead of raped and poisoned by modern techniques. It is of utmost importance to our very survival. It's more than just finding more sophisticated agricultural methods that make corporations rich . . . it's about actually feeling the life of the soil and hearing your own soul speak. And it's about consumers boycotting the big company players who don't nurture our planet. That is when real change will occur.

'When we get a farm again, Mum,' my son said, 'I'm going to run the land like Colin Seis does.'

I smiled, a little sadly. A farm. *Oh, for another farm in a new place!* I knew our visit to Colin Seis's property was etched in my boy's mind and within his young man's heart. Col's farm was not just a benchmark of ecological beauty, but of what is possible for the future of farming. My son could see that. When he is at home begging me for more 'outside jobs' when there are none, he turns to the internet to seek out information about other farmers who use regenerative techniques. With such a keen young steward of the land, I know there is hope for the future. But for many of us adults without the plasticity, purity and clarity of a young person's mind, open-mindedness and adapting to change is not so easy. Often it takes a crisis, a big life-dumping crunch, to find our diamonds within.

As the kids and kelpies queued with me at Devonport in lines of cars, utes and bikes waiting to board the ferry to the 'mainland', I saw how detached we were from nature. Life for most of us there was plush. There were rows and rows of shiny fancy-pants gigantic caravans with satellite dishes, solar power and signage that read '*The great Australian adventure*'. It didn't look like adventuring to me. But because of media conditioning we travel these journeys of life in this way without question. Like the crowd at the cricket, we all flow where we are told to flow. To hardware stores and supermarkets, to theme-park holidays and appliance stores. Do we really need all this stuff? Does it all need to be bigger and better? Bigger houses? Bigger caravans? Bigger ag machinery? Bigger farms owned by bigger corporations? Bigger irrigation schemes? Bigger-sized animals? Do we really need to keep doing the things we do when we innately know it is failing? Failing awfully.

The next morning, still rocking from our Bass Strait bashing, we made our way out of the belly of the boat, along the ever-increasingly wide freeways out of Melbourne towards Ballarat for breakfast, catching up with an old mate, a rodeo clown and clown in general called Kelpie, then on to Hamilton. Full of pancakes, in a rain haze, my little boy was sitting in the front seat of my ute with his head bent over my iPhone, trying to plot a course to dog school at Ian O'Connell's, near Hamilton. He ignored the physical signs at the roundabouts that pointed us to our destination, and insisted on adhering to the computer version that took us on the shortest route. I let him make that call, knowing there would be lessons to be learned. We found ourselves travelling on a back road, the computer taking us the shorter but slower way as we dog-legged across soldier settlement patchwork farms and bumped along a sometimes single bitumen strip. As the fuel gauge got lower and the phone signal weaker, I wanted my darling, curious boy to learn that technology will fail us every time if we rely on it solely. When we depend on it so heavily, we lose our own senses, and as a society, I believe we are losing our senses. We are falling into screens like when Alice in Wonderland fell down the rabbit hole, and we are forgetting to really see the world around us. It will be a crisis that will wake us all up, like a slap in the face, when the systems crash.

It's not just navigation systems where technologies are befuddling us, but also agricultural systems. We farmers look at data and apps on phones to monitor the land on which we stand. We log into software programs on our home computers to monitor irrigation flow, weather, manage animals, calculate fertiliser and sowing rates and finances and commodity prices, and yes they help us make decisions, but are we losing the feminine art of *feeling the land*, truly sensing what it says to us in slow cycles and seasons. By focusing entirely on technology, we lose focus on what's real: soil, water, air, trees, food, connectivity between living things and, above all, *love*. Yes, *love*. It is the touchstone to everything.

To teach my kids that smartphones aren't the only way to navigate, I'd bought us a paper map of the state of Victoria. When unfolded it caught in the wind from the opened window and it wrapped my son up like a gift. After laughing and wrestling his paper map into order, I could see his face turned to the landscape more often than it had been when he was on the phone. He was now looking outwards for signs in the landscape. So much better than a screen! He was also not just seeking signs on metal poles to tell us which road to take, but he was also reading the landscape in the way I had taught him.

He, like his sister, now sees overgrazing and erosion, and knows the answers for how to counter that. Everywhere we travel he sees what the roadside vegetation looks like compared to what's in the paddocks. He can see where councils have sprayed and when stock don't have enough diversity in their diet. He knows tiny creatures by the billion exist beneath his mini-man farm boots and that unless we give them a rich life, we can't have a rich life either. He knows that the way us whitefellas see the world is not the only way. I showed him and his sister how people from our culture place grids across the earth. Straight lines drawn with rulers, overlaying the landscape of cities, states, parks and farms. Land divided with straight fences and lines and more lines. This is how most of us think too – in straight lines. As a contrast I reminded the kids of the map of the 250 Aboriginal nations we'd recently seen on a documentary. That map had flexible borders that squiggled over the entire continent, following rivers, creeks, gullies, mountain ranges and ridge lines. There was not one straight line on that map. Those ancient peoples farmed the continent with no fences and they lived within the landscape, not imposed upon it as we do. We are so used seeing the world our way that we have forgotten how to read the signs the land is giving us that She is in trouble.

Whilst staying in the Hamilton region, we saw the landscape's warnings were the same as in our home state. We could feel its sickness and its decline. A decline that moves so slowly most don't see it. We could also feel its beauty though. A tenacity that says to me that Mother Nature will win in the end. Just give Her time. It was crop-stubble burning month and as we drove along, I saw the ribbon rows of black that swept across the landscape in straight lines. Organic matter all gone to the sky through the lick of flame. Tidy.

A few days into our stay, Ian told me he was going to be on hand to help his neighbours when they fired up the brittle stems of a harvested wheat crop over the fence. It was Ian's job to patrol the boundary and make sure the fire didn't jump onto his farm. He asked me along for the ride. Pump and water on the back of the ute in case of runaway flames, Ian and I set off. In the paddock he introduced me to his local neighbours. Lovely blokes. Ian, masterful in his way with handling people, knew I had a book to write on landscape and the changes in how we manage it. He was always up for a bit of a ribbing too, so he set off prompting a conversation between me, the starry-eyed future farmer, and the practical old-school male farmer who exuded blokeyness.

'Tell Rachael why you burn the stubble,' Ian poked at his friend. The farmer's eyes slid across to me. Was he summing me up as one of those 'greenie' types? From his tone I think he was.

'We do it because of the problem we have with the slugs,' he said, a little defensively, perhaps. 'We have a moisture problem in the winter months, so we're prone to slug attack.'

A moisture problem, I silently repeated, looking around at the blank paddocks. I saw it as a soil structure problem, not a moisture problem. There was our point of difference in how we read the land.

'They've stopped stubble burning in the lighter country,' he continued, 'but we have heavier soils here, so we still burn.'

My mind ran off down the farming pathways I'd learned. The 'lighter' country was that way not just because of soil type, but also because of management. I knew that right across Australia our 'heavier' soils were getting lighter and lighter . . . and with it, losing the ability to hold moisture. Looking around, it was hard to see the district had a moisture problem. Rainfall events are altering dramatically around the country. Climate is changing. As it has done for millennia.

'I don't know a lot about cropping in this area. We do things differently down in Tassie,' I said, hoping to let him know he wouldn't get an argument from me. I wasn't judging him in any way, because I'd learned long ago there's no point in judging others. I wanted to switch off his defensiveness, but Ian was on a roll. I caught the twinkle in his eye.

'Rachael, tell him why the slugs are a problem,' Ian prodded again. Stirrer.

How could I say to that proud and now prickly man that the slugs are only a problem because the ecology is out of balance, without him taking it personally? That's the problem with change. It makes us feel that what we have done is wrong; that *we* are wrong.

With this man, I got the sense that his tension came from within – a deep knowing that what they were doing was actually harming the microbiology of the soil. He was simply yet to seek other ways, ways that were kinder to the soil, and ways that, over time, offered more profit.

It was funny-bugger Ian who kept digging, not me. I won't tell you where the man went with his comments but just know it was a blunt racist jab at the genocide this country has at its heart. Even if said in jest he clearly had no time for cross-examination by a woman about his farming practices, even though it was being conducted by my shit-stirring interpreter Ian. I smiled at Ian when the man got up into his truck and roared away to set the landscape to flame.

'That went well, Ian,' I said. 'Thanks.'

'He's actually a really good bloke,' Ian said.

'I know,' I said, 'I could see that.' And I meant it. He was a good bloke. A contributor to his community. His family. His farm. He just didn't see the colour of the world the way I did. Nothing wrong with that.

We do what we do because of those unconscious roads that stretch back as far as time that condition our way of being. We forget why we do things. We don't question it. Yes, fire is a cleanser. We innately love it – the controlled version of fire at least. The practice of burning things lights us up within. And we love big, red, shiny fire trucks that used to send us into a frenzy of excitement when we were little. Burning is a ritual. It's a right of passage for a man to burn. And as a woman it gets my blood pulsing. I loved fire as a child, lighting up tussocks, and later on farms burning stubble.

How could I say to that bloke what I really wanted to say? 'Have you ever thought about not doing it? Have you ever thought about new ways?'

It would get me nowhere. Some are just not ready to hear it, particularly from a woman. I accept that. Nowadays, I get to dance away and sing my new tune and leave others to their song.

As the smoke billowed across the landscape, birds bolted across the sky and hares hot-footed it towards the shelter of trees alongside the highway, I watched as the slivers of ash spiralled across a grey haze sky. They eddied up and over, across the boundary fence, settling like confetti onto Ian's paddocks.

'Look! What lovely neighbours,' I said to Ian cheekily. 'They are top-dressing your paddock for you with pot ash and organic matter – for free!'

He laughed.

The next day I walked the dogs to that boundary paddock and slipped through the fence so as to get the feel of the baked soil in my hands and study more closely what remained. The crunch under my boots of exposed, torched soil felt sickening to me, like walking on the brittle bones of babies. Quickly, I went back into Ian's paddocks. A conventional high-input farmer, Ian is a good caretaker. He locks up 90 per cent of his land in dry times, sacrifices 10 per cent to hold his stock on and feeds them well so they look fully in bloom, no matter the season. I walked his pastures that had life, and a good level of plant diversity ready to bolt when moisture arrived. Colin's is one way. Ian's is another. Both men know, though, to put their soil and plants first so their animals thrive.

In the last few days of the trip, with the kids off visiting their East Gippsland relatives with their father, I farewelled Ian and Kay, and drove the back roads from Hamilton through Ararat across to Auntie Whiz in Bendigo. She is my Granno Joan Wise's eldest girl. As the landscape changed, the overgrazing was a constant. Once I was out of the striped land of burnt stubble, I moved through places that were scarred with mining, and into semi-rural fringes where horses were double-stacked on barren blocks.

In Bendigo, my auntie greeted me with tea, and my kelpies settled into the backyard, going from window to window to perve intently on the elderly cat within the cottage. The cat rubbed up against me as I sat on Auntie Whiz's lounge room floor. Scattered about me were my grandmother's photo albums and papers of her published stories, the cat walking over them and dribbling as she purred.

'Puss! These are heritage documents!' I chided. The dogs at the window whined a little, ears pricked.

I peered at the picture of Granno Wise – Joan – sitting in her tweeds with her golfing gal pals. Hair tightly curled, all in sensible woollen skirts, they wore ladylike pearls, brooches on cardigans and dollops of formal hats.

'They are dressed so conservatively!' I said to Whiz, who sat twining her homespun wool on the lounge.

'Oh, don't let that fool you,' Whiz replied, 'they were all absolutely wicked.'

As I lifted and turned the pages of the giant cardboard book that my grandmother must have bound together with her own hands, I saw the legacy of many lifetimes' work within. Not just of farms and favourite horses, like Rainbow or Black Sammy, but cows too, in particular three stud jerseys, one silver, one black and one golden, brought from Runnymede House in Hobart. I also found a long-forgotten collection of my grandma's fictional writing. As I flicked through the documents I saw just how our compass on the earth stretches in time both forward and backward. There on the pages of the history books, I discovered my great-great-great-grandfather William Wise. I learned that around 1834 Mr Wise owned most of Richmond Town, right to the paddocks where I now rent that flystrike-green house! It seems my natural compass point did take me to some kind of home after all. In a strange twist, when I turned the pages of the book my own grandmother had created, I saw the black-and-white image of one of the Richmond buildings that William Wise once owned.

'That's Czegs, the coffee shop where I've been writing this book after school drop-off!' I exclaimed to Whiz. For the past year-and-a-half, I'd sometimes escape the scattering of crumbs and dirty plates left hastily on the kitchen bench, turn my back on the silent piles of broody washing and walk my son to school with the two kelpies and my daughter's bouncing yo-yo poodle. For an hour or so, I'd tuck myself away in the corner of that very same building William Wise once walked through. As I sat looking at the hand-split boards of the ceiling above and the trapdoors hinged on the floor to the cellar below, I had wondered about the history of the place. The deep-set windowsills were crafted from beautiful wood and as I took in how low the door frames were I would ponder about the people who once inhabited the rooms. I had no idea that the plot of my own story was tangled with a great-great-great-grandfather of mine who once carried out his daily life here in this very same building where I typed on my laptop computer.

In Granno Joan Wise's writing, I saw that she too, like me, wrote of landscape and of the people in them, drovers, rabbiters and the island's sea. She wrote of burning the stubble too. A practice that my own grandfather Archie did.

Sometimes I don't want to look too closely into the past. Did my forebears in the 1880s shoot thylacines for the government bounty? Or, God forbid, did those relatives who arrived here first and who are now barely traceable on my fraying family tree target the original people of this place? Is my quest for the restoration of native grassland in this continent born out of a deep saturation of guilt from some dark travesty that lurks in my early settler blood?

As I ponder this question, I arrive at the deep truth that comes to me in a loudly singing conclusion. My passion to inspire us to regenerate our Australian soils, grasslands and food systems comes absolutely from a place of love. Love is the same place that I entered a marriage. Love is the same place I set up a farm business for my father. It's the same place I bore children. Love. My love for land. Despite my past hurts, I still love. I still believe utopia can be achieved. Fiction and life intertwined. It's only the diamond crunch of my own crisis that has delivered me to this one glorious conclusion. Love is everything.

Christmas Wishes for
Rain and Change

It was Christmas Eve and late in the day, the kids and I, droopy with heat, decided to drive to the supermarket. We were singing 'Rusty Holden Ute' to the tune of 'Jingle Bells' and we were excited by the prospects of the magic that Christmas brings. In typical fashion, I'd left our Christmas food shopping run a little too late. I noticed the apricot roadside stall at Midway Point had shut up shop, the seafood van man was turning customers away due to empty freezers and the new-season pink-eye potato stall had diminished to just one bag. My son spotted a sign painted on a wooden board that read 'unsprayed cherries' and instantly I veered my old red ute into the rocky drive. The lady selling them in the shade of a tin shed, and from beneath a floppy hat, said apologetically, 'There are only some seconds left. They're fresh but not-so-perfect.'

'Oh! We are good with not-so-perfect,' I replied. To me, when it comes to cherries that have never seen a chemical spray, there is perfection right there! They are a rare find in the cropping area where we now live, where spray rigs hooked to the three-point linkage arms of tractors are frequently seen driving over the oldest still-in-use convict bridge in Australia. Booms folded up like vehicles from a *Star Wars* film, they cruise right past the primary school, on towards the lettuce farms or stone fruit orchards. The kids and I celebrated our spray-free find by chomping on the cherries as soon as they were bagged. There was no waiting for Christmas with this lot. The plump orbs of dark juicy fruit that gleamed with reflections of silver when held up to the light were just too tempting. There was nothing 'second' about those beauties! With stained fingertips, we rolled on and into the concrete prefab space of Coles in our nearest major rural township.

The new supermarket sits beside exhausted ploughed paddocks and a repainted and made-to-look-classy KFC. Wind turbines above the concrete, treeless carpark and massive truck bays gave the slightest suggestion that maybe, just maybe, the people who design these sorts of places in Australia are taking small shuffles towards more enviro-friendly principles. The heat from the tarmac rose up to hit us like a furnace. Through the parting automated doors into air-con iced air we ventured and were captured within the fluoro-lit world that promised low prices. It was almost identical to the type of mega-store food shopping offered across the road with 'the fresh food people'.

It was here on the eve of Christmas I saw a scenario that would be replicated across this whole nation in the giant cavernous spaces that hold our food supplies that we now accept as 'normal' . . . supermarkets. The shelves had been stripped bare, as if one day of closed shops would somehow cause starvation. As my son and daughter cruised alongside me with the trolley, we discovered there was no turkey left. The strawberries had sold out. At the bakery section there were no more loaves of bread, save for a lonely Dutch loaf. As a writer, I often watch people as if seeing them from above, like a lone bird, looking down on a vista . . . a vista that is becoming increasingly ravaged by human greed. So as we encountered this Christmas 'food shortage' I used it as a chance to teach my kids that supermarkets aren't really about food filled with good in-season nutrition, or about helping Aussie farmers. They are about money-making and marketing, and mostly conditioning humans to behave as consumers. Then I began my spiel about branding and labelling. Poor kids. They just wanted an ice-cream from their mum on such a hot day. But there I was standing in front of the milk section, where there was only supermarket-branded milk left . . . stuff I won't buy. I'd just been employed to write an article about the importance of healthy gut microbes in cattle and had attended a cow autopsy to see it for myself. The dairy cow's owner said it was standard practice in his area to give the milking cows a dose of antibiotics mixed daily into their feed ration – a practice that kills gut microbes. He said he had stopped the antibiotics, but despite his management change, his vats of milk still ended up in the generally branded milk that we buy in the supermarket that is from cows that have the antibiotic ration, and that in turn ends up in my kid's bellies.

As we drove home with our Christmas shop of possibly antibiotic-infused milk and a present for the emotionally tumultuous poodle, the kids and I knew we wouldn't starve at Christmas, even though there'd been slim pickings at the supermarket.

At home we had eggs that our chickens had gifted us. There was stone-ground flour from the Oatlands' Callington Mill in the pantry and we could call into Sophie, who has fresh strawberries on her Littlewood Berry Farm down the road. Plus there were lemons in the fridge, grown in a pot on the balcony of my mum's townhouse. We summed up what we had, and it was decided . . . we would make pancakes for Christmas! An all-day breakfast! I wanted to teach my kids that Christmas was about love . . . not the pressure of a set menu and gorging yourself just because the religious texts said Jesus was born on this day over 2000 years ago.

While I don't take my children to church, I do teach them that we exist in a blue-sky cathedral and that the message of Jesus, if we are to have a day of celebration for him, is all about love. Not just love for other people, but for all living things. I've never understood the stress-filled consumer frenzy of Christmas in Australia when so few of us are religious in any way. Do people ever ask why we do it? To escape the grind of Christmas obligations with my immediate family after our eviction from the farm, I told my mother jokingly to let the family know Christmas was against my religion. I was now a practising Wiccan. A white witch. My mum could see the humour written on my face and got the joke.

She promptly told me where I could buy some nice plants for my witchcraft friends.

On one level I had been joking, but when I thought about it, I wasn't far off the truth. I was teaching my children witches weren't as they are potrayed in modern fairytales. They were medicine women and midwives. I treat ailments with nutritional medicine – be it garlic, lemons, turmeric or honey, or simple chicken soup that feeds the soul. I also can't do dates and calendars, and instead time my life with seasons and sunrises. Essentially that's all witches were . . . medicine women who worked with and worshipped Mother Nature's cycles to find plants to balance or cleanse the body. They didn't work with antibiotics. They worked with onions that had antibacterial properties, long before modern medicine came about. My children have always enjoyed their home remedies from mother – concoctions I call 'medicine' drinks filled with all sorts of goodies and my love. They have also heard their mother speak of eating food in season, only choosing meat where the lives of the animals have been honoured, and being grateful for what the planet gives us. They are rarely ill, and when we do go to see a doctor who is familiar with modern medicines, they are ones like Dr Tomato Plant who ask questions like, 'Are you getting enough sleep?' or 'Are you drinking enough water?'

On my family farm I had the ability to live more directly from the land but now we are living in a semi-rural area, the children are witness to their mother sometimes being weary and frustrated as she searches fruitlessly (pun intended) for organic or holistically produced food. Some days I feel like a modern hunter-gatherer mother, constantly on the lookout for food for my family that isn't weighed down with the toxins of manmade sprays, fertilisers or hollow foods grown in depleted soils so the food itself offers no nutrition whatsoever. Based on that, I feel as if I live in a time of famine . . . a pure-food famine. There is a deficiency in our society of food literally grown from a place of love.

That is why I am tenacious in keeping a vegetable garden going no matter where we live so I can at least offer my kids some homegrown clean food. After witnessing one of the hottest, driest summers on record for Tasmania, I'm also compelled this Christmas to wish for change. There was such a chilling disconnection from that supermarket with its artificial lighting, fake air and faux food with what was going on outside its prefab windowless walls. Outside where the farmers are.

It's been so dry here in the lead-up to Christmas. Hot and windy. Crops have failed. Dams are empty. Stock are being sold off. Or kept on to stagger about and die. Minds are being twisted towards despair as the hollow promise of grey clouds in summer skies above are still failing to deliver any rain. It seems as if it's all we have been speaking about lately. The dry. The heat. The scarcity of hay. The terrible shortages of grass – possibly for years to come. All due to the weather. For months, the talk has been going around like this:

'How much did you pay for your hay? The rural merchandise blokes are selling it for $22 a bale for small squares. It's crazy!'

'I saw one round bale on the back of a ute advertised for $200 parked near the grocers. Two hundred bucks. For *one* bale. It's a wonder someone hadn't torched the bale and the ute along with it. That's wrong. It's daylight robbery.'

'There's going to be a shortage for years now.'

'We just need rain. There's no grass anywhere.'

It's a conversation I've heard repeated on loop every few years all my life during drought times. But isn't it time we asked ourselves, Is it really the weather? Is it really lack of rainfall, or is it something else? Something to do with how we have shaped our landscape and our soils since white man's settlement and how we manage it? Even when the conversations are going on around me amidst my friends, my mind says, *But there is grass*. You only have to look at the roadsides in the driest of times to see the benchmark of what banquet Mother Nature has on offer, stimulated by the lightest of dew on beautifully protected soils. Mother Nature is a modest lady . . . she likes to cover up. Roadsides are where I get my eye in on what is possible to grow in dry times. But only if the land is grazed right.

Christmas Day turned out to be scorching 36 degrees – probably higher out on the barren ground of denuded paddocks. My cousins would be skiing on the river that flows through their farm, a day off of sorts wedged in between grain harvests and hay-carting duties and livestock care. The kids and I had opted to leave them to their water worship and simply stay home and lark about in the floppy inflatable pool we'd set up in the backyard. It was an Aussie classic. The best yet. Super-soaker guns, an inflatable crocodile, Lee Kernaghan blaring on the CD player, and the pancakes of course! I just felt blessed I had such gorgeous kids and we had water.

Later, in the evening, I drove from the flystrike house to feed my horse Archie, who was not far away on agistment. On the drive, I passed farmlets and hobby blocks that looked like desert landscapes. I saw our precious soils blowing away over fencelines from paddocks like rain squalls. The paddocks looked as if they'd been sliced dry by iron ploughs, but they hadn't been ploughed at all. Instead they lay bare because they were chronically, unrelentingly overgrazed. It was land that never knew rest from hungry mouths and land that had been abused. I watched life-giving soils hurtling towards the sea. My heart bled at the sight of it and the neglected stock on barren paddocks.

Cattle with ribbed sides like xylophones desperately pushed their heads through barbed wire, grabbing what they could from roadsides. Miserable hot sheep, despondent with hunger and tattered and mangy with lice, hung their heads and panted in treeless paddocks. I wished I could doorknock on all the houses of the people who owned the hobby blocks and animals, not to berate them . . . but to show them another way. It's a way I've discovered from meeting and following the visionaries who are revolutionising farming and the way we think about our connections to animals, soil, land and food.

I bet the people within those houses had eaten well on

Christmas Day and sought shade. But their animals hadn't been able to. I thought to myself, if only the people who owned those small acreages knew the possibilities and importance of nurturing land to life so that not only would their animals be more comfortable but they too could help reverse climate change by sucking carbon out of the air, through their grasses and into the soil so it stabilised there. Heck, they could even surround themselves with beauty, not barrenness. All those semi-rural land parcels could begin sequestering carbon back into the soil by giving life to it. If only I could write a book that would inspire all that . . . then our Christmas vista could be vastly different!

I made a Christmas wish then and there in the gale-force furnace winds, not just for rain, but for change . . . change in direction towards an Australia that is wonderful, not just for every person, but for every living thing. Not just man, but also microbes. A new vision that would see the life in the soil stable and fecund, no matter the amount of rain. And the water systems too, nurtured back to the crystal-clear tree-lined rivers Aboriginals must have once enjoyed. Like all Christmas wishes, you make them once and send them out, then comes the hard part . . . waiting with a sense of trust and inner knowing that they will come true. It's the same as the concept of Santa, in that sense that if you believe, you receive. So it is with life. It's the Law of the Universe. Your beliefs become your reality. And hopefully by you reading my words now, the reality of our place, our Australia will change.

After arriving home from my barren drive, as if on cue after my wish, the sound of rain could be heard landing on the corro roof. A moment later a text arrived from my mate Jackie in the north of the state.

'It's raining – proper rain,' she texted excitedly. As I typed a reply, it started to 'rain proper' on the roof above me too and raindrops covered the glass and began to converge in silver rivulets on the window. 'We three', the kids and I, from the front windows of our rental house, are witness to the saddest of paddocks across the dirt road from us. It's a landscape more reminiscent of outback Queensland. It has the pallor of the sick. It is yellow and grey. Starlings are trawling the compact bare soil surface for seeds and insects. The sheep, instead of being camped, are up, haunting the ground, nibbling what is left of the grasses, roots, soil and all. In my fictional world, I imagine I am gazing out the window and can see a biodiverse paddock that has been strip-grazed with different species of livestock. The creek would not be the bare, washed-out gully that it is, but instead, in my imaginings, growing with blackwoods, shrubs, native grasses, forbs and herbs that used to thrive here before the settlers arrived. The sheep would be camped under a shady patch, chewing their cud and they would be content. The frogs too would be singing.

Fortunately for us all there are real-life farmers achieving this kind of vision from the windows of their homesteads. There are people waking up to the possibility of new farming and food-selling systems that sit outside the norm of that bleak drought-scarred landscape and Christmas-ravaged concrete supermarket.

These new-age farmers are travelling down the dirt roads of thought to new places. They are the people who are no longer willing to simply race at high speed along the concrete highways of collective thought. Unchallenged beliefs about an economic-based society that turn us all into 'consumers' rather than 'citizens' are funnelling us towards our own extinction. As a race, we have become so used to looking at bare landscapes of farms, coal and gas mine sites and accepting the massive developments of commercial sites and housing and industrial estates, that we assume this is how Australia should be. That this is somehow normal. *It's not.*

We have forgotten how this continent was once teeming with life and vegetation under a different management regime – that of Aboriginals who had mastered this entire landmass and its islands and ran it as a grassland farm, without the ravages that money brings. I, along with many agricultural change agents, believe that women are an untapped potential of the mightiest power to make the changes in food production systems that humankind so desperately needs. I see it will be the balanced, conscious, fully awakened woman who can coach the men to awaken too, so our brotherhood moves with us. As we women heal on a deep ancient level, so too shall the earth heal.

I'm hoping that this book has graced a place beneath your Christmas tree, and that more people will be waking up to the fact we need to make changes in how we perceive and manage our land, and the importance we place upon the richness of our lives that comes from landscape, not bank balances. All it takes is just one wish from you. One special Christmas wish. As you journey forward, remember to use your seven-point compass to guide you . . . North, South, East, West, Above, Below, Within. This year, may the spray-free cherries find you.

Postscript

It's the first day of spring and a journey down a new dirt road is about to begin. I have just signed a contract to buy 'we three' a house on a pretty postage stamp patch of land that happens to be nestled in a dirt road cul-de-sac on a quiet country road! It was six years ago on this very same day, 1 September, that we got the keys to our Heavenly Hill. Now here we are sowing new seeds to our dreams based on our vision for 10 acres near the children's school. The house feels solid and friendly and has the potential to come to life with the ramble and rumble, tumble and play of children and dogs. There are sunny spaces for me to write, and views to bush covered rolling hills. Only a novelist could dream up such a tidy and happy ending to a story, but here it is in real life.

Whilst there are still some hillocks to climb with the bank and the sale of the Heavenly Hill, I can feel the stars aligning. The real estate agent in charge of selling our Heavenly Hill has a family very keen on buying the place. I'm certain they felt the energy of love that we had infused there, and I'm sure they sensed the thrum of life in the soil that we had loved back to life in the paddocks.

Now we have the chance to love more land to life. With a loan yet to be approved, it's a matter of faith, trust and detachment from the outcome. There is only room for peace in the process and daily taking the step-by-step moves that will lead us to holding the keys to the place in our ready-to-work hands.

Imaginings of great potential have been prompted in all three of us as we fell instantly in love with the honest brick house and the easy 'flat as flat' land. It has freed up our minds.

For my son, he sees the good sturdy dog kennels and his dream of training collies and kelpies to kindly and quietly work sheep comes to life. It's an art that will gift that young man with a lifetime of opportunity to seek wisdom via each pup he trains.

For my daughter, the sight of busy ISA Brown chooks at the property has fuelled her dream to deliver 'Czeg's eggs' to the Richmond café, using chook tractors that we shall move behind the areas grazed by the horses and half a dozen dog-training sheep.

There's also fruit trees and vegetable garden beds aplenty, so my pure food famine as a mother can end and I can again gift fresh produce to family and friends, or use our surplus as barter, just as my grandmother did.

On the flat land we have already imagined the direct drilling of oats to kickstart soil function and how we will test the soil, before and after our grazing management begins. The little place, we can see, could become a showcase of what is possible on small acreage. In my head I'm already hosting our first field day, with Col Seis, Annabel Walsh and Graeme Hand in our midst.

We three are discussing where we shall put our portable horse round yard and house our saddles for Archie, and our golden pony Jess, who has just won the 2016 National Horse of the Year for Riding for the Disabled. Bless her gentle soul.

On the quiet road into the place we noticed plenty of unsprayed roadside grasses. It will be little pony Gemma's job to harvest the native seeds on her tether and then manure them onto our land.

We have already discussed which directions we will strip-graze the paddock, and if the land becomes too burdened by mouths, how the agistment place is just up the road, within sight of the house, and we can rest the land by taking the horses off it for a time. Once again my children will be learning to look at species diversity, to monitor pastures and assess when to move livestock on with me by their side.

It's where I belong. With them in a paddock. Moving the fences so the animals can enjoy fresh pick, watching the plants respond to the grazing. Sky above. Earth below.

In my heart too, I know now I'm healed and ready to open up to others once again. I can see this patch of land and the warm house receiving weary farm women, who have come to learn about soil and their connection to it. A place where they can again discover the feminine power they hold within. It's a power that, once embraced within one's self, has the opportunity to spark the most positive transformations for our society, in particular in agriculture.

The best thing though is that, with the future of this new road spreading on deliciously before us, I now barely even think of that old place. That old farm. Instead, I just feel love for those I once knew there and seek out fond memories, not dark ones. The excitement about my power within to create a version of an agricultural world that gifts us all is too strong in me now to look back.

I know this story is far from over. I just know, the next non-fiction book I share with you shall be the story of a patch of land that has been loved to life again, and can sustain not just my family, but many. When that time comes, I will write you a new love story about children flying high and happy from the nest, and the blooming of a woman's soul and her soil, along with the willingness to impart that wisdom to others.

For me, being in a paddock means anything is possible.

Acknowledgements

I have Penguin's Publishing Director, Ben Ball, to thank for this book! It was Ben who provided the creative spark for this writing journey. Ben not only offered me lunch, but also the opportunity to write my story about food and farming, so a big hug of thanks for his vision in what was possible, and his faith in me.

Beside me the entire way has been my long-term mainstay literary agent Margaret Connolly. Thank you for helping me to hunt out the old demons and turn the page to a new chapter in life.

And to my wonderful friend and colleague, Penguin's Ali Watts, thanks for seeing the importance of what I needed to say. Thanks to the entire Penguin Random House team, from editors to proofreaders, to sales and marketing, who have assisted in bringing this book to life so it glows! Thanks especially to cover designer Alex Ross, and to Tassie photographer Natalie Mendham for the 'natural Rach' saddle-blanket back cover pic.

A big thanks to all the sales reps who have taken *Down the Dirt Roads* into bookstores around Australia . . . especially Tassie rep Debbie McGowan. I know you 'felt' my book, as well as simply reading it. Your caring hugs meant so much!

A massive thank you to my fantastic network of fellow school mums who helped me juggle work with kid commitments, especially Di Sawford aka Flipper. You rock! Ta to Ma for the tucker and the help with washing. Thanks to my lovely neighbours in our street for your warm welcome to your community. For Jackie, your ever-present friendship sustained me throughout the arduous journey of finding the loving balance in this book! Thanks to Lucy and her beautiful boys at the café Czegs in Richmond for giving me a refuge away from my housework to write my manuscript . . . and for great food and coffee. Thanks to my admin helper Heidi and my new business buddy Polly McGee who is encouraging me along new dirt roads in life.

Big thanks to all the friends and family and agro-ecology activists who appear in the book, from Col, to Annabel, to Ian, to Graeme, and to those who don't appear in words, but are there in support and spirit for this fantastic grassroots movement.

A massive thank you to my immediate family and my former husband for the lessons in life you gave me, that I now see I came to this earth to learn. You have been remarkable teachers and I send you my eternal love for the gifts you gave me. And speaking of eternal love . . . my two divine children and my cheery animals . . . you are my everything! Thanks for making my life an ongoing comedy that is chockers with love and laughter.

Thank you to YOU, who have read this book and are now committing to change for our Mother Earth – even if it's simply by shopping at a farmers' market ahead of a superstore. I thank you and I send you love. If I've forgotten to mention anyone, apologies, but you know me . . . the sun's shining and I'm off to find a paddock. May we all go forth and share our love with our soil microbes, for they are the lungs of our Earth! Let's love them to life! Breathe!

References and

Further Reading

'A Singular Woman (Annabel Walsh)', *Australian Story*. ABC Television,
    13 August 1998.

Cameron, Julia. *The Artist's Way*. Penguin Putnam, New York, 1992.

David, Marc. *The Slow Down Diet*. Healing Arts Press, Vermont, 2005.

Diamant, Anita. *The Red Tent*. Allen & Unwin, Sydney, 1998.

Dyer, Wayne. *The Virus of the Mind*. Hay House, Brighton-Le-Sands, 2009.

Gammage, Bill. *The Biggest Estate on Earth*. Allen & Unwin, Sydney, 2011.

Grandin, Temple. 'Livestock Behaviour, Design of Facilities and Humane
    Slaughter'. www.grandin.com

Hay, Louise. *You Can Heal Your Life*. Hay House, Brighton-Le-Sands, 1984.

Hicks, Esther and Jerry Hicks. *The Law of Attraction*. Hay House, Brighton-Le-
    Sands, 2006.

Hunt, Scott. *The Black and White Dog Book*. Lateral Media, Hobart, 1999.

MacPhail, Paul. Beloka Kelpies Working Dog Education.

    www.belokakelpies.com.au

Mama Gena's School of Womanly Arts. www.mamagenas.com

Meuret, Michel and Fred Provenza (eds). *The Art & Science of Shepherding: Tapping the wisdom of French herders*. Acres USA, Texas, 2014.

Miller, Daphne. *Farmacology: Total Health from the Ground Up*. Harper Collins, New York, 2013.

Mollison, Bill. *The Permaculture Book of Ferment and Human Nutrition*. Tagari Publications, Sisters Crek, 1993.

Norton, Robert. 'Soils and Our Nutrition'. International Plant Nutrition Institute, 2014. http://anz.ipni.net/article/ANZ-3224

O'Connell, Ian. Working Dog Training. www.facebook.com/Ian-OConnell-Working-Dog-Training-795038373905521/

Ohlson, Kristin. *The Soil Will Save Us*. Rodale Books, Pennsylvania, 2014.

Pinkola Estés, Clarissa. *Women Who Run with the Wolves*. Ballantine Books, New York, 1997.

Pollan, Michael. *The Omnivore's Dilemma*. Penguin Press, New York, 2006.

Polyfaces: a World of Many Choices, Regrarians Media, 2015. www.polyfaces.com

Purvis, Andrew. 'It's supposed to be lean cuisine. So why is this chicken fatter than it looks?'. *The Guardian*, 15 May 2005. www.theguardian.com/lifeandstyle/2005/may/15/foodanddrink.shopping3

Rees, Graeme. Low Stress Stockhandling. www.lss.net.au

Rural Industries Skill Training. www.rist.edu.au

Salatin, Joel. *Fields of Farmers: Interning, Mentoring, Partnering, Germinating*. Polyface Inc, Virginia, 2013. www.polyfacefarms.com

Sams, Jamie. *The 13 Original Clan Mothers*. HarperCollins, New York, 1994.

Seis, Colin. *Pasture Cropping*. www.pasturecropping.com

Tabernaberri, Carlos. *Through the Eyes of the Horse*. Moonrise Media, Melbourne, 2006.

The Man from Snowy River. 20th Century Fox, 1982.

The Sunny Cowgirls. 'Kelpie', *Dust Will Settle*. Compass Bros Records, 2008.

The Wolfe Brothers. *This Crazy Life*. ABC Music, 2016.

Treasure, Rachael. *Dog Speak*. Rachael Treasure Pty Ltd, Sorell, 2010. www.rachaeltreasure.com

——*The Stockmen*. Penguin Books Australia, Melbourne, 2005.

Wallach, Joel. 'Dead Doctors Don't Lie'. 2005. www.youtube.com/watch?v=ARB73jV4mro

Wise, Joan. *Trapped on Tasman*. Illus. Helen Sallis. Rigby, Adelaide, 1971.

——*The Silver Fish*. Illus. Marilyn Newland. Cassell Australia, Melbourne, 1972.

——'The Conquest of Emmie'. *The Bulletin* vol. 71 no. 3649, 18 January 1950.

Wood, Danielle. *The Alphabet of Light and Dark*. Allen & Unwin, Sydney, 2003.

——*Deep South*. With Ralph Crane (eds). Text Publishing, Melbourne, 2012.